APPLYING SELF-DEVELOPMENT IN ORGANIZATIONS

APPLYING SELF-DEVELOPMENT IN ORGANIZATIONS

Edited by

Mike Pedler
Sheffield Business School

John Burgoyne
University of Lancaster

Tom Boydell
Transform Ltd

PRENTICE HALL
New York   London   Toronto   Sydney   Tokyo

First published 1988 by
Prentice Hall International (UK) Ltd,
66 Wood Lane End, Hemel Hempstead,
Hertfordshire, HP2 4RG
A division of
Simon & Schuster International Group

© 1988 Prentice Hall International (UK) Ltd

Printed and bound in Great Britain by
A. Wheaton & Co. Ltd, Exeter

British Library Cataloguing in Publication Data

Applying self-development in organizations.
1. Executives – Great Britain
2. Career development – Great Britain
I. Pedler, Mike II. Burgoyne, John,
1944-   III. Boydell, Tom
658.4'09   HD38.25.G7

ISBN 0–13–043407–8

---

1 2 3 4 5   92 91 90 89 88

ISBN 0-13-043407-8

Contents

Preface

The idea of self-development as applied to the education and training of managers has been in currency in the UK for ten years or so. This book consists of field reports and essays on management self-development being used and applied in a variety of organizational settings. Some of these are straightforward accounts of self-development applied to appraisal, career planning or company-wide resources networks. Others define particular approaches such as self-managed learning, open and distance learning or self-development groups as well as providing illustrations and examples of these.

This book comes about as a result of a conference on self-development sponsored by the Manpower Services Commission in May 1986. At this conference we were impressed not only by the degree of interest shown in the topic but by the widespread involvement of the participants in applying self-development in their work. Many of these chapters owe a debt to the contributions made by the participants in workshop sessions at the conference.

In its four main parts, this book follows the conference themes beginning with the concept of managing one's own learning, then dwelling on 'differences at work' and especially gender, as a particularly powerful focus for efforts at self-development in recent years. The third part is concerned with the linking of careers and assessment, and the final part considers organization-wide applications.

The seventeen contributions in the four parts follow these divisions. Some chapters could have been placed in other parts and we could have used some alternative divisions – for example, four chapters are concerned with self-development groups. The broad divisions are best seen as starting points – if you're interested in careers start here etc. – and not as compartments.

An introductory chapter overviews the current state of the art, tracing the origins and the main dimensions of the idea as well as noting the limitations and drawbacks.

As with any book which makes its contribution at the frontier, this is incomplete in that it does not report all the applications of self-development being tried out in work organizations, and is also likely to be overtaken as practitioners continue with their developments. This book signals a stage where people are not only arguing the merits and de-merits of the idea but are using it as an increasingly widespread tool for management education and training.

We hope it moves you on.

M.P.

J.B.

T.B.

List of Contributors

Janet Atkinson has come to her own understanding of self-development from her experience as a group work specialist within a variety of organizations within the public and voluntary sector in this country and in the USA. Much of her work continues to be undertaken as part of the programme of the Division of Continuing Education within the University of Sheffield. She has a background in community work and group dynamics and is currently working both as an independent trainer and consultant and as a student training officer for Sheffield Family Service Unit.

Don Binsted was a founder member of the Centre for the Study of Management Learning (CSML) at Lancaster University. He has a background in industrial management, management training and organization development in ICI. He is currently involved in designing and running workshops, and directs CSML's open and distance learning research programme and associated activities.

Tom Boydell spent a short time as a practising engineer before finding he was more interested in learning and training. He worked at Sheffield City Polytechnic, and is now a member of Transform (Individual and Organizational Development Consultants) Ltd. For some time he has been actively involved in a number of approaches to self-development, and has written extensively in this field. He is married with three children.

John Burgoyne is a Professor and Head of Department in the Centre for the Study of Management Learning (CSML) at Lancaster University. He has previously been Research Director in CSML, and Lecturer in Management Development at the Manchester Business School. John has published, researched and consulted on managerial behaviour, management development policy, self-development, the nature of the learning process, and career management.

Simon Cooper has worked within the Texaco organization since 1970. For the past six years he has been involved in management training. This is after several assignments in both marketing and sales management capacities. His role of Co-ordinator of Training involves the development and implementation of a variety of management training programmes for the European division of Texaco.

Keith Cope, Sheila Davies, Mike Garton, Barbara Harris, Andrew Jarvis, David Pearce, Ann Simpson are all managers in various departments of Nottinghamshire County Council who joined together in a managers' self-development group and in an evaluation of their activities towards their own management development.

Rennie Fritchie has been active and proactive in working in the field of Women's Development for more than ten years. She works from her own consultancy company in a range of organizations, (public, private, voluntary sectors), in a variety of areas related to organization, management and personal development, including a range of self-development programmes. She is a self-developer and a single parent.

Calvin Germain first began to work with career development in Abingdon eight years ago. He was then an Organization Development Adviser with the £450m Fife Ethylene Project for three years, before taking a similar post with Esso Chemicals UK. He is now an independent consultant.

Jan Hennessey joined the Anne Shaw Organization in 1978, after previous work experience in the Health Service and as a recruitment consultant. She has worked extensively in training, focussing primarily on self-development, project management, and effective work relationships. She also specializes in the design of assessment centre models for management selection and development. She is an experienced counsellor with a particular interest in career development for women managers.

Martin Hughes worked in line management in textiles before spending five years in personnel management in the engineering industry. He now works as an independent consultant specializing in self-development and action learning, using these methods for both career and business development. Since 1981 he has worked as an associate consultant with the Anne Shaw Organization on self-development, career counselling, and assessment centre programmes.

Janice Leary is 41, a working mother, adult education tutor, consultant and volunteer art therapist. She works with individuals and groups on their development in a variety of settings from community associations and local authorities to miners' wives and open prisons.

Malcolm Leary is 43 and a father of three teenage girls. He is a consultant with Transform (Individual and Organization Development Consultants) Ltd. and is involved with a wide variety of development projects. He has a special interest in handling conflict, taking initiatives, self-development and biography work.

Peter Martin worked in personnel management for a number of years before becoming a senior lecturer in the Department of Management at Bristol Polytechnic.

David Miller has worked in recruitment and training for fifteen years, the last six of which have been with American Express. He is currently Director, Personnel Services, American Express (Europe) Ltd.

Alan Mossman is a member of the Self Managed Learning Unit at North East London Polytechnic and has a small private consultancy. His first degree was in architecture, he then went on to do research at the Manchester Business School before working in the Policy, Research and Intelligence Unit at Trafford MBC. His research is on how managers learn from experience and his particular focus is on outdoor management development using a neuro-linguistic programming framework.

Alan Mumford is Professor of Management Development at the International Management Centre from Buckingham. He was previously involved for twenty years in management training and development in industry. His publications include *Making Experience Pay* and, with Peter Honey, *The Manual of Learning Styles* and *Using Your Learning Styles*.

Mike Pedler is Senior Lecturer in the Department of Management Studies at Sheffield City Polytechnic, and is Director of the Business Management Development Programme at the Sheffield Business School. He has worked and written extensively in the fields of self-directed learning, self-development, and self-management, and he is currently applying these concepts to the development of new businesses.

Cynthia Roobottom started her career on a short service commission in the Royal Air Force, and then gained experience of direct selling with Proctor and Gamble. She worked with PER before joining Pedigree Pet Foods, where she was Training Manager for five years before becoming an independent consultant. During that time she developed and practised a wide range of approaches to behavioural training, counselling and personal development.

Jane Skinner is Director of the Post-experience Programme at the University of Aston Management Centre. This includes the *Women and Work* programme, which was started in 1984 and has gained a national reputation for developing and running a range of pilot positive action programmes focussed upon women, management, and equal opportunities in working life. Jane undertakes consultancy work in a number of organizations. She has a background in managing social community services, and is herself a working mother.

Rory Stewart is a member of the Learning Systems Division of Shell Internationale Petroleum in the Netherlands. From 1981 until August 1985 he was Head of Development Training for Sarawak Shell Berhad in East Malaysia (Borneo). Prior to Sarawak he was five years in Shell's personnel function which he joined from Life Insurance and Pensions Sales and Planning. He has a degree in business studies and is a Fellow of the Chartered Institute of Insurance.

Tony Winkless runs his own business, providing management assessment and development services to the private and public sectors, based on his previous career in training and personnel in industry, which included five years with Kodak and ten years with the Geest Organization.

1

Self-development and Work Organizations

*   *   *

MIKE PEDLER

As an approach to the training and education of managers, self-development has been an idea in increasingly widespread currency over the last ten years. Ideas are rarely entirely new and self-development is no exception having emerged in recent history at several points. In this opening chapter we will note some of these earlier expressions and sketch out the dimensions of the current incarnation. Of particular interest is the question of why self-development is seen as appropriate for managers in the 1980s and 1990s. Further to this, in what ways can manager self-development be organized and in what ways is it inherently anarchic? This is one of a number of unanswered questions and dilemmas of self-development which we pose at the close of this chapter.

Nevertheless, it appears that, for many management development practitioners, matters have progressed beyond toying with the idea of self-development to seeking to apply it within their work organizations. The battle for the idea being over, energies are being focussed upon linking the self-development impulse with organizational processes, structures and systems. Some of the chapters in this book contributed by managers and project workers with a variety of commercial, industrial and public service organizations give examples and evidence of this pragmatic trend.

Hitherto these pioneering efforts have remained largely unknown outside their immediate setting, yet, taken together they indicate a 'critical mass' illustrating the widespread acceptance and application of self-development ideas. The purpose of this book is to take stock of the current status of management self-development within work organizations, and to make more widely known the various applications and expressions of the idea and some of its pitfalls.

The aim of the opening chapter is to present an overview of management self-development. First, what does the idea consist of and where does it come from? We then look more closely at the central idea of

1

development and consider how this is related to the desire to improve the quality of management. Finally we consider some of the limitations of the self-development idea and comment upon the type of organization in which it is most likely to be fostered.

What is Management Self-development?

Management self-development is a term used for those approaches to management training and development which seek to 'increase the ability and willingness of the manager to take responsibility for him or herself, particularly for her or his own learning' (Pedler, Burgoyne and Boydell[1]). As such it is a reaction to, and a rejection of, the notion of expert-based management development manifested in the courses run for managers by those who allegedly know better, which still form by far the bulk of our provision. As we said in our earlier book, the implicit message of expert-based courses is – don't try to solve your own problems, somewhere there is an expert who knows the answer and can do it for you, all you need to do is to find him or her. Management development is largely done *to* managers rather than done *by* them, socializing them into existing organizational norms, practices and values, and treating them very much as 'patients' rather than 'agents'.

Management self-development draws upon the ideas of many people over the last twenty years or so who have emphasized the need for learner-centredness and learner control in training and development. Chris Argyris,[2] Carl Rogers,[3] Reg Revans[4] and Malcolm Knowles,[5] among many others, have taught that it is the learner who can take prime responsibility for deciding what to learn, when and how to learn, including when to stop and how to value what has been learned. The teacher is assigned the role of 'facilitator' – a helper or enabler rather than initiator. Teachers and trainers can help learners choose goals, resources, methods for learning, but they can no longer assume that they know best in defining another's needs or directly teach another what they need to know.

Many self-development designs use tasks as learning vehicles. Instead of working on abstract cases, learners work on actual tasks and then reflect upon their efforts, perhaps with the help of coaches, counsellors, support groups – what have they learned about managerial work? What have they learned about their strengths and weaknesses? What have they learned about their own preferences and style compared with that of their colleagues? What do they need to learn next? Work and learning, indeed life and learning, are brought back together and not separated as they are on the training course.

From the process of learning from the task – teasing out the lessons from personal experience – we may also learn how to learn, that is, we begin to understand how to make sense of, and draw conclusions and lessons from, our own experience. Done in this self-aware way, all learning can have two 'payoffs' – learning about the thing itself, e.g. budgeting, negotiating, and also learning about learning, i.e. this is what I did to learn about budgeting, negotiating etc., and I can apply this 'second loop' learning (as Argyris calls it) to any other learning task I have. The vision of the self-developing manager is one who is continuously converting everyday experience into learning and thereby continuously improving practice and performance.

In a rapidly changing world where techniques and custom and practice date soon after discovery, where the environment is unstable and unfriendly, and organizations are constantly changing shape and style to cope with rapid technological change from without and altered expectations from within (the argument runs) we need managers who know how to learn, who are self-aware enough to know when they don't know, and who have the confidence and personal substance to be able to initiate the required learning activities when necessary.

The self-development school holds that this ability, including, most importantly, the willingness to take the responsibility and initiative to learn from experience, can only come via a process in which the learner does these things for her or himself. They cannot come from a teaching situation in which the learner may be active in the physical sense, but is essentially passive in terms of responsibility and choice. A central dimension of self-development are the two meanings of 'self' in the term. The 'of-self' aspect makes self-development a goal or a series of ascending goals concerned with the expansion and development of the self – Maslow's 'self actualization' or the Bhudda's 'way of enlightenment'. The 'by-self' aspect is that which we have discussed above where self-development is essentially 'manage-it-yourself', sometimes involving one's friends or colleagues, but with the learner taking responsibility. These two meanings explain why some of the proponents of 'self-development' don't understand each other. As Don Binsted discusses in his later chapter, 'true' self-development requires both of-self and by-self components. However, there are various paradoxes if we insist that the of-self process must be entirely by-self, and the by-self process is also of-self, including the one Don points out that we don't always know what our own learning needs are – we need a best friend to tell us sometimes. Also, would we allow submission to some great teacher or yogi as self-development? Or that learning by correspondence course about motorcycle maintenance must also lead to the sort of expansion of the soul as it apparently did for Robert Pirsig? These are good paradoxes and there are yet others.

Where Does the Self-development Idea Come From?

In essence it has a long history, but the most obvious source is perhaps the notion of 'individualism' which Steven Lukes describes as a 'Nineteenth century word originating from around the time of the French Revolution'. Conservatives and Liberals took turns to castigate or extol individualism – by and large the French were against it, holding with the British conservative Edmund Burke that nation and collectivity are more important than the mere individual and that the exercise of individual will leads to spiritual and civil anarchy. The Romantic Germans, however, were for it: Goethe appealed to the 'theory of the right and duty of self-development' and Marx saw 'man' as a 'species being' whose 'own self-realization exists as an inner necessity, a need'. John Stuart Mill did not agree that the notion of self-development need be antisocial and held that through the development of the person, each becomes more valuable – to self and to others.

Clearly the roots of the idea go back farther – for example, Lukes quotes Lindsay in concluding that it was the New Testament which made the great contribution to individualism in balancing the Old Testament notion of the state (Israel) as the prime concern of God, with a new conception of a direct relation between God and the individual. (See Lukes[6].)

In the nineteenth century, more direct forbears can be seen in Samuel Smiles, whose *Self Help* first appeared in 1859 celebrating those who had pulled themselves up by their bootstraps and made an example and contribution to society. (Interestingly, a new edition of *Self Help* appeared in 1986 with a foreword by a prominent apostle of economic individualism, Keith Joseph, and was criticized for omitting much of Smiles's commentary on how these nineteenth-century individuals had contributed to community and society.[7]) The North Americans picked up naturally from the great Victorians and the written homilies of industrialists such as Andrew Carnegie and Alfred Sloan became bestsellers. Dale Carnegie's *How to Win Friends and Influence People*[8] summarizes the USA self-development creed as applied to the ordinary person and which still persists strongly to this day. The 'Business and Management' shelves in any bookshop in the USA tend to be dominated by books echoing this philosophy.

The short history of organized management development in the UK accelerated rapidly in the 1960s even as the economy entered increased comparative decline. Retrospectively those were years of hope, of never-ending growth and prosperity for all and in sharp contrast to the situation facing managers in the 1980s beset by problems of low growth, high unemployment, increasingly fierce overseas competition, rapid technological change, increasing social divisions at home and abroad and so on. Management self-development, as an idea, has gained momentum in these straitened times, not always for honourable reasons, but in contrast to two earlier ideas which dominated the 1960s and 1970s.

At the risk of some over-simplification the 1960s was the era of systematic *training,* fuelled by skills shortages in a full employment economy and encouraged by the Industrial Training Act. Training is outer-directed; training needs stem from 'organizational goals'; skilled training officers diagnose individual needs, set measurable objectives, devise programmes and so on. 'Individuals' are trained in squads, cohorts whose training needs are all the same. Systematic training was effective (and still is) for much training, especially in manual skills, but when the approach was applied to management development, a critical problem known as the 'transfer of training' problem emerged. Programmes were excellent and trainees learned a lot – according to post-course evaluation instruments – but their actions and behaviour back at work did not change.

This problem led to a focus on *learning.* Instead of concentrating on what the trainer does, let's see what happens when people learn. The late 1960s and 1970s saw the discovery of the learning cycle of Revans,[4] Kolb *et al.*[9] and others, and the pursuit of the art of 'learning how to learn' became the new Holy Grail. Carl Rogers provided an inspiration for the learning movement with his 'non-directive' or 'learner-centred' views in remarks like 'that which can be taught directly to another is relatively trivial, whereas things of significance can only be learned.'[3] Learning was inner-directed, concerned with the feelings and thoughts of the individual, was relatively unrelated to 'organizational goals' and was successful when the learner said that he or she had learned.

The Idea of Development

Development as an idea embraces both the outer reality of environment and 'organizational goals' and the inner reality of the emerging self. Each of us is a unique being in the process of becoming a person – as Rogers and Maslow taught – but we can realize that in the company of others and in a world where restraints and pressing problems are only ignored by the blind and self-indulgent. We do have more control over whether we choose to develop or not in this direction or that, than the trainers allowed, despite the obvious limits of individualism. It is this realization – of the power we have to choose – which lends the impetus to the idea of self-development.

Methods such as 'action learning' and 'self-managed' learning stress the interaction of inner and outer where the acquisition of managerial

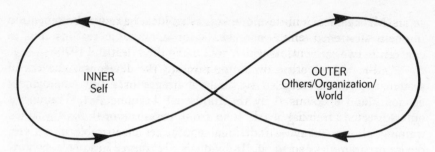

skills requires *both* an inner choosing and 'transformation' *and* a changed outer performance. Self-development as an idea is then a synthesis of earlier ideas being neither this or that but *both* ... *and* ..., where development involves a continuous passing from outer actions (experience) to inner processes (reflection) back to action and so on.

It is to development rather than learning that we attach the prefix 'self—'. When we think of the times we have developed – as managers or human beings – we may think of particular points in time when 'something happened' which eventually led us to see and do things differently from before. These points stand out and sometimes obscure periods or phases when things seemed to stay the same. Even within this apparent continuity we are moving towards a point where things will change, where we become dissatisfied with how things are, when we will be ready to develop, to take our next step. When the step comes it is always a surprise, a shock, a perturbation in the hitherto smooth flow. It may start with a question entering the mind, from an increasing feeling of boredom and dissatisfaction, from the comments of a colleague – indeed from anything which happens and which we take notice of. We cannot take a step in development until this point is reached. It is both the 'happening' and our admitting of it that makes up the experience. It is what we then do about that experience that forms the nature of this step in our development. When we develop in any aspect we feel different from before and, looking back, there is a break, a discontinuity with how we were then. For this reason we have sometimes used the term 'step-jump' to describe the always surprising, discontinuous nature of development. Of course development is not inevitable – if we are unable to admit any given 'happening', but forget it or deny, repress or avoid thinking about it, then development cannot take place. Equally, if we admit the experience but are unable to make sense of it – as in the case of some severe shock – then we cannot develop. We all of us have *blockages* of various sorts preventing us from developing in various directions usually as a result of receiving unassimilable shocks to our current level of functioning. Usually these are relatively unimportant or even valued parts of our personalities. The twists and turns, the quirks and idiosyncrasies which make us the individuals we are today are as much to do with what we haven't developed as what we have.

Any development, however, requires a 'little death' or disintegration from an earlier smooth stage of functioning. The development event is a crisis which both disorganizes us, renders us confused and uncertain, 'all at sea', and opens us to something new, to that state of having 'an uncommitted potentiality for change' in Bateson's words. Fostering this process in oneself may seem risky enough, but to encourage others to do it seems to pose all sorts of problems for management developers in organizations. However, we should remember that this development is largely a 'naturally occurring' process and that when we ask managers when they developed the skills and abilities which they consider essential to their jobs, they cite all sorts of instances and events, many of which are unconnected either with work or with organized training events. It seems we choose to develop most of the time when we can and the question for any management developer, perhaps, is not whether she or he should assist another to 'disintegrate' in the hope of future re-integration at a superior level of functioning, but whether they want to assist in what is largely a naturally occurring process.

Nonetheless to work with development we must be prepared to accept a decrement – a falling off in performance from the old level – before any increment is likely. If, as an adult, we change our way of doing something we are likely to experience an initial period of errors and confusion before we get it right. How many management development systems do actually support this process in managers and how many organizational environments encourage individuals to take a decrement in current performance in order to achieve a possible step-jump in performance? If this is the definition of development, then we would probably have to conclude that most of the activities going on under this label at the moment are not true development.

To sum up, then:

(a) The notion of development is both continuous and discontinuous and can be seen as a process occurring in a series of phases each marked by a set of characteristic principles, structures and values, each of which ends in crisis . . .

(b) . . .which is experienced as shock, surprise or perturbation and causes the disintegration of the old phase of functioning and creates the conditions for the discontinuous 'step-jump' to a new phase. This succeeding phase incorporates yet transforms the repertoire of principles, values, etc., of earlier phases and adds to them. The new phase is therefore not entirely new – it is a transformation. Each succeeding phase is more complex, integrating what has gone before.

(c) Development is a progression of phases which is irreversible, although regression may take place in times of crisis. This development 'curve' may be compared with this familiar learning curve and its continuous progression, albeit with plateaux:

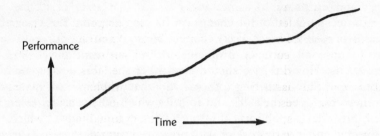

The phases and step-jumps of development may suggest a 'staircase' like this:

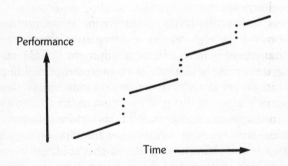

but a broken spiral may be more apposite, where we 'spiral' to greater understanding, performance, etc., periodically revisiting old problems and dilemmas now seen in a new light, but having that vague feeling of having somehow been here before:

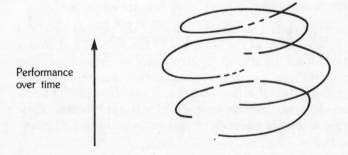

(d) This sense of 'having been here before' is sometimes felt as frustration, such as when someone, being asked if they understand now, says, 'Yes, I've learned something . . . but I'm still confused – but at a higher level!' This is partly because we only ever solve puzzles, while problems worth their salt remain with us, to use Revans's dichotomy.

By example let's take a manager who, at one point, feels herself unable to speak to her boss about something. When she understands that it is a lack of confidence which stops her, she somehow finds the pluck, only to find during the interview that she lacks some skills of expression. She has solved a puzzle, but the problem remains. She acquires the necessary skill after being coached by a friend and confronts the boss, only to find that the boss is unwilling to make the decision . . . and so on. Each time she solves a puzzle, the situation is transformed but the essential problem – in this case, the manager's relationship to authority – will probably remain with that person in some shape or form. Nevertheless, she has developed if she has learned from this experience that she can summon up courage and learn new skills. Hence the 'spiral' has an ascending dimension.

Most models of development ascend from lower to higher stages, as Tom Boydell has shown in assembling an impressive array of theories on many aspects of human development.[10] The 'spiral' also has a circling dimension in that the crisis preceding development comes when a hitherto governing principle or idea is opposed in dichotomy with a new idea – the Hegelian notion of thesis/antithesis. The challenge in development is to find the 'third position' or synthesis which contains elements of both but transforms them into something new – which is the break point of the 'spiral'. To put it another way we may quote Boydell's Law: 'Development is decreased duality; increased unity'.[10]

(e) Development takes place over time, and is a long-cycle process extending over the life cycle. Some developmental crises or tasks occur partly as a result of age – adolescence, leaving the parental home, having children, reaching mid-career, retiring and so on. Development is necessarily a whole person concept and these crises and the development which proceeds from them are just as much a part of the manager as anything that happens at work. The training approach assumes we can deal with the manager-at-work in isolation.

(f) Development is obviously a matter of 'readiness'. We cannot develop until we are ready to do so – it is then that we 'choose' to attend to the crisis or developmental task. We cannot be forced to develop, only encouraged. Each of us has a natural right *not* to develop until we're ready and also not to develop at all along a particular dimension if we so wish.

(g) Finally, development is not easy or inevitable. We all get stuck in certain aspects of our lives, choose to stay put in others. There are times for survival and maintenance as well as development and, as Roger Harrison reminds us, to a large extent, we are our defences.[11] When we do want to develop it will often happen 'naturally', but at other times we will need help and support. In another Revans phrase, the best sort of help perhaps comes from 'comrades in adversity' – people in the same boat, tackling similar crises and tasks, yet prepared to lend a hand. Other help can be found via 'speaking partners', counsellors, coaches, support groups. Development can be difficult and painful and, even when triumphant, is marked with the bereavement of giving up and letting go some of the past.

In adopting the idea of self-development rather than or as well as training, management developers are taking on a more complex idea which demands more of those who would foster it. The prime requirement is to understand how the process of development works in people. While the hands-off simplicity of the still present Dale Carnegie school of thought may be a regression from the bold interference of the trainer, the development facilitator needs to think about both strategies in determining whether and how to intervene.

Self-development and the Quality of Management

As concepts of management development have moved on, so have those about what constitutes quality in management. While there is still concern in some quarters to establish what the great men have in common – the 'trait' approach – by and large the quality debate can be seen as following two directions. The 'horizontal' approach attempts to define the range of qualities which makes up the repertoire 'of the 'effective manager'. A number of models of these qualities have been put forward, for example, by Stewart,[12] Burgoyne and Stuart[13] and Mintzberg.[14] Such models suggest that all managers need certain skills, abilities or qualities such as command of basic facts, social skills, conflict resolution skills, emotional resilience, self-awareness and so on. Some form of assessment, by appraisal, assessment centre or questionnaire for example, against the model, is followed by planned training and development opportunities. The self-development idea has had considerable impact here and a number of practitioners are seeking to make appraisal, career planning, assessment centres and so on much more by-self (and perhaps of-self) than formerly. Some examples of these attempts can be found in this book.

The limitations of 'horizontal' models are that they tend to be context-specific and rather static. They are relevant to particular people, in particular jobs, at particular points in time and in particular cultures, and their adoption and institutionalization in any organization will be oppressive for some people and eventually dysfunctional for the whole. 'Horizontal' models are static because they tend to be represented as a series of goals, often linked to the appropriate training course. Over time, attendance on the course provides the necessary evidence that one has 'learned' or acquired this quality. This is not to knock the idea, for example, that managers in organization X need budgeting skills and that they should be given opportunities to acquire them. This is typical of the 'training approach' and is laudable where opportunities are created which did not exist before. However, it represents a limited stage of development. A 'vertical' dimension is required in order to overcome the problems and is more in tune with the idea of development – that we are always in a state of becoming rather than arriving – there is always further to go. Only a vertical dimension can encourage the striving for excellence beyond competence.

As we noted earlier most models of development are 'age' or 'stage' models, taking the form of a ladder of development stages. Most of us are familiar with Abraham Maslow's theory of human motivation – the famous 'hierarchy of needs' – which he held to be universal in terms of its application and which shaped so strongly his own development. From his first articulation of it in his 20s to the end of his life, he worked to take it further, particularly with regard to his 'top rung' of 'self-actualization'. His later work on the 'further reaches of human nature' has much in common with mystical and religious ideas about human development, perhaps especially those associated with Bhuddist thought with its 'eightfold path' of enlightenment. 'Vertical' theories of human development tend to depict the human being moving from the primitive and instinctive, with limited control and awareness, to the advanced and enlightened state of 'oneness' which denotes not only self-awareness but union with all living things. Interestingly such beings in their wisdom often choose to refrain from action in favour of contemplation, despite a hard-won repertoire of skills and responses gained on the path of development. It seems clear that a model of manager development which will encourage the manager towards 'excellence' or further enlightenment rather than 'satisficing' or 'mere competence' does require a vertical dimension.

Tom Boydell and others have recently developed a vertical model of managerial quality based upon the archetypal ideas of Rudolf Steiner.[15] Initial testing of the model with managers is encouraging.[16] There are various versions of the model, including the five stage one given in Table 1.1.

Table 1.1

Developmental stage or mode	Benefits of this way of managing	Effect of being blocked at this stage	Nature of next developmental step
1 Rules and procedures	Set procedures etc. can be of use in certain types of emergency, where it is particularly important to do the 'right' thing quickly and correctly. They are also useful for beginners, because they provide a reassuring base from which to start.	In fact, not many managers are stuck at this stage. Those that are can only operate in a limited number of 'standard' situations, and are likely to be most ineffective at anything that might be described as 'truly managerial'.	To move on, you need to start querying, modifying or deviating from standard procedures, seeking explanations and reasons rather than mere instructions.
2 Norms and conventions *Influenced mainly by external factors*	Enables you to behave in an 'appropriate' way – i.e. in the way that is in accord with accepted reasons, rationales and explanations, and is socially and politically respectable. In so doing you are likely to be popular with the powers that be, keeping your nose clean and being considered safe, acceptable and reliable.	Many managers remain at this stage, and are quite happy to do so, since it can lead to a reasonably content existence. On the other hand, these managers are likely to find any unexpected change most unpleasant and difficult to cope with. Should they be forced to leave the organization (e.g. through redundancy) they will have a particularly bad time adjusting to their new situation. Also, of course, there is often a long-term price to be paid for not being oneself – a certain malaise, doubt, 'surely there's more to life than this?' begins to creep in. They suffer from all the effects of not managing themselves that were outlined in [Chapter 1] – i.e they are stuck, become bored, lazy, timeservers etc.	You need to start questioning and challenging the established and accepted ways and reasons for doing things. Start to think for yourself: do you really think this is the best way of doing something? Is this really a good, acceptable or valid explanation or reason? How can you find out for yourself, come to your own conclusion or decision?

Table 1.1 (cont.)

Developmental stage or mode	Benefits of this way of managing	Effect of being blocked this stage	Nature of next developmental step
3 Thinking for yourself *Enter the self: now internal factors have a big influence*	Much more likely to be creative, and to be able to manage new, ambiguous, changing situations, both within your organization and in other aspects of your life. Also greater feelings of self-confidence and self-worth. The price to pay for this is that you may well be unpopular at times with those who like to maintain the status quo and do things in the 'proper' manner.	Being stuck at this stage means that you are so keen on thinking for yourself that you become too self-directing, completely ignoring the ideas, feelings, values and goals of other people, and the effect of your actions on them. You are also likely to distort your confidence into a form of arrogance.	You need, therefore, to start to temper your arrogance with humility, and to synthesize or combine self-management with management by and of other people, particularly by becoming aware of their views etc., and of the effect of your actions on them before coming to your final decision. It is also useful at this stage to start thinking about what you have to offer others, to contribute to their development.
4 Awareness *Now it's both internal and external factors, in a synthesis of the two*	You are now thinking for yourself, making your own decisions etc. in full awareness both of yourself and of others and their goals, ideas, feelings: this leads to what is often seen as 'intuitive behaviour'. To do this involves ' . . . both . . . and' thinking, and requires open-mindedness and suspension of judgement: in addition, of course, this awareness enables you to choose which of these modes to operate in – i.e. you now have a repertoire	Not a bad stage to be 'stuck' at! However, you may now find an increasing need and desire to use these skills, this ability to manage yourself, to a particular purpose, that you yourself feel to be important. There is also a danger of abusing these abilities, this high level of consciousness, to further personal ambition, manipulate others	Start to look for this special purpose: ask. 'Why on earth am I here? What am I doing with my life?'

Table 1.1 (cont.)

Developmental stage or mode	Benefits of this way of managing	Effect of being blocked at this stage	Nature of next developmental step
	available to you, from which you can choose consciously. Thus, this is the stage of effective management, as outlined in [Table 1.1].	and gain power over them, or for other negative, evil ends.	
5 Purpose *Now you apply this synthesis, this art of managing yourself, to a particular purpose – to your purpose in life*	Now you are managing yourself with a full awareness of your purpose in life, of the task you want to achieve. Hopefully this task isn't something just for yourself, but in some way makes a definite contribution to the development of your organization, profession, area of expertise, community, affinity group, family, or whatever it is that you choose to commit yourself to. However, there is also a great danger that this commitment will be to some negative or evil cause – this is where we find fanatics, despots, tyrants (sometimes obvious, sometimes posing as great saviours).		

Source: *Managing Yourself*, Eds. Pedler M.J. & Boydell T.H. Fontana/Collins, 1985, p. 70/71.

Of course, horizontal and vertical models of managerial quality are not mutually exclusive. They can be used separately or together. For example, managers in a given organization can aspire both to a range of particular qualities and to depth in taking a particular quality or ability further. The vertical model exampled above is a general model, but it is likely that a specific model of say, negotiating, would follow a similar path. While managerial job descriptions, on the whole, imply horizontal models only, there are some recent attempts, especially within graded salary structures, to illustrate what level of performance is required in a given skill or ability at a given level of pay or seniority. Taken too far in our current way of thinking, of course, this might result in a sort of martial arts grading of managers – green belts or seventh Dans in counselling perhaps – but used more carefully, the concept of vertical quality within horizontal repertoires gives a much richer picture of what is possible.

It may be that it is this contribution of the essentially 'vertical' nature of human development to the largely 'horizontal' managerial qualities that explains why self-development is an important idea at this stage of management development. To make more explicit the contrast between the ideas of 'excellence' and 'competence' which we have referred to above, the debate about managerial quality reflects the wider debate and crisis in the 'developed' economies. In the UK, our manufactured goods have tended to suffer in comparison with some of the competition, not so much on price as on quality. Our sometimes neurotic concern for excellence is an aspect of our acceptance of this. We have further concluded that the quality of our products reflects upon the quality of labour and therefore upon the quality of management – and the buck stops here. At the level of the person we might say that excellence cannot be achieved without some vertical notion of development. Carl Rogers pointed out that what is 'personally significant' can only be learned and not taught, and personal excellence cannot be arrived at via a training approach. Training can only aspire to competence in the person – a most useful quality – but one which stands short of excellence.

Much of the current burgeoning 'excellence literature' is in fact retrogressive. We are rather encouraged to believe we can all achieve excellence all of the time. The 'Great Corporation' has replaced the 'Great Man' of yesteryear but the tune is the same old one Dale Carnegie sang. We can aim for quality and excellence without falling for this rehashing of the heroic ideal with its consequence of confirming us at our low-level stage of development of 'hero worshipper'. Here is where we came in, for self-development is precisely about passing beyond expert prescription and increasing our ability and willingness to take responsibility for ourselves and for our own development.

Current Problems and Dilemmas with Self-development

As we noted earlier, the application stage of self-development is more conductive to revealing pitfalls and limitations. Here are some very knotty problems, some of which are very practical, such as the one which Don Binsted raises in his chapter – on the fact that we don't always know what some of our own learning needs are and that sometimes these can only be spotted by other people. This nice little paradox need not trouble us too much if we remember that the spotting of another's need does not confer the right to take responsibility for that person's learning. However, Don draws different conclusions which may be more realistic in many work organizations.

Other problems are more philosophical. Is all development 'good'? What does 'highly developed' mean, and do I – you – want to be like that? (The image that comes to mind is of the 'overdeveloped musclemen'.) Such questions are not easily resolved. When we look at our own development, and particularly in the context of management development, we tend to focus overmuch on what we may have successfully wrought, rather than what remains fixed, unexplored, underdeveloped or repressed. In this we are all clearly unbalanced –

overdeveloped here, underdeveloped there, our capacity for self-delusion most obvious perhaps to those who work under or for us. If development is 'good', then does it not also bring with it awareness of the ease with which 'good' acts have 'evil' consequences? How often in literature have the great ironists used simple, courageous folk to trigger holocausts and disasters? These and other questions are of crucial importance once we commit ourselves to development rather than, say, training, but this is perhaps not the place to dwell upon them. We finish this chapter by commenting upon three pitfalls for self-development which are easily observed in work organizations, and a suggestion as to the future direction for those wishing to give self-development a good home.

The most obvious of these pitfalls lies in the looseness and width of the idea. In 1978 we noted that, among practitioners the idea of self-development had a wide range of meanings – from correspondence courses to T-groups; from self-improvement to self-actualization.[17] While this width has helped in the establishment of the idea, it now threatens its integrity as, increasingly, various exponents fail to recognize each other's efforts – are self-development groups and distance learning for a higher degree really part of the same thing?

This is perhaps the major stumbling block to the continued development of the idea as applications reveal differences in philosophy. As noted earlier, these differences can usually be seen along the two underlying dimensions of 'of-self' and 'by-self', which, used as crude measures show clearly that some 'self-development programmes' are more learner-directed and managed than others.

There are great dangers in being too purist about ideas, especially in this most pragmatic field of endeavour. Management development is characterized by a steady, some would say torrential, flow of ideas, methods and techniques, most of which pass quickly on leaving only faint traces behind. Defending the integrity of ideas may easily spiral into 'laager-building' if the time is wrong. Equally, if an idea is too loose then it may be 'hijacked' and there are already plenty of self-development 'courses' on offer with the ubiquitous training department marking out the pitch and setting up the goalposts. All self-development designs should be subjected now and then to the acid test of certain key questions – who sets the goals? ... decides the methods? ... designs the programmes? ... evaluates the results?

The ease with which the idea of self-development may be 'hijacked' leads to the second pitfall. The very acceptability of self-development offers a golden opportunity to those concerned to cut training budgets and put in the place of training courses a self-development approach in the Dale Carnegie self-improvement sense. The former are expensive and inefficient; the latter cheap and easy – too easy of course, for sometimes managers are simply charged with the duty of self-development in addition to their existing workloads. Responsibility is devolved downwards but without the encouragement, the resources, and above all, the example of senior people. Such a 'self-development philosophy' will quickly lead to a Hobbsian state of nature in training and development terms, where only the fittest survive. There is some evidence of this cynical or simply mistaken approach to self-development being taken.

The third pitfall comes about sometimes because people try to avoid the second. To safeguard the training provision, self-development programmes are pronounced as 'advanced' or suitable for managers ready for 'further development', i.e. after having run the gamut of courses laid on for managers in the organization. Experienced people who have worked with the idea of self-development sometimes suggest that it doesn't work for everyone, but this recognition of the 'readiness principle' should not lead automatically to the élitist assumption that self-development is for senior people, 'high flyers' or already well-developed managers. On the contrary, we have evidence that self-development is especially powerful in releasing the energy and potential of 'oppressed' people – those stuck in limited and disadvantaged positions. This is why self-development designs have been used so much to increase opportunities for women managers and also for other groups such as redundant managers, supervisors and even, in one case, short-stay prisoners.[18]

Following on, there are obvious reasons why the notion of self-development is inextricably entwined with the concept of 'career' as an upward, hierarchic progression within the organization. Development implies advancement in many workplaces. This coupling should be resisted as another 'hijacking' – the process of self-development, in itself implying no 'arriving', is turned into a product, e.g. the 'developed manager'. The assumption is that those who are 'developed' must also rise to the top; those who are at the top are therefore by definition the most developed. It is an easy step from here to justify unequal resource allocation in favour of these 'gifted children'.

The élitist tendency needs to be balanced. The 'room-at-the-top' school of managerial career planning is based upon a view of organization strongly influenced by 'Great Man' theories of leadership. This seems seriously at odds with the testing and insecure conditions with which many organizations are faced and which require high quality at all levels and from all employees. What is more appropriate to today's conditions is a significant shifting of resources into creating training and development opportunities for all personnel. Self-development is appropriate for all workers in the organization as one strand of this effort because it is an approach capable of creating excellence that is beyond competence.

There are people in some organizations who are working towards this vision, adopting strategies such as making all employees 'staff' or 'managers' together with the appropriate conditions and terms and expectations. They are increasing the numbers of trained trainers at large in the organization and not just in trainer roles, stipulating a number of 'training days' per person per year for all employees and offering all sorts of resources for learning, including those not directly connected with work but concerned with home, leisure or general interest. Learning and development thus becomes a normal part of work and learning anything develops the capacity for learning anything. This ultimate vision here is what we might call the 'Learning Company' in which all members regard continuous life- and career-long development as part of what work means. Personal and professional development of oneself, and of one's fellows, becomes a true product of that work.

This vision of the Learning Company is not a Utopian one. The extent of the capacity for learning within the organization as within the individual is the key to survival and development in unfriendly or rapidly changing conditions. The proper place of self-development as a management development strategy is perhaps not as a replacement for other strategies, but as a companion to many other opportunities within the environs of the Learning Company.

References

1. Pedler, M.J., Burgoyne, J.G. and Boydell, T.H. (1978; 1986) *A Manager's Guide to Self-development*. McGraw-Hill, Maidenhead, UK.
2. Argyris, C. (1960) Do-it-yourself executive development. *Think*, **25**(6), pp. 9–11. May. Argyris, C. (1957) *Motivation and Personality*. Harper & Row, New York.
3. Rogers, C. (1969) *Freedom to Learn*. Charles E. Merrill, Columbus, Ohio.
4. Revans, R.W. (1971) *Developing Effective Managers*. Longmans, London.
5. Knowles, M. (1970) *The Modern Practice of Adult Education*. Association Press, New York.
6. Lukes, S. (1973) *Individualism* pp. 3–72. Blackwell, Oxford, UK.
7. Smiles, S. (1986) *Self Help*. Penguin, London. (Abridged by George Bull with an introduction by Sir Keith Joseph.)
8. Carnegie, D. (1953) *How to Win Friends and Influence People*. Worlds Work, Kingsworth Tadwood. New York.
9. Kolb, D.A., Rubin, I.M. and McIntyre, J.N. (1971) *Organisational Psychology: An Experiential Approach*. Prentice-Hall, London.
10. Boydell, T.H. (1978)
11. Harrison, R. (1962) Defenses and the need to know. *Human Relations Training News*, **6**(4). Winter.
12. Stewart, R. (1967) *Managers and their Jobs*. MacMillan, London.
13. Burgoyne, J.G. and Stuart, R. (1976) The nature, use and acquisition of managerial skills and other attributes. *Personnel Reivew*, **5**(4), pp. 19–29.

14. Mintzberg, H. (1973) *The Nature of Managerial Work*. Harper & Row, New York.
15. Boydell, T.H. (1982) Development. *MEAD*, **13**(1). Spring, pp. 10–32.
16. Leary, M., Boydell, T.H., Van Boeschoten, M. and Carlisle, J. (March 1985) *Levels of Management Performance, Learning and Development*. Manpower Services Commission, Sheffield, UK.
17. Burgoyne, J.G., Boydell, T.H. and Pedler, M.J. (1978) *Self-development*, pp. 4–5. ATM, London.
18. Boydell, T.H. *et al.* (1986) *Self-development Groups for Women Managers*. Manpower Services Commission, Sheffield, UK.

SELF-MANAGED LEARNING

Three of the chapters in Part One are by management educators who seek to make explicit the assumptions behind their particular approaches to management and self-development. The fourth chapter is unusual, being co-written by seven people who are also managers in a large local authority. These seven 'consumers' of management education have conducted their own rigorous evaluation of their own development programme. The story of their life together in a management self-development group illustrates much of what is properly a managerial perspective showing concern for task, for people and for resources used.

In the opening chapter of this part, Alan Mumford contributes a lucid explanation of why 'learning to learn' remains for him the fundamental feature of any designed self-development process. Building from this basis Alan Mossman and Rory Stewart give individual and organizational examples of the self-managed learning approach developed at North East London Polytechnic since 1979. They focus particularly upon the design principles for developing in-house programmes.

Don Binsted clarifies some of the ambiguity surrounding the term 'open and distance learning' and creates a matrix for helping us decide what is from what is not. Linking this to the principles underlying self-development Don is able to show some of the possibilities as well as the difficulties in delivering open and distance learning which creates new opportunities and freedoms for self-managing learners.

2

Learning to Learn and Management Self-development

* * *

ALAN MUMFORD

Introduction

My personal experience is that learning to learn needs to be a fundamental feature of any designed process which is called self-development because:

(i) the right of the individual to choose *what* is to be learned can be extended to *how* it is to be learned;

(ii) the design of the process needs to be built on effective learning principles;

(iii) individual capability to learn from particular processes varies;

(iv) the capacity of the learner to benefit from any self-development activity needs to be itself addressed as something capable of development;

(v) continued capacity to learn after the designed event is enhanced if it is treated directly on that event.

This latter point is especially important. Managers who take charge of their own learning need to be enabled to do so outside the activities which have introduced them to the principles and some of the processes of self-development.

No distinction is drawn here between learning and development. The processes described are equally effective in enabling both, though they might be seen as even more important for what are sometimes described as the more fundamental processes implied in the word 'development'.

This chapter is based on a survey in the UK and USA of management educators and trainers[1]. They described the processes they used, and the concepts behind those processes. The sequence of this chapter, following a definition, is to describe the benefits of an explicit approach to learning to learn, and then to set out the different approaches used. The design of the chapter moves therefore from general principles to detailed specific cases – a design which itself illustrates a crucial feature of learning to learn. Some readers (learners) might have preferred a different sequence!

A Definition

Learning to learn involves:

(i) helping managers to know the stages of the learning process and blockages to learning;

(ii) helping them to understand their own preferred approaches to learning;

(iii) assisting managers in making best use of their existing learning preferences or building additional strengths and overcoming blockages;

(iv) helping managers to carry their understanding of learning from off-the-job to on-the-job opportunities.

It will be seen from these definitions that I take the view that learning to learn has to be a clear overt part of any programme which claims to be providing such an experience. I recognize that this is setting a higher standard than some providers of learning experiences would accept. I am clearly setting out the case for a formal approach (although the formality can be presented in a very informal way). In addition, I do not accept that learning to learn can be treated as an implicit, unstated activity. Some tutors have argued that managers may have secured a better comprehension of their learning process through a learning experience, although that experience and that learning process have never been explicitly discussed with them. This is like arguing that managers learn from the experience of mock selection interviews, although the interview is not discussed. Of course some learning may occur – but clearly it will be in many cases more limited, more accidental than it needs to be.

Benefits

A substantial list of specific benefits can be identified:

  (i) an increase in the capacity of individuals to learn;

 (ii) a reduction in the frustration of being exposed to inefficient learning processes;

(iii) an increase in motivation to learn;

 (iv) a recognition that unwillingness to learn from one particular kind of activity is not generalizable as an unwillingness to learn from all kinds of activities;

  (v) development of learning opportunities well beyond formally created situations;

 (vi) a multiplier effect for managers in their developmental relationship with their subordinates;

(vii) the reduction of dependence on a tutor;

(viii) the provision of processes which carry through beyond formal programmes into on-the-job learning;

 (ix) the better identification of the role of learning in an effective managerial behaviour, for example in problem-solving or team work;

  (x) the development of more effective behaviour in relation to the crucial subject of change.

A careful analysis of learning needs, the preparation of learning objectives and a plan for learning are also all major contributors to whether a manager learns something effectively or not. These remain essential stages in learning. Interestingly, however, experience shows that discussion on learning to learn brings out a better understanding and often a wider understanding of learning needs and learning possibilities inherent in management jobs.

This general experience was confirmed in a second Report for the Manpower Services Commission[2]. For this 144 directors were interviewed about the processes by which they had learned on the way to the top of their organizations. Among other things, the discussions showed that most of their learning had occurred within real life rather than from their infrequent management training or education experiences.

In itself, this was an unremarkable finding; of greater significance was the recognition by directors themselves of how inefficient the process of learning from real life had been. Opportunities to learn had rarely been recognized in advance, and the processes by which they might learn, for example, in carrying out a project had not been understood. The new model of management development proposed in the Report brings out the significance of understanding learning processes as a necessary feature of effectively combining task and learning.

Prime Factors Influencing Learning to Learn

A large number of factors can be identified which are likely to influence the totality of a manager's learning effort and the specifics of how he or she approaches learning how to learn. Even on specialized programmes about self-development a complete list of potential influences seems not to be discussed.

Two prime factors have been the central focus for those few people who were working directly on learning to learn – blockages, and learning styles. The work of Temporal and Boydell[3] on blocks to learning is a major contribution in this area and could be at least a main part of the content of structured learning to learn approach.

I have used their analysis to draw up my own review of blocks to learning:

Perceptual	Not seeing there is a problem
Cultural	The way things are here . . .
Emotional	Fear or insecurity
Motivational	Unwillingness to take risk
Cognitive	Previous learning experience
Intellectual	Limited learning styles
	Poor learning skills
Expressive	Poor communication skills
Situational	Lack of opportunities
Physical	Place, time
Specific environment	Boss/colleagues unsupportive

In some circumstances this might well be the major focus of the effort to help managers. The original Temporal and Boydell analysis was developed further by Roger Stuart[4] in a very interesting form in which he combines an analysis of blockages with Kolb's definitions of learning styles (referred to below) so that the two can be seen together. Among the many virtues of directing attention to the issue of blockages and personal motivation is that this operates on the reality of why managers learn and do not learn in a way which is easily recognizable to the managers themselves. In addition work on helping to identify the social and emotional issues involved is one of the ways of avoiding any temptation to deal with learning purely through a well designed input and discussion which revolves around neat analysis rather than personal awareness.

Another major approach to this subject has been through the work of David Kolb[5]. His learning cycle theory appears regularly in articles and occasionally on courses:

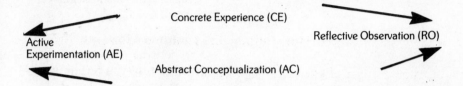

Concrete Experience (CE)

Reflective Observation (RO)

Active Experimentation (AE)

Abstract Conceptualization (AC)

However, the cycle describes an ideal learning pattern; his great discovery was that individuals differ in their interest in learning from the different stages of the cycle. His learning styles inventory (LSI) was the first, and for a long time the only, available diagnostic tool through which it was possible to approach the likely differences in the way in which individual managers learn.

The LSI initially establishes the extent to which an individual will approach learning with a preference for one of the stages of the learning cycle by scoring questions based on each of the stages. These scores are then converted by combination into your learning style:

Converger (combines AC and AE):

Finds practical uses for ideas and focusses on specific problems.

Diverger (combines CE and RO):

Sees/views concrete situations from different points of view; adapts by observation rather than action.

Assimilator (combines AC and RO):

Interested in abstract ideas and concepts.

Accommodator (combines CE and AE):
Learns primarily from hands-on experience.

Honey and Mumford in the UK developed their own learning styles questionnaire (LSQ). This starts from a similar view to Kolb about the fact that there are often substantial differences in learning preferences between managers, and that these different preferences will largely determine the effectiveness of any learning process to which they are exposed.

As with the LSI, the LSQ identifies four styles, the characteristics of which are:

Activists	learn best from activities where they can engross themselves in immediate tasks (e.g. business games, team tasks).
Reflectors	learn best from activities where they have the opportunity to review what has happened.
Theorists	learn best when what is offered is part of a system, model, concept or theory.
Pragmatists	learn best when there is an obvious link between subject matter and a problem or opportunity on the job.

It is, of course, difficult for me to be objective in commenting about the usefulness of either of these instruments in general, or about the particular properties of them which makes one or other a more suitable choice. A major advantage for both instruments as compared with any of the other processes discussed here is that detailed guidance is available for the prospective tutor on how the instruments can be used. In addition to Kolb's book[5] and recently revised inventory (1985) he has published a user's guide[6]. The combination of his book and this guide would assist any tutor in setting out a session or sessions based on his particular approach. In addition to their *Manual*[7] Honey and Mumford have also published *Using Your Learning Style*[8] which, like Kolb's guide, is directed at the individual learner.

Objective data on the differences between the two approaches and the two instruments can be secured by using the comments made during the course of the 1985 survey. Several participants in the UK had used both instruments and were therefore able to compare by direct experience (though the LSI users were all referring to the original version). The major advantages of the LSI were seen to be the fact that it could be completed very quickly, that the results could be mapped directly on to the Kolb learning cycle, and, of course, in some cases that the tutors using it were very familiar with it and could easily respond to questions.

The advantages of the Honey/Mumford LSQ were seen to be the direct rather than two-stage route to styles, and that the questions were also more clearly about managerial behaviour and provided a more credible base for managers. The associated statements about preferred learning processes were seen to give a direct entry to the subject of learning. The variety of norms available for different kinds of manager and managerial functions was a useful extra. In terms of the guidance available in the books and other material, the significant difference is probably that the Kolb guide is explicitly directed at training situations, whereas the Honey/Mumford approach covers a much wider range of potential uses on and off the job.

The LSQ would, whatever its other features in comparison with the LSI, seem to be particularly appropriate to self-development activities for this latter reason. The Kolb book, however, gives much more substantial treatment of conceptual issues about learning.

The Choice of Approach

There has been much more emphasis on the use of material about learning styles than about blockages. Although I may have been influenced by my own work, it was the case in the survey that most people had worked through learning styles and not through blockages. A review of the literature also shows that styles not blockages appear in articles by practitioners.

It was also the case that most people had used either the LSI or the LSQ rather than not using an instrument at all. Those people who had used an instrument saw it as a useful starting point for discussion which could then be used as a basis for shared data and language. Like many questionnaires it was seen as a relatively low-level, low-risk starting point which was necessary before some of the more personal and perhaps higher-level issues could be discussed. It was found that for some managers the revelation that they were not poor learners as such, but rather sometimes ineffective learners in certain activities because of their style, was both a relief and a starting point for improvement. The availability of norms which provide comparative data was found to be helpful in providing some fixed bench-marks. This also leads to further useful discussion, particularly on issues which might be less individual and personal and more about organizational or cultural factors.

However, some participants in the survey did not find the use of either instrument helpful, either in prospect or in actuality. They felt that the reduction of individual complexity as a learner to four styles was an inappropriate simplification. Sometimes they also felt that individuals might reject learning opportunities without considering them seriously simply because they did not fit what they had learned about their own learning style. When faced with these disadvantages, those who had used instruments confirmed that such issues might exist and certainly had to be resolved by careful discussion of the detail of descriptions and of action. The dangers referred to were believed to exist more in those circumstances where people filled in the questionnaires with no significant further discussion.

Some descriptions of ways in which these instruments can be used are now gradually appearing in the literature, extending beyond or sometimes confirming the description given by the original authors.[9,10,11,12] The basic processes mainly follow a tutor-led pattern (which some might find in conflict with some self-development preferences):

(i) Tutor distributes the instrument before or at an early stage of a programme.

(ii) Tutor analyses scores, shares results with the students and shows norms.

(iii) Tutor leads discussion on the results and perhaps gives formal input on the model or theory behind the results.

(iv) Individuals break into small groups for exchange of discussion on results or consequences.

(v) Students prepare some plan for further development of their learning processes.

This sequence may be accompanied or followed by sessions updating the discussion, or alternatively the trainer may bring out issues arising during the programme as a means of reinforcing the learning that has occurred. This latter process can, of course, be particularly powerful since it brings out issues which are both very specific and very real and usually clearly known to members of the programme. Equally, however, they may be additionally risky since they can well involve issues affecting other members of the tutorial staff.

Most of the contributors to the survey discussed the application of these instruments in a course context. It is possible to use both LSI and LSQ with individuals outside a course as part of the process of identifying their personal development needs, a particularly important feature for self-development. This might arise during an appraisal discussion or as a precursor to a discussion of development needs or before a course. Some advisers may even have the satisfying but relatively luxurious opportunity to help managers by observing their behaviour at work and relating this to learning styles.

Non-instrumented Approaches

It is quite feasible, and for some people may be preferable, to approach learning to learn through a general discussion rather than through an instrument. Students can be asked to go through a four stage process such as:

(i) identifying their most successful past learning experience;

(ii) identifying their least successful past learning experience;

(iii) reviewing barriers to personal learning;

(iv) developing personal learning plans.

Clearly this approach has an advantage where either the tutor or the prospective participants are not enamoured of questionnaires. The information can be discussed in pairs, trios or small groups and the group exchange can lead to the development of a learning contract between individuals or within the group or with the tutor. This approach clearly has strong connections with, and probably was first used in the UK by, the originators of the self-development philosophy and some illustrations are given in Pedler[13]. It has the substantial advantage of not working to predetermined definitions of style, of not requiring that people are placed in apparently over-neat descriptions. It has the major philosophical advantage of placing the major responsibility on the learners themselves to identify their answers, rather than imposing predigested issues and statements from outside. Some tutors, and some learners, may prefer this approach. It may lead in some cases to a deeper approach to learning – or in others to a relatively superficial discussion, if the learners are not in fact able or willing to work in depth.

Combined Approaches

Clearly the use of instruments can be combined with a variety of other forms of discussion. The instrument could precede or follow the kind of approach outlined above as a general discussion. A particularly powerful combination can be produced where the learner is asked to complete a learning log or learning diary. A significant virtue of this approach is again that it leads naturally to, and indeed often depends on, experience on the job and its learning lessons rather than relying purely on course-based phenomena. Learning logs have been around for quite a long time and it is perhaps surprising that more has not been written about them. The learning log may be used as shown by Peter Honey[14] in relation to learning styles. However, it could also be used as a means of reviewing and attacking blockages to learning other than those revealed through learning styles.

A learning log requirement is built in to the Master of Business Administration programme run by the International Management Centre at Buckingham. Although this demonstrates the importance we attach to learning, our experience has shown that participants have to be given substantial guidance and encouragement to record and monitor their learning processes in the most useful way. We have to remember that for most managers, let alone most managers with particular styles of learning, the process involved in writing down experiences and reflecting on them is not one which managers will see naturally as valuable, nor one for which they will receive either internalized or external rewards. The learning style predictions are confirmed: strong Reflectors appreciate the process, strong Activists do not. However, establishing the requirements helps the Activist to take more seriously a process he would otherwise ignore.

This last point brings out an issue of great significance both generally and in the self-development context. It is of prime importance to establish and relate to the different learning style preferences held by individuals. If, however, they are offered only those activities congruent with existing preferences, then their learning will be limited. Far better then that they should be helped to build their skills around the whole learning cycle.

The point made here, however, is that this will not be achieved, as some course organizers apparently hope, simply by providing a mixed menu of different kinds of learning activities. Unless individuals are made conscious of their own approach to learning, and are given opportunities to work on their abilities, some parts of the mixed menu will remain undigested.

Combining Learning and Reality

Learning logs reveal a fact of life which we have to bear in mind for the whole learning to learn process. The results of learning are often difficult to determine, and the rewards from having learned effectively are often perceived as either minimal or uncomfortable. For all these reasons the application of learning to learn as a matter of principle and designated time on programmes is not necessarily high on the list of issues to which managers will give high priority. It is therefore desirable to attach the learning to learn process to a more strongly felt need. I was impressed with two examples of how to do this in work done in the UK[9] and USA[15].

Some Specific Applications

Substantial guidance on what to do and how to do it is available in the references, and I strongly recommend that anyone moving into the field for the first time does read the books and articles, not least because there are so few that this does not represent an intensive burden. However, it may be helpful if I add to that material by quoting four cases from my survey.

Case A

Participants on an MBA programme are given the LSQ before they are accepted on the programme. The results are used in the following sequence:

  (i) Individuals with strong learning preferences are identified and 'shared' between small groups who will work together during the programme.

 (ii) During the first few days of the initial residential period participants are asked to review their own learning preferences following an introductory description of the theory and the detail of learning styles. They are asked to exchange in their small groups information about their learning preferences and to discuss the likely impact of this on them as individuals and on the group.

(iii) Information about learning styles is related then to two experiences of learning. First, participants are asked to review their past learning experiences, establish which were the most significant and useful and to try and identify a relationship to learning styles. They are also asked to review the learning experiences they have had so far on the programme, and again to relate these to the predictions made through learning styles.

(iv) Finally they are asked to note personal action points, which they may do as part of a general learning log or through the booklet *Using Your Learning Styles*.

Case B

  (i) Participants are issued with either the LSI or the LSQ on the first day of a management programme. They complete the questionnaire immediately and then their results are charted in front of the whole group. The results and what they mean in relation to the description of the styles are then discussed either in the full group or in small groups. Participants are given the task of discussing what the results mean and what action individuals should take during the programme and later.

(ii) All small groups later in the programme are chosen openly in relation to the individual results.

(iii) It has been found more effective to provide a good mix of results rather than to provide groups dominated by one style. Individuals have been found to learn more from exposure to other styles than they do from being placed with predominantly similar people.

(iv) As a further element in the programme, participants are placed in pairs during and at the end of the programme to review their exhibited learning preferences and to identify future action plans.

Case C

(i) Flip chart descriptions of the four Honey/Mumford learning styles are put up in four corners of a conference room. Participants are invited to stand next to the description which most accords with their self-perception. Their preference is recorded and they may even be given labels showing this.

(ii) They then complete the LSQ, score it and compare their score with the prediction on the original description. The benefits of this are said to be that participants are motivated to discuss in detail the reasons for differences and to identify the specific behaviours which they now believe to be predominant and valid.

(iii) This process has the advantage of getting away from the somewhat cold introduction by means of early completion of the questionnaire.

Case D

In this example neither of the instruments is used.

(i) The tutor waits during a programme for experiences and problems to emerge which can be used as a factor for focussing discussion of learning issues.

(ii) The tutor may take, for example, a group which has either improved on performance on a task compared with earlier experience, or one which has done no better and use that as a vehicle for talking about learning.

(iii) The tutor will discuss with group members what is happening within the group in terms of those members who seem to be particularly involved and turned on by the activity being undertaken, and again use that as a means of generating discussion on learning processes. He will use analogies from the need to be creative and develop an understanding of learning to learn from these particular experiences within the programme.

(iv) Such an approach obviously requires great flexibility, deftness in analysis and real commitment to introducing the subject.

A major virtue of the 'learning biography' approach is that it enables the designer of learning activities to integrate current learning processes with previous events and activities. This has been well described for a particular workshop by Robinson [16]. The same virtue, of integrating learning with felt managerial needs, exists in the process of using reality through an assessment process such as that described by Daloisio[15] or Honey and Povah[17].

Physicians Healing Themselves

The final issue arises with the tutor's own preferred approach to learning, since this will almost certainly express itself in a preferred approach to how others should learn. Those who are offering to guide others in self-development ought to be particularly conscious of their own learning preferences, in case these are in any way limiting what they are offering. Facilitators of self-development ought, however, to be not only effective designers through this self-consciousness, but also effective exemplars of the processes of learning – see Honey[14].

A Checklist for Action

The following points should help in providing guidance on what to do.

(i) Are you aware of your own learning experiences and preferences? How do you use this knowledge in developing yourself and others?

(ii) Do you have a definition of learning which you use in designing or recommending learning activities? Does it need to be changed?

(iii) Do you include 'learning how to learn' as an explicit subject and process in your self-development work?

(iv) What is your view on the significance of organizational and personal blockages to learning? Do you need to do more to help overcome them?

 (v) Do your present processes take sufficient account of different preferences in the learner's approach to learning?

(vi) If further action on learning to learn is desirable who has to be convinced and how may this best be done?

(vii) Would it be appropriate to work on the skills of learning on any of your programmes?

(viii) How could you engage managers on a real commitment to learning to learn? What activities can be used to generate this commitment?

(ix) Which of the strategies (theory first or activity first) would be most appropriate for which of your programmes?

 (x) Which of the processes, e.g. with or without diagnostic instruments for working on learning to learn, will be most appropriate for which programmes?

(xi) How would you monitor and evaluate actions on learning to learn?

References

1. Mumford, A. (1986) Learning to learn. *Journal of European Industrial Training,* **10**(2).
2. Mumford, A. *et al.* (1987) *Developing Directors.* Manpower Services Commission. Sheffield, UK.
3. Boydell, T. and Temporal, P. (1981) *Helping Managers to Learn* Sheffield Polytechnic, Sheffield, UK.
4. Stuart, R. (1984) *Maximising Managers Day-to-Day Learning in Management Development* Cox, C. and Beck, J. (eds) Wiley, London.
5. Kolb, D. (1983) *Experiential Learning.* Prentice-Hall.
6. Kolb, D. (1985) *User's Guide.* McBer and Company, Boston.
7. Honey, P. and Mumford, A. (1982) *Manual of Learning Style.* Honey.
8. Honey, P. and Mumford, A. (1983) *Using Your Learning Style.* Honey.
9. Richardson, J. and Bennett, B. (1984) Applying learning techniques. *Journal of European Industrial Training,* **8**(1,3,4).
10. Canning, R. (19) Management self-development. *Journal of European Industrial Training,* **8**(1).
11. Scriven, R. (19) Learning circles. *Journal of European Industrial Training,* **8**(1).

12. Rae, L. (1986) Application of learning styles. *Industrial and Commercial Training,* **18**(2).
13. Pedler, M., Burgoyne, J. and Boydell, T. (1986) *Manager's Guide to Self-Development* (2nd ed.). McGraw Hill, Maidenhead, UK.
14. Honey, P. (1984) Learning styles and self-development. Training and Development (UK) Jan.
15. Daloisio, T. and Firestone, M. (1983) Speaking from experience. Training and Development (USA) Feb.
16. Robinson, L. (1984) Supporting self-help in management development. *Industrial and Commercial Training,* **16**(1).
17. Honey, P. and Povah, N. (1986) Self-development – overcoming the paradox. *Industrial and Commercial Training,* **18**(4).

3

Self-managed Learning in Organizations

*   *   *

ALAN MOSSMAN AND RORY STEWART

Introduction

An Organizational Example

For some years now British Airways has had a Mission Statement for the business as a whole. Each manager has his or her own key results which contribute to achieving that Mission. BA's Young Professionals' Programme is designed to enable the airline's top graduate entry to:

(i) specify, agree and revise as appropriate their key results;

(ii) sort out what they need to achieve these;

(iii) enable them to satisfy those needs;

(iv) review and assess their performance and learning as they work on their key results.

An Individual Example

Three years ago Pat Russell (not her real name) was acting head of residential care for the elderly in a local authority social services department. Her former boss, an autocrat, had just retired early on medical grounds. Pat had just started a management course which allowed her to design her own curriculum. She chose to develop two things:

(i) the autonomy of the heads of homes who reported to her; and

(ii) the quality of the dignity and respect experienced by the elderly in those homes.

Working on these areas required her to develop a range of related skills and knowledge – in her *learning contract* she committed herself to developing a more participative management style and improving her budgeting, delegation, team building, training, liaison with other departments, relations with the trade union and marketing. During the course, Pat also worked on disciplinary issues and acted as a consultant to other managers in her learning set on topics such as interviewing, time management, micro-politics and the management of change.

Pat was appointed Head after she had been acting in that role for a year and her staff threw a party to celebrate her appointment. At the end of her course she and her learning set had to agree whether or not she should get a post-graduate diploma. Prior to that stage she chose to involve her boss and other senior officers, her admin. officer, heads of homes, as well as a trade union rep, in assessing appropriate parts of her learning so as to provide evidence to her set of the progress she had made.

Self-managed Learning

Both the British Airways programme and Pat's course use the principles of self-managed learning* developed by Ian Cunningham and his colleagues at North East London Polytechnic. Pat was on the Post-Graduate Diploma in Management (by SML) at NELP. The PGDip has been running since 1980 and SML principles have been explicitly used as the basis for in-house programmes in both the public and private sector since 1983.

*We will use the following abbreviations throughout the chapter:
  (i) self-managed learning = SML;
  (ii) North East London Polytechnic = NELP;
  (iii) Post-Graduate Diploma in Management by SML = PGDip.

Our purpose in this paper is to give our view of what self-managed learning is and to outline some of the problems and some of the advantages associated with running SML programmes in-house. As SML can be used to enable a wide variety of people to learn new skills, knowledge or ways of being, in this chapter we shall generally refer to learners rather than managers, participants, professionals or other traditional titles. (This is because SML is 'content free' – there is no prescribed curriculum for the learner to follow.) Instead SML offers learners a structure and a process with which to pursue whatever it is they need to learn or develop.

We perceive the need in many organizations for people to relearn how to be creative, independent and inter-dependent. To do this people need to develop their ability to learn from experience, to survive in the existing environment and to grow. (We recognize that this process *may be difficult* for both the individual and the organization to manage in the short term and yet we feel that the rewards are likely to far outweigh the costs.) We believe such people will be more fulfilled and effective in their jobs, more entrepreneurial (or intra-preneurial), and set higher standards when appropriate.

We see SML as one of a number of initiatives which an organization might take to develop *itself* as a learning system.

What is SML?

Self-managed learning (SML) is an approach to management development which enables managers to be more aware of:

(i)   how they achieve key results using live work issues . . .

(ii) while controlling the content, processes and pace of their own learning . . .

(iii) with a group of other managers who are collectively responsible for assessing their own progress . . .

(iv) within a structured programme facilitated by an adviser.

Principles

The approach is based on a number of principles. These are expressed as an agreement between learner and trainer (or set adviser):

Learners:

(i) are responsible for their own learning;

(ii) have the *right* to and are responsible for identifying their own learning needs, and for changing them over time;

(iii) have the *right* to and are responsible for negotiating how they meet their learning needs within the available learning resources;

(iv) are responsible for evaluating and assessing their own learning.

Set advisers:

(i) are responsible for helping the learners realize their individual responsibility for their own learning;

(ii) are responsible for providing access to the available learning resources;

(iii) have the right to and are responsible for determining their own personal involvement in the provision of learning resources (referral is acceptable);

(iv) have the right to and are responsible for evaluating the whole programme and their own effectiveness.

These principles give rise to the *process* of self-managed learning through which the learner personally works out *what* is to be learnt and *how* it is to be learnt, in conjunction with others.

Applications

SML has been used with board-level managers as well as recent graduates, with *ad hoc* groups and existing teams (see Fig. 3.1 on this and the following page). What is important is that they are all volunteers, understand the processes involved and have the necessary commitment before starting. Evolved over the last decade, its roots are in humanistic psychology, self-development, action learning, and independent study.

NELP *North East London Polytechnic* where it all started back in 1979. Since 1980 the Poly has offered a Post-Graduate Diploma in Management (by SML) run along these lines (see NELP[1,2,3] and Cunningham[4]). This programme is included because a major part of the learning goes on at work and as the original and longest running SML programme it is a useful source of comparisons.

XPC   *Xylem Polymer Corporation* (not its real name) – the first attempt to run a totally in-house programme. The one XPC set ran for 12 months with the six sales and service managers of one division who worked from 4 locations from Strathclyde to Surrey.

GEC   The software engineering division of one of the *GEC* companies has run a number of SML type groups beginning while the training manager was on the NELP PGDip.

SSB   *Sarawak Shell Berhad* is a Shell operating company in East Malaysia (Borneo). SSB's first set (Satu Tenaga) began in 1984 as a self-development group and has now spawned two more sets. Satu Tenaga celebrated its 100th meeting in October 1986.

ABC   The *Aberleigh Borough Council* (not its real name) set involved all six members of the top finance team – director, deputy and 4 assistant directors.

BA   *British Airways Young Professional's Programme* is aimed at new graduates recruited into the airline. The 6 month YPP is their induction course. Their focus for the first six months is the airline and how they can operate effectively within it.

LBN   The *London Borough of Newham's* housing department have combined with two other London borough housing departments to offer SML style sets for housing managers.

MEHA   *Mid-Essex Health Authority* are currently (April '87) setting up a joint programme with Essex County Council social services and involving housing and voluntary organization staff who need to work together. The focus for the first programme (24 managers working in 3 sets and starting in April 1987) is 'Joint Care Planning', management and personal development. (There are also two other SML initiatives currently being pursued in NE Thames Regional Health Authority.)

Figure 3.1 **Organizational applications of SML referred to during the paper.**

Issues for In-house SML Programmes

Running SML programmes in a single organization poses a number of special problems concerning process and outcome. On the PGDip programme the managers come from a wide variety of corporate cultures. This is valuable as each cultural perspective tends to throw up a different range of questions and challenges. In addition the different backgrounds of managers has lead to some interesting cross-fertilization of ideas such as local government officers like Pat Russell using a marketing perspective to help them think about what they are doing. On an in-house programme these effects are likely to be muted unless it is decided to open the programme up to managers from other local organizations with different cultures and objectives. One of the things that excites us is the recent crop of multi-organization in-house SML programmes (e.g. MEHA, LBN).

The comments which follow are based on our experience in organizations of different sizes and cultures. We shall group our comments under four headings (see also Fig. 3.2):

(i) *Getting in* – negotiating the programme;

(ii) *Getting started* – the initial meetings of sets and contract forming;

(iii) *Getting on* – subsequent meetings, resources and so on;

(iv) *Getting out* – assessing achievements, celebrating the group's successes and winding it up.

Getting in

Access to run an in-house SML programme is likely to be negotiated like any other approach to developing managers. From some there will be demand, from others resistance, and from most indifference. The resistance is likely to come from those senior managers who prefer to use their personal or organizational power to get things done. They will perceive, we think correctly, that this particular approach is likely to develop staff who know their own minds and are prepared to stand up for what they believe in. Others will recognize that it might show up their own weaknesses. The demand will come from managers who want to develop the autonomy, initiative and flexibility of their staff (for whatever reason).

Finding set advisers could be a problem in some organizations, at least initially. Working as a set adviser (SA) on an SML programme requires a very different set of attitudes and skills from those required of a traditional lecturer or trainer (see Fig. 3.3), and is not something

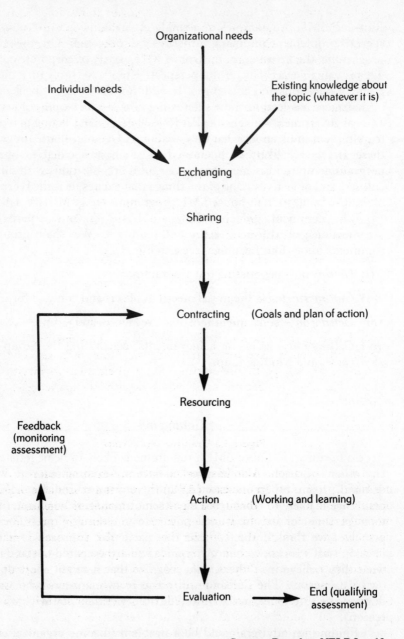

Figure 3.2 A map of the process of SML.

everyone can do. It is very difficult for those who are used to 'telling' or lecturing to stop doing that and to allow managers to muddle through, to wallow, etc. – in other words to allow and enable people to learn from their own mistakes. Cunningham[4] (p. 161) sees the staff role generally as the crucial determinant of the success of SML programmes.

Alan and his colleagues at NELP have been running workshops for set advisers for some years now. They have noticed that some line managers can often learn to be set advisers more easily than many college tutors. Such line managers are generally among the more competent and sensitive in the organization. They:

(i) find it easier to avoid being trapped in their 'subject';

(ii) are less likely to try to manipulate the problem to fit their particular subject speciality;

(iii) are less threatened by not having any subject expertise; and

(iv) are motivated by the realization that set facilitation skills can help them back on the job as well as in the set.

Experience at NELP suggests that being a self-managed learner is a good way to start learning how to set advise. This has provided a good experience base for getting the most out of a set adviser training workshop. Before starting sets in their own organizations some learners have become co-set advisers with an experienced staff member.

Figure 3.3 Training set advisers.

On two occasions Alan has worked with pre-existing teams trying to use SML principles. In one case (ABC) there was a reasonable degree of openness and they got through a significant amount of business. In the meetings they tended to work on corporate issues in preference to personal ones though the boundary between the two was somewhat blurred. That team subsequently reported that they could operate more effectively even though they lost two out of six members for a period.

In the second case (XPC) improved team working was reported as the prime benefit. This group reported to a general manager whom they perceived as autocratic and who they felt had insisted on their participation in the programme. There was very little personal development apparent from this group. It is not clear to what extent their perceptions of the divisional culture influenced this. We outline another explanation in Box 4 below. XPC set members were happiest working on collective problems. This was the first in-house programme Alan ran and he chose not to insist on formal contracts. Alan now feels that contracts would have helped him to clarify what were personal and what collective issues. He could then insist that the agenda be related to individual learning goals so that any topic is fully 'owned' by at least one set member and covered by a learning task in that manager's contract.

Getting started

An important part of getting started is defining the needs, setting a bench-mark and writing the contract. A number of things can make that process more difficult. Having the members of a set all from one organization may lead to problems around self-disclosure, trust and confidentiality (see Fig. 3.4). All three are important to successful SML.

At XPC at least one member, Jo, did not feel safe to talk about issues in her territory because of the presence of someone else from the same territory. She believed that this person, given half a chance, would sabotage ideas which he didn't like, so she didn't talk about any ideas she was developing that might be jeopardized in this way. It was only at the end of the programme that Alan learned that other members of the set knew of this situation and refrained from raising similar issues so as not to put their colleague under pressure. It seems that the group members used the confidentiality ground rule to block *any* discussion of what went on in the group with outsiders, including their general manager – this was not helpful.

Figure 3.4 Confidentiality at XPC.

In our experience SML has not worked very well where there has appeared to be an element of compulsion to attend the programme. For a start there is likely to be far less self-disclosure by those who feel compelled and this could affect the degree to which the volunteers are willing to risk disclosing things about themselves.

One of the key ideas underlying SML is that people learn in different ways – and it is important to remember that there are many other ways to learn than SML and that some people may prefer them. Others may well prefer to work only on cosmetic changes rather than deep ones affecting their personal attitudes and beliefs.

There are various ways to begin the process of working towards a contract. Some are given in Fig. 3.5.

1. *Beginning with biography.* The opening residential of the MEHA programme will have a strong focus on content – 'Joint Care Planning'. To counter this and to establish the emphasis in the sets on individual learner-centred programmes, some detailed biography work based on the ideas of Malcolm Leary and others[5] is being used as part of the contract development phase.

2. *Self-disclosure.* In SSB the key 'icebreaker' was the 'Coat of Arms' exercise. This worked much better than the Woodcock and Francis[6] 'Blockages Questionnaire' with a predominantly Malaysian group.

3. *Self-rating.* Working with fairly homogeneous groups of software engineers in GEC, Libby Arnold had participants list the skills and knowledge required in their type of job. When these were typed up, set members were asked to rate the items in terms of importance for their own job and in terms of the extent to which they had the relevant skill and knowledge. This has worked well as the basis for discussion and for individual contracts. As the GEC sets have tended to be existing work groups set members have been able to get significant feedback on their self-assessments.

Figure 3.5 Three beginnings.

Many learners have found the following five questions a useful next step from their starting point:

(i) Where have I come from?

(ii) Where am I now?

(iii) Where do I want to get to?

(iv) How will I know if I have arrived?

(v) How will I get there?

These five questions use a journey metaphor which might not be right for everyone and it is quite easy to reinterpret them in terms of a different metaphor – working with an architectural practice a design metaphor might be appropriate.

Managers seem to like to start by focussing their attention on learning 'hard' skills and on work tasks – focussing on the 'skin' in the diagram in Fig. 3.6. This is not surprising as it is what most other courses and programmes claim to do: it fits their expectations and they feel safer.

Then, as their feelings of trust and safety in the group develop, they revise their learning tasks so that they review and involve an increasing proportion of their personal 'core' so as to promote congruity between themselves as people and their managerial selves. It is in this way that SML is, in Pedler's terms, 'whole life and job related' (see below).

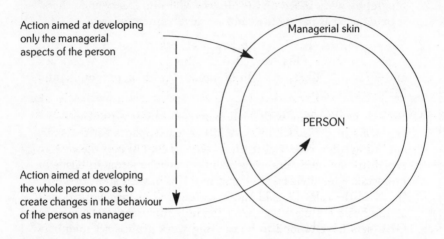

Action aimed at developing only the managerial aspects of the person

Managerial skin

PERSON

Action aimed at developing the whole person so as to create changes in the behaviour of the person as manager

Figure 3.6 The person as manager – two distinct types of learning activity.

In addition to the gradual shift of focus as illustrated in Box 6, sets have to learn how to operate effectively together. They have to learn what works for them. To some degree the set adviser can help them choose the right direction though it is often important for the set members to discover some things for themselves (see Fig. 3.7).

Early in the life of the first SSB set members spent a lot of time choosing what they wanted to do and, through this, learning how valuable such a focus could be. Halfway through this process Fred Young discovered the acronym 'SMART' as a way of testing objectives:

Specific
Measurable
Achievable (i.e. 'Can I do it?')
Reasonable (i.e. 'Should I do it?') and
Timely (i.e. 'Have I both got time enough to plan it and will it happen soon enough to stimulate me?')

When Fred Young used SMART to test his own objectives he realized how unfocussed he was. His experience encouraged others in the set to sharpen up their own objectives and gave them a mechanism for challenging each others'. This has been used by the group ever since.

Figure 3.7 Learning in SSB.

Getting on

One key role for the set adviser at this stage is to get the set members to recognize both the progress they have made and, most importantly, the processes they used to get there. This helps them become more aware of how they learn and gives them an opportunity to do it more effectively. As they transfer these learning skills to other situations their awareness increases and they become increasingly independent of the set adviser.

Running an SML programme within a smaller organization is likely to lead to *resourcing* problems. It may be possible to deal with these through an arrangement with a local management centre, but we do not believe that it is possible to rely on a local public library alone. They are very unlikely to have an adequate range of audio-visual material. BA's idea for 'mentoring' younger managers (see Fig. 3.8) could well be used in other and smaller organizations.

Each of the young professionals has a mentor – an older more experienced person in the organization to whom the learner can turn for advice, counselling and so forth. BA mentors are chosen specifically because they are likely to provide a good role model. The mentor's specialism is the organization, what makes it tick and *how* to make that happen. (This has similarities with the specialist tutor notion.) In BA it is intended that the relationship between the mentor and the young professional should continue well after the YPP and probably into their early 30s.

Figure 3.8 'Mentors' in BA.

During an SML programme some sort of *monitoring assessment* helps set members to keep track of their own and each others' progress. It is a way for the learner to get feedback on work in progress so that 'mid-course' adjustments can be made in good time. It also increases the likelihood that projects will be completed successfully. In programmes with a qualifying assessment stage, monitoring assessment provides an opportunity for a set to develop, experiment with and fine tune its assessment process.

In SSB wives of set members (Yeo Wei is the only woman involved) have also started meeting in their own self-development groups. This developed following a joint weekend meeting facilitated by Rory and his wife Diana and has contributed to the development within the parallel sets as husbands and wives are able to grow and develop at the same rate. We find this development interesting as it emphasizes the 'whole life and job related' nature of SML.

Getting Out: Assessment and Closure

'How am I doing?' is a question frequently asked by managers, particularly younger ones. It seems to us that more mature managers are generally better able to answer this question for themselves and we feel that the ability to evaluate one's own performance is an important step towards personal (not just managerial) maturity.

Assessment is likely to be problematic in most contexts – we think it will be particularly so in smaller organizations bearing in mind the comments we have made about confidentiality. There could be particular problems if promotion is tied to the assessment. Assessment in SML, as we have seen with Pat Russell, is managed by the learners in the context of the set (see Fig. 3.9). This adds to the duration of the process, but the extra period tends to be one of extensive and rapid further learning.

BA's experience suggests how this might be done. The YPP sets agree their assessment process with the airline's management development manager who was in effect the 'external examiner'. He has monitored the process and in the event of sets failing to agree assessments he would be asked to arbitrate. This is in a large company and the learners are newly qualified graduates whose future in the airline depends on their own self-assessment and that of their peers (set adviser and other young professionals) in the set. As in the NELP PGDip the requirement is for concensus within the set so that all set members have equal power (in theory at least).

When more senior managers are involved the confidentiality issues may be more significant. It will be interesting to observe what happens at MEHA.

Figure 3.9 Managing assessment in-house.

Three further differences between SML and 'traditional' programmes become apparent in the final phase of a programme. *First*, closure is not prescribed as it usually is on more traditional courses; *second*, closure may be more like ending one chapter and starting another; and *finally*, within the holistic framework closure is typically more explicit.

Closure is important because, in our experience, many managers live predominantly fire-fighting jobs and rarely experience explicit closure, let alone celebration of accomplishments. This final step in the SML process therefore provides an important model for project completion/ celebration/closure with direct managerial and organizational applicability:

(i) at the organization level it signals progress and opportunities for organizational learning;

(ii) at the managerial level it allows focus by minimizing the number of 'unfinished' items around, giving the chance to move on to the next challenges with minimum distractions;

(iii) at the individual level it provides positive recognition so frequently missing from managers' motivational styles.

For any SML group planning its own ending the key tasks can be summarized:

(i) *Looking back* – reviewing achievements, growth and development.

(ii) *Looking forwards* – thinking about what comes next and relating past learning to it.

(iii) *Being here* – being in touch with the feelings associated with the 'wake'.

For example:

(i) Learners may develop new contracts with themselves. Returning to the journey metaphor they might ask:

'Where am I now compared to when I started?' (*Being here* and *Looking back*);
'Where do I want to get to from now?' (*Looking forward*);
'How will I get there?' (*Looking forward*);
'Who and what has helped me to get here?' (a summary of the key learning (*Being here* and *Looking back*) and particularly useful when planning similar tasks in the future).

(ii) Decisions on any continuing meetings: one NELP set has continued for nearly five years since they got their diplomas with the set adviser now a full set member, and the XPC group continued to meet as a self-development group after the programme (*Looking forward*).

(iii) Feedback to each other based on the substantial knowledge and insight built up over time in the group (*Looking back* and *Being here*).

(iv) A time for appreciations for all group members, and a time to recognize and celebrate the 'movement' and progress that individuals have made (*Looking back* and *Being here*).

We believe that it is useful, from very near the start, to negotiate some criteria for ending. These may include dates, events, group membership, etc., and are as open to review during the set meetings as are the learning contracts (see Fig. 3.10).

SSB celebrated the closure marked by the departure of an early member on transfer, and built on this experience to mark their next transition on Rory's departure. They did three things for closure and reincarnation:

(i) Worked on the business issues in the group by:

   (a) completing a questionnaire about the progress in the group so far,

   (b) deciding on the issue of continuing with another set adviser,

   (c) deciding how to manage the closure;

(ii) held a farewell party with partners;

(iii) ran the two final meetings, with the new set adviser, giving a round of feedback and appreciation from each member to every other. They also gave Rory a memorial gift.

Figure 3.10 Closure at SSB.

The Organizational Benefits (and Where They Come From)

(i) *Managers work on issues, problems and opportunities particular to their situation and their employing organization.* These are both the starting point for deciding what they want to learn, and the acid test of their success.

(ii) *Managers are offered opportunities to explore and take considered risks with the support and challenge of their set.* This follows from benefit (i) and from the climate developed in the set. The set members will compare the manager's outcomes with his or her progress to date, and one frequent discussion centres on helping him or her to identify areas where he or she can take risks, but manage the level of risk appropriately.

(iii) *Learning and working are integrated – a lot of learning takes place on the job and a lot of work gets done in the set.* One of the set adviser's roles is to make the connection between work and learning visible, and to assist set members to explore the learning available to them in commonplace or unusual work situations.

(iv) *Managers review their own progress and can change direction as they develop, or as their organization itself changes and develops.* This comes out of point (iii) and from the focus on setting and reviewing outcomes against which progress may be measured.

(v) *Managers meet at mutually convenient times.* Unlike conventional 'timetabled' training, the set is responsible for agreeing their own meeting times, duration and frequency.

(vi) *Managers learn more about how they learn so they are able to go on learning new things and developing their flexibility after the course.* Because they improve their skills both at spotting learning opportunities at work and at generalizing that learning to wider contexts.

(vii) *Learning is long term, broad based and at a variety of levels as it tends to take place over a number of iterations of a do-review-adjust cycle which requires the learner to consider a variety of initially peripheral issues connected with the successful imple-mentation.* This stems from the emphasis on reviewing and challenging in the group, and from discovering that the original outcomes either need to be reset, or cannot be achieved without taking the peripheral issues into account.

(viii) *Learning is often shared with the manager's staff and other colleagues.* Being used to discussing learning in the set, the manager will feel freer to talk with others. He or she is also much more likely now to see staff difficulties, problems or mistakes as opportunities for mutual learning rather than recrimination.

(ix) *Managers develop consultancy and meeting management skills which they can use back on the job and particularly in the development of their own people.* The need to advise and challenge other set members builds these interactive skills.

(x) *Managers are generally better able to integrate their home and work lives.* The holistic approach in the set, the 'getting started' activities, and the extension of the set over a substantial time, make it OK to raise and work on these issues.

An issue for trainers to recognize is that SML programmes may result in a small number of managers deciding that they do not fit in the organization and so leave. * It may well be that the people who do this are good at their jobs, yet they come to realize that they could be more fulfilled elsewhere. At one level that is a loss to the organization. At another the organization has an opportunity to promote someone who is suited and committed. It is not yet clear whether the SML approach is more likely to lead to this outcome than other programmes. On the face of it, it would seem that the holistic emphasis within the programme is more likely to encourage people to review their life and work together.

The Structural Elements of SML

An SML programme offers individual learners a clearly articulated structure designed to help them learn, become conscious of their own learning processes and to assess their progress and effectiveness. They do this while dealing with current responsibilities at work. We believe that to be successful the necessary elements of that structure are:

(i) *Sets:* groups of four to six learners with a set adviser. Sets meet regularly – say every two or three weeks (less frequently and continuity is lost) – to develop individual learning contracts (or key results) and then to review learning and assess progress against the criteria set out in contracts.

(ii) *The set adviser:* a trained facilitator who provides the initial structure for the set and helps the set members learn how to support and confront one another and how to be advisors or consultants to each other.

The key role of the set adviser is to *assist the learner.* Set advisers are likely to:

(a) offer set members a degree of structure (e.g. frequency and duration of meetings, ground rules for working within the meetings);

---

* By the same token organizations who recruit people who have been involved in SML programmes are likely to encounter people who know more about who they are, where they are going and how to manage the synergy between their personal and their work lives.

(b) offer ideas about how to begin the process of identifying learning needs (e.g. diagnostic exercises);

(c) do some personal disclosing in the early part of the programme as a way of modelling behaviour which is generally helpful in the context of SML;

(d) provide support to set members if others in the set are not doing that; and

(e) offer supportive confrontation if that is not forthcoming from others.

Set advisers will not normally direct the set. Rather they will make clear that the learners can take leadership roles in the set, take the initiative and above all take responsibility for managing their own learning.

Often course members who themselves want to be set advisers serve an apprenticeship as a *co-set adviser,* working alongside an experienced set adviser. This is generally valuable for both parties.

(iii) *The learning contract* in which the individual learner specifies his or her own learning 'task(s)'. Learning tasks can range from conventional study, research and/or personal growth work to 'action learning' style projects. It is common for learners to set out with one goal in mind and then to *learn* that they need to change goals and hence to change their contract.

(iv) *Resources*: workbooks, films, colleagues and specialists in the workplace, courses, study guides, books, technology, etc., which the learners can use to help them achieve whatever they have specified.

Every self-managed learner has access to his or her own personal and organizational networks. Different organizations have supplemented these resources in various ways, ranging from providing personal budgets to contacts with educational or training institutes.

(v) *Assessment.* Learning contracts will usually specify the criteria for the assessment of each topic, task or item. In addition to this, each set can develop its own criteria and standards for assessing its members *overall* performance. Overall (or qualifying) assessment is an important part of the NELP, BA and MEHA programmes. It is externally refereed and, among other things, helps the learners to sharpen and develop their personal criteria for success (and as we have seen with Pat Russell this can involve reference to others).

Ian Cunningham has argued that some form of overall assessment is necessary for effective self-managed learning as it focusses the mind and creates closure.

The above will be features whether there is just one set or many. There are advantages for the learners and the set advisers if there are a number of sets linked into a 'learning community' – a community of people who temporarily work together to further mutual learning. In that case some additional structure will help to promote the learning community and to enhance the learning opportunities for learners, set advisers and others. These additional features include *community meetings, special interest groups, networking* (see Fig. 3.11) *residentials* and *specialist tutorial (or mentor) support*. Almost all of these features contribute to the cross-fertilization of ideas between course members and between sets.

One of the critical learnings in Satu Tenaga, the original SSB set, was the value of asking for help. This is most clearly evidenced in what happened when the MD asked Selva, Chair of the Malaysian Senior Staff Council (and a member of the set), for ideas on how to reduce costs (SSB had a directive from Head Office to reduce costs by at least 17%). Selva used Satu Tenaga to brainstorm ideas and then to help him make a presentation to the management team. The presentation team 'fishbowled' their presentation with the rest of the set and then used four groups of outsiders to provide a critique on their presentation as they developed it.

Figure 3.11 Networking in SSB.

Conclusions

In this chapter we have outlined the process and key features of SML and connected it to current thinking about management development. We have provided some specific examples of its application – totally in-house, in multi-organization SML and via the NELP PGDip (all of these involve substantial learning on the job and for our purposes are 'in-house') – to illustrate some of the issues involved in running in-house SML.

We have particularly focussed on the need for and role of set advisers, the principles which support their agreement with the learners and the ability that SML offers to each learner to tackle almost any topic, opportunity, problem or experience.

What we have said seems to add up to two things:

(i) first that SML 'reaches those parts that other programmes cannot reach'; and

(ii) second that the approach is one way to enable the 'organization' to reflect on and learn from its own development; organization members (the learners) do this and feed the information back into the organization.

References

1. NELP (1980) *Post Graduate Diploma in Management (by Self Managed Learning) Course Submission.* North East London Polytechnic, London.
2. NELP (1986) *Manage Your Own Learning: Post Graduate Diploma in Management (by Self Managed Learning) Handbook* (SML Handbook) North East London Polytechnic, London.
3. NELP(1987) *Writing about SML – Articles and Letters about the Self Managed Learning Programme at NELP.* North East London Polytechnic, London.
4. Cunningham, I. (1986) Self managed learning. In Mumford, A. (1986) (ed.) *Handbook of Management Development*, 2nd edn., pp. 145–162. Gower, Aldershot, UK.
5. Leary, M. *et al.* (1986) *The Qualities of Managing: A Report on a Project Sponsored by the Manpower Services Commission.* Manpower Services Commission, Sheffield, UK.
6. Woodcock, M. and Francis, D. (1982) *The Unblocked Manager.* Gower/ Wildwood House, Aldershot, UK.

4

Open and Distance Learning and the Use of New Technology for the Self-Development of Managers

*   *   *

DON BINSTED

Open and Distance Learning

There is some ambiguity about the meaning of 'open' learning and 'distance' learning, and in current common usage the two expressions might appear to be synonymous. Should the Open University really be called the 'Distance University'? This prompts me first to suggest some clarification of open and distance learning based on the work of Coffey[1] and Holmberg[2] and my own research.[3]

The fundamental characteristic of distance learning is the separation of the tutor and the learner (hence the distance). My colleague, Vivien Hodgson,[4] identifies two different types of distance learning programme: those which are based on materials and those which are based on learner-groups. These can be distinguished as follows:

(i) Materials based programmes:

   (a) involve the use of at least one form of media (print, video, computer output on a VDU, etc.);

   (b) are often designed for solo learners (although use by two or three learners together may be advantageous);

   (c) need some sort of delivery system;

   (d) can be used anywhere (but only if delivery hardware is available).

(ii) Learner-group based programmes:

(a) are based on learner groups or 'sets'[5] (where learners take responsibility not only for their own learning but for others in the group);

(b) nevertheless, for most of the time learners work on their own;

(c) learning has a strong base in work activities.

Learner-group based programmes are not always recognized for what they are, and in this chapter the use of technology will be in the context of materials based programmes.

Open learning is mostly to do with choice. For example, it involves learners having:

(i) choice about the learning goals they wish to pursue;

(ii) choice about the sequence or depth of learning they wish to pursue;

(iii) choice about learning process and pace;

(iv) unrestricted access (i.e. not dependent on previous learning attainment).

It is this last property of openness which accounts for a restricted view of the meaning of open learning.

In reality most programmes are neither entirely 'open' nor 'distance', based on the definitions suggested. For example, a programme which offers open access to learners may not allow any choice about learning goals or sequence of learning once the learner has engaged with the programme. Similarly a programme which is 'distance' and materials based may include some face-to-face tutor contact or weekend workshops. It is thus useful to consider 'distance' and 'openness' as dimensions of a programme.

The distance dimension can be expressed in terms of tutor interaction and proximity as in Fig. 4.1. Programmes may be entirely distance, or many include some elements which make it overall mostly distance learning.

Not distance   Distance

High tutor interaction   No tutor interaction
and proximity to learner   other than through
                                                media, nor proximity to
                                                learner

Figure 4.1 The 'distance' dimension.

The open dimension can be expressed in terms of tutor prescription and learner choice as in Fig. 4.2. Totally open programmes can be found, generally associated with learner-group based programmes, but many so called 'open' programmes are only open in terms of access. Such programmes might rate high on the distance dimension, but overall rather low on the open dimension.

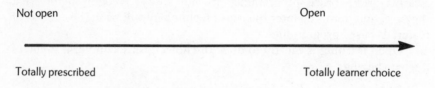

Not open   Open

Totally prescribed   Totally learner choice

Figure 4.2 The 'open' dimension.

If these two dimensions are combined in a map, then programmes can be identified as predominantly open or distance or neither or both, as in Fig. 4.3. Traditional education and training falls into the 'Not open nor distance' quadrant. Tutor led workshops based on learning communities would fall in the 'Open not distance' quadrant. Much so-called open learning falls in the 'Distance not open' quadrant. Programmes which are both predominantly open and distance are harder to find at this point in time (January 1987).

Self-Development

Burgoyne, Boydell and Pedler[6] identified ten different meanings of self-development. If examples of these ten different types of self-development are plotted on the map in Fig. 4.3 they scatter over the four quadrants. This would suggest that there is no direct correspondence between self-development and open and distance learning. Self-development can be open or distance or neither or both. Burgoyne et al. also distinguished between development which is 'by-self' and that which is 'of-self'. This distinction appears to be much more meaningful in relation to open and distance learning.

Development 'Of-Self'

As a goal, I interpret this as learning about or changing one's self to some extent. Burgoyne[7] identifies an 'onion skin' model of personality where

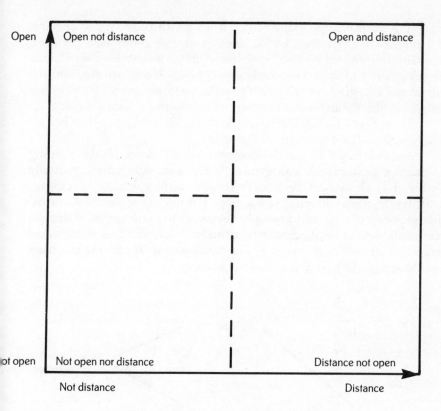

Figure 4.3 The 'open' and 'distance' model.

self is in the inner core. Thus development 'of-self' implies a deep rather than a shallow type of learning, something of significance to the learner.

There was a great emphasis in the 60s on the development of self both as an end in itself and as a means of improving personal effectiveness. For example, many managers became familiar with Maslow's model of the 'hierarchy of needs'[8] and the idea that the highest level of attainment is 'self actualization'. Vitz[9] explores the notions of other self theorists and traces the development of 'selfism' which he describes as secular humanism with a devotion to 'self' to the point of becoming a religion.

My own position is that development 'of-self' as an *end in itself* may well develop into selfism, which is both seductive and unsatisfactory, seductive because as Vitz states 'The tendency to give a green light to any self-defined goal is undoubtedly one of the major appeals of selfism', unsatisfactory because of the destructive consequences which can result from an *exclusively* self orientation. Some of these consequences are resulting in societal problems which will be with us for many decades. Examples are the effects on children of changing marriage partners, sexually transmitted disease, etc. However, as a *component* of human development and as a recognizable part of psychological growth, learning about and changing our self (inner core) and becoming more aware of our effect on others is an essential element of management development.

There is at least a prima facie case that open learning approaches are likely to fit with self orientated learning goals.

Another factor in the development 'of-self' concerns the learning domains associated with management.[10] These are shown diagramatically in Fig. 4.4. This model identifies three main learning domains: cognitive, skill development and affective learning. The model suggests that in areas like problem-solving the learning has elements from the cognitive domain and skill development. Similarly attitudinal learning has elements of cognitive and affective learning. For development 'of-self' the emphasis would appear effective and attitudinal learning.

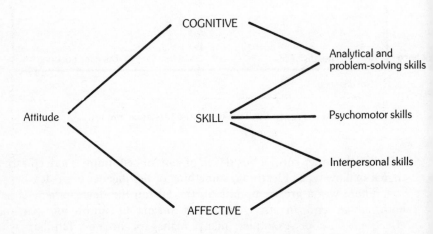

Figure 4.4 Learning domains.

Development 'By-Self'

Development 'by-self' is defined by Burgoyne *et al.*[6] as 'implying that self (the learner) as opposed to some other person, or persons or force in the learner's environment is "responsible for" or "initiating" or "controlling" the learning process.' This concept matches very well with the ideas of what constitutes open learning. One could suggest that the more open the learning, the closer it accords with development 'by-self'. However, this is not the whole story, since self direction and self choice is, I would contend, not always wholly possible or even desirable. Some examples may clarify this.

Consider the question of choice of topic or goals by a learner and consider the situation of a learner and another person who I will call 'other' who has knowledge of the learner. The situation can be described using a variation of the Johari window.[11] There will be learning goals that the learner recognizes and those which (s)he does not. Similarly 'other' will recognize some goals and not others. The model is shown in Fig 4.5.

LEARNER

	Recognizes	Does not recognize
cognizes	Open agreement	Blind = ignorance
OTHER		
oes not cognize	Secret need (weakness)	Hidden

Figure 4.5 Learning goals and areas.

The choice of learning goals in the 'open agreement' area is not problematical. The learner will be aware of these. In the 'blind' area the implication for the learner is that help is required to identify goals. This is the 'not knowing what you don't know' problem. Also in the 'secret' area the learner may be reluctant to admit to a need. There is evidence that open and distance learning systems may contribute to solving this problem by offering the learner not only choice but maintaining confidentiality about performance during learning. An example is a computer-based learning package which does *not* record details of learner responses.

Another question which is raised by offering learner choice results from choice of the learning process. There may be a conflict here between what the learner prefers and what is effective and feasible. For example, in the interpersonal skills area, some practice and feedback is essential for skills to be developed (whether the learner recognizes it or not). Again from an economic point of view it may not be feasible to provide several programmes based on different learning processes covering the same ground. The same sort of issue arises over learning styles. It is feasible to make open the distance learning programmes in any of the four styles,[12] but the dilemma is this: should the learner use the programme which matches his/her style, thus reinforcing an already unbalanced style, or should the learner use a less familiar style and thus help to balance up his/her learning ability? I would argue that the latter would be more developmental.

'Of-Self' or 'By-Self'?

The reader will now be aware that I am not buying in unreservedly to the idea that a total dedication to self-development is universally a good thing. The positive and negative aspects in my view are as follows:

	Negative	Positive
'Of-self'	When it becomes an end in itself which develops into selfism.	Learning about self as a component of management development.
'By-self'	The pretence that it is wholly possible.	Up to a level where choice is appropriate.

In all cases an appropriate infrastructure to support the learning will be essential.

The New Technology

New technology is taken in this chapter to be computer-based learning systems, generally using micros and interactive video systems. Workbooks, linear video and audio tapes are old technology (which does not imply obsolescence).

The new technology offers the facility for distance learning but of itself does not imply openness or non-openness. The key issue is this: Do we know how to design programmes (courseware) which are 'open' and suitable for self-development using the new technology?

I will now attempt an overview of the current state of the art highlighting the key issue above. It should be remembered that development in this field is at an early stage, particularly in the application to management.

Computer-based Programmes

Computer-based programmes fall mainly into two types: those which set out to teach something fairly specific in a didactic way with the learner taking a rather passive role, and those which require a more active response and simulate some management situation from which the learner can learn.

The didactic programmes utilize the principles of programmed learning (tell and test) and are based on conditioning theories of learning. They utilize presentation screens, multi-choice, missing word or open answer questions, use scoring of some sort, remedial loops, hints, etc. In their worst form, they get close to electronic page turning, use 80 column text and attempt to enliven the screens with colour and graphics. Although not denying that this form of design may be very effective for teaching procedures (e.g. operational procedures) they do not accord with the principles of openness, nor either definition of self-development ('of-self' or 'by-self'). Although the learner can control the rate of progress through the programme, (s)he may have no other choice nor lattitude of interpretation. This situation is quite contrary to the principles of openness and self-development, and indeed the notion of conditioning seem both incompatable and inappropriate for management self-development. This does not imply that managers would learn nothing from such programmes, but that from our limited testing such designs lead to frustration and a generally poor reaction to computer-based learning in general. If you have seen such a programme you may well have formed the opinion that this is an inevitable function of the technology, but this is not so, as will be commented on later.

The simulation type of computer-based programme are of two types, situational and numerical. The situational are specifically non-numerical and computerized action mazes and in-tray exercises. These involve a greater degree of interaction from the learner, and contain substantial elements of discovery learning. In the better examples the feedback is not in terms of simple right/wrong responses but is of consequences. There is scope here to create more open-ended designs. In practice the learner is presented with numbers of choices, and depending on his/her response, will follow differing paths through the maze. Again these designs can be based entirely on conditioning theories of learning, in which case there may be only one way out, or the design may contain gates at various stages through which learners *have* to pass. Such designs do not seem to enshrine the principles of openness or self-development. However the designs can be opened up by, for example, leaving more 'ways through', explaining why consequences occur, or allowing learners to exercise judgement based on their work experience.

The numerical types are based on a mathematical model which simulates such things as production lines, stock control situations, marketing or business plans. The learner can create or alter various parameters and the computer will work out a set of results. The underlying learning process is again discovery and in most cases learners have a wide choice to input a variety of values, and can have as many goes as (s)he wants. This sort of design is intrinsically more open. The issue of how developmental the learning may be, is another issue. This would appear to be influenced by the extent to which the learner is making rational and informed inputs and can understand the numerical results, or to what extent (s)he is putting in any number (s)he can think of and not really understanding the results that follow.

The Video Dimension

The addition of a video element provided by interactive video systems opens up a whole new world of design possibilities. Currently the video element of programmes is being used for:

(i)   giving verbal inputs of content (talking heads);

(ii) giving the learner instructions/demonstrations;

(iii) providing surrogate support, e.g. encouragement (talking head of your friendly tutor);

(iv) providing a context for learning, e.g. a case study, dramatized or real;

(v)   providing human interactions (dramatized situations).

(vi) presenting situations or problems (dramatized or documentary).

As with the computer-based programme types already described, the technology does not define the openness. It does, however, give scope for more imaginative designs. Currently available programmes are similar to the computer-based ones already described in that didactic and simulation types can be found, both situational and numerical. The video element greatly improves the impacts of situational simulations. Our research shows that the video element gives considerable advantages from the learner's point of view.

Future Developments

Radically different designs need developing and testing with the specific intention of creating more open designs which will be more in tune with the principles of self-development already explored in this paper. This will include both 'of-self' and 'by-self'. This calls for research rather than production. Currently a programme of research at CSML at the University of Lancaster is undertaking some of this work, funded by a consortium of 11 large and diverse organizations. The research methodology is to design and make a short programme, test it on managers (not trainers), revise the design, and re-test.

Some of the designs which are showing signs of achieving more openness in interactive video programmes are:

(i) giving the learner choice at every possible opportunity;

(ii) letting learners make their own interpretation of situations from video material (not written case material);

(iii) giving learners encouragement to reflect;

(iv) providing for learners to make significant inputs of their ideas which they can retain;

(v) providing criteria for learners to evaluate their own observations, answers, etc.;

(vi) providing facilities for learners to integrate their live interpersonal behaviour into the programme.

More research needs to be done with the aim of producing designs which are open and suitable for self-development of managers. Three key areas come immediately to mind:

(i) much cleverer design of open and distance learning programmes in affective, attitudinal and reflective learning. Some interesting straws are in the wind, e.g. the work of Boot and Boxer[13];

(ii) development of courseware that offers choice of learning style and control of learning process;

(iii) support structures which enhance learning but which might reduce dependence on self alone, extending the work of Hodgson.[4]

Conclusion

Overall I am optimistic that the new technology has the potential to contribute to self-development for managers involving open and distance learning. There are warning signs that in some areas, notably video disc systems, development is technology led. The exciting developments, however, are stemming from experimentation and innovation with the learning process. Although the technology does have real limits, it does not imply openness or non-openness, *per se*. I feel fairly convinced that the long-term development and ultimate survival of new technology-based open learning in management will depend on the quality of design, *and the appropriateness of support structures*.

References

1. Coffey, J. (1977) Open learning opportunities for mature students. In Davies, T.C. (ed.) *Open Learning Systems for Mature Students*. CET Working Paper 14.
2. Holmberg, B. (1977) *Distant Education*. Kogan Page, London.
3. Binsted, D.S. (1986) New ways of learning. In Mumford, A. (ed.) *The Handbook of Management Development*, 2nd edn. Gower, Aldershot, UK.
4. Hodgson, V.E. (1986) *The Relevance and Effectiveness of Distance Learning for Management Education* FME/CSML Report.
5. Casey, D. and Pearce, D. (eds) (1977) *More than Management Development*. Gower, Aldershot, UK.
6. Burgoyne, J., Boydell, T., and Pedler, M. (1978) *Self Development*. ATM, London.
7. Burgoyne, J. (1985) Self-Management. In Elliot, G.K. and Lawrence, P.A. (eds) *Introducing Management*. Penguin. London, UK.
8. Maslow, A. (1970) *Motivation and Personality*, 2nd edn. Harper.
9. Vitz, P.C. (1981) *Psychology as Religion: The Cult of Self Worship*, 2nd edn. Lion.
10. Binsted, D.S. (1986) *Developments in Interpersonal Skills Training*. Gower, Aldershot, UK.
11. Pfeiffer, W. and Jones, J.E. (eds) (1974) *A Handbook of Structured Experiences for Human Relations Training*, Vol.1. University Associates.

12. Kolb, D.A. and Fry, R. (1976) Towards an applied theory of experimental learning. In Cooper, C.L. (ed) *Theories of Group Process*. John Wiley.
13. Boot, R. (1979) *The Management Learning Project: Final Report of the Director*. London Business School.

5

Personal Experiences of a Manager's Self-development Group

* * *

KEITH COPE, SHEILA DAVIES, MIKE GARTON, BARBARA HARRIS, ANDREW JARVIS, DAVID PEARCE AND ANN SIMPSON

Our management self-development group was formed in November 1983 and originally consisted of eleven middle level managers from a variety of disciplines within a large local authority – Nottinghamshire County Council. Initially the group was tutored by Mike Pedler, from Sheffield Polytechnic. This particular group was part of a continuing programme of self-development groups set up by the training function of the County Personnel Division, with the emphasis on self-selection for membership and self-motivation for development.

The following is a summary of the evaluation which the group undertook of its activities when our series of organized meetings were drawing to a close. To set the scene we have outlined the composition of the group, our expectations on joining, our objectives, the format and content of meetings and the various phases in the group's development.

The most important part of our evaluation were our own experiences, which have been included in their entirety, and the reports of our own line managers, which are summarized. The case study which follows these includes line managers' and work group views in full. As a conclusion we identify why the group worked and compare this form of self-development with other methods of management training.

The Group

Membership of the Group

Members came from widely varying backgrounds both in terms of work experience and training. Originally there were two members from the County Treasury, two from the Architects Department, one from Personnel and six from the Social Services Department. All of us had some management training, but the members from Social Services and Personnel had a knowledge of group processes which was new to the other group members. This divide was very marked in the early stages when the members from Treasurers and Architects were known as the 'nutters and bolters' because of their preoccupation with facts, figures and objectives.

During the life of the group the initial membership of eleven has been reduced to seven. Members left at the second, fifth, eight and fourteenth meetings (two to move to other posts outside the authority and two because they felt the group no longer met their needs).

Expectations of Group Members

There was a wide variation between the expectations of the group members when they joined, but they can be put into the following categories:

  (i) wanting a bolt-hole from pressures of work with space and time to think;

 (ii) wanting to become a more effective manager;

(iii) wanting to gain insight into their own management techniques and find out about group processes;

(iv) wanting to review their managerial tasks and to plan organizational changes in their workplace;

 (v) wanting to continue management development by trying something different;

(vi) wanting a refuge because of an unhappy work situation, and career counselling and support;

(vii) wanting career counselling and support.

Group Objectives

The group objectives were formed in its early stages, although these were not formalized until later. Broadly, these were to provide facilities for the self-development of the individual within the group through:

  (i) allowing space and time for individuals to bring personal and managerial issues;

 (ii) experimenting with experiential techniques of management;

(iii) sharing management experiences;

 (iv) assisting members to carry out managerial, personal career and personal development plans through stimulation, support and monitoring;

  (v) developing the group as an effective unit, i.e. team building;

 (vi) analysing group processes.

Format and Content of Meetings

The first meeting in November 1983 was a two-day residential session at which the future organization was determined. It was decided that the meeting should be residential at intervals of 4–6 weeks. Each meeting consisted of an evening and the following day, and a regular pattern was established starting with the evening meal followed by three hours' work before adjourning to the bar. This session was used for winding down from work, picking up the 'minutes' containing issues from the last session, dealing with new issues brought by individual members, and broadly planning for the following day's work.

Flexibility and the opportunity to deviate from this pattern when the need arose was extremely important. The following day's agenda would vary depending on the needs of the members, but generally any new work such as management games, role playing exercises, tackling members' problems, etc., would take place during the morning session and the afternoon would be spent reviewing what had happened and summarizing our conclusions. Topics often continued to be discussed over a number of sessions.

During the life of the group a number of different exercises were used to investigate the management issues which were under discussion. These could be broken down into the following broad categories:

  (i) management games;

(ii) role playing exercises;

(iii) use of visual aids.

Management Games

A wide variety of games were tried for three main reasons: to illustrate group processes, to assist individual developments, and to illustrate management processes.

Group Processes

These were very important in the early stages of the group's development. Exercises were carried out in a number of different formats: individual, pairs, threes, splitting the group in half, as a whole group. There was always a feedback session to make sure the whole group benefitted.

Splitting the group in its early stages caused a lot of conflict, but as members' trust in each other grew the changing of formats proved to be stimulating rather than disruptive.

Another finding in the early period of the group was that members varied in the format they found most comfortable to work in. This was fully discussed and was a great help to those who had not been involved in group processes previously.

Exercises carried out included the following:

Glimpses	Individuals listed ten items which they felt reflected their identity.
Needs	Individuals tried to identify what they hoped to get from the group.
7 key developments	A pairs exercise where group members helped each other identify the key development periods in their career.
Work biography	A pairs exercise to increase group trust, support and commitment.
Needs and offers	When the group was six months old individuals listed what they needed from the group and what they felt they could contribute. This was compared with the earlier 'Needs' exercise.
Fish tank	Carried out with a male/female split to illustrate differences in attitude and approach to problems.

Individual Developments

These exercises were used to help individuals identify their management styles, methods, strengths and weaknesses and included the following:

Say something nice	Feedback on individuals by other group members. It illustrated the effect of inadequate positive feedback. Some found it difficult to receive compliments.
Group make up	What other members felt individuals contributed to the group. The principles could be transferred to the work environment.
Why are we here?	Review of reasons for attending the course and the benefits which are being obtained.
How have we changed?	Group impressions on how individuals have changed since the group formed.
What are our weaknesses?	Group helping individuals to identify areas for improvement. Carried out during later development period demonstrating the trust which had developed within the group.
Insecurity	A pairs exercise to identify individual's weaknesses.

Management Processes

Various exercises were carried out to illustrate management principles including:

Age chart	An exercise to show the effect of age on performance.
Rectangle game	An exercise to illustrate the need for clear communications.
Leadership style	An exercise to see the different management styles which can develop and how they are related to individual personalities.
Group evaluation	Major exercise to identify and reinforce benefits obtained from the group.

Role Playing Exercises

These were used to illustrate to group members some of the management techniques, by giving them an opportunity to participate in an exercise designed for the purpose, and to receive feedback from other group members on their performance. It proved very enlightening to some group members that they did not appear to other members of the group as they intended, and the exercises always promoted a lively discussion.

Some of the exercises were drawn from publications or members' previous experiences, but others were specifically written for the group by one of the members:

'I want what I asked for'	An exercise showing the need for clear communication and flexibility in approach to a problem.
'Cave rescue'	Illustrated communication problems and group processes.
'Assessment interview'	Used to illustrate to participants the impression they made without being aware of it themselves.
'Audit interviews'	Illustrated the need for thorough preparation and clear objectives in the formal interview situation.

Visual Aids

The main visual aid used was films, primarily on the topic of personnel management. All the films were followed by discussion sessions and in some cases they were then used by group members in their own team training. The films used were:

(i) motivation of team members;

(ii) the annual assessment interview;

(iii) the disorganized manager.

The group also used a video camera to record one of its role playing exercises and used the film in the discussion session. Members were not inhibited by the camera and found the playback facility useful in their discussions.

Phases in the Group's Development

The nature of the topics discussed and issues raised varied with the various phases in the groups development. We can now see we progressed through four main phases:

(i) Initially, under the guidance of Mike Pedler, we had seven meetings at roughly six week intervals.

(ii) We then progressed to an entirely self-directing group until late 1985.

(iii) At which time, in drawing to an end, we decided to carry out an evaluation of the group's achievements.

(iv) An informal meeting and a meal after work every two or three months is the final and current phase of the group – we still cannot bear to part!

In the early stages of the group, the most important underlying subjects for discussion were group membership, processes and trust. At this stage there were three main developments happening concurrently to group members:

(i) learning from the experiences of other members;

(ii) development of group processes;

(iii) development of the group character, its objectives and the expectations of trust and support it put on its members.

By the time the group leader left, the group had been well prepared to manage independently. Although the structure and organization remained largely unchanged, there were significant differences in the way the group operated. No one individual emerged as a leader, although all the members at different times took on a leadership role. The absence of a formal leader removed what had become a constraint in terms of independence and growth. Without someone to refer back to all the time, the group moved forward at its own pace.

Membership as a topic for discussion continued to be an important issue throughout the life of the group, but because it was stable and a high degree of trust existed, many other topics were raised and these can be grouped into the following broad categories:

(i) membership;

(ii) workplace issues:

    (a) individual,

   (b) general;

(iii) personal;

(iv) effect of the group on individuals.

Membership

After the early departure at the second session of one group member, we lost only one other member while the paid leader was part of the group, and this was for the positive reason of career progression. Membership was stable therefore until the first meeting after the paid leader's departure, when one member left because the group could not meet her needs. This immediately brought the issue of membership up again, and helped rather than hindered the development of the group in its new format because it provided a focus for discussion.

   Individual members of the group were very conscious of their responsibilities to the group, and we were also aware of the pressures which could be put on individuals. It was always emphasized to any individual who raised a personal item for discussion that no matter how strongly the group felt, the decision always rested with the individual and the group would support that. We always expected feedback, however, so that once an issue was raised by an individual, there was pressure from the group to resolve it.

   The group felt very protective towards itself and if there was any sign of a member becoming isolated, great efforts were made to find the reasons and resolve the problem if one existed. During the second phase of the group without the paid leader, only one other member was lost – leaving the authority under totally unpredictable circumstances.

Workplace Issues

These can be broken down into issues personal to group members and the more general workplace management concerns.

(i) The personal issues tended to be in reaction to events at the workplace, e.g. internal reorganizations, staffing reviews and personal motivation. One of the biggest benefits to group members has been the facility to discuss work problems frankly with colleagues who are not in any way involved. Support, through analysis of the problems and discussions of possible solutions, has given some members the confidence to follow their natural instincts when dealing with problems. Not all workplace issues were discussed in reaction to such events – positive steps were planned to introduce new methods and training opportunities.

(ii) The general management topics we discussed were very wide ranging – the need for a senior manager to have detailed professional/technical knowledge, management style, discrimination, motivation, power and the responsibilities that go with it, relationship between the personality of an individual and the role filled (square pegs in round holes), how to deal with disruptive office influences, employee specifications (identifying the right person for the job), integration of new members into the existing structure, management for retirement, stress and the effect of too much work, organizational politics, staff development interviews, communications and core messages, technical innovation, and the effects on individuals and organizations.

Personal Issues

Probably the most common personal issue has been the career development of individuals. Since July 1984, three members of the group have changed their jobs (one unsuccessfully) and three others have considered, or are still considering, a move. There were also discussions on the effect that stress has on individual group members and where they obtained their support at these times. The home was very important, but the group also figured prominently. These discussions developed into reviews of personal weaknesses as seen by the individual and the group.

Effect of the Group

A continuing item for discussion has been the influence and pressure created on individuals by the group. Members were happy to create pressure on themselves by bringing issues for discussion, and we talked about whether the group helped to identify members' problems which may have remained dormant without its catalytic effect, but it was generally felt that the group just made members more aware of issues which affected them.

The work of the group has been workplace orientated, but the topics were varied and always related to how they affect individual members of the group. There was always time available for any item a member wished to discuss and the structure of the group has meant all individuals have been treated equally.

Evaluation

As our series of organized meetings were drawing to a close we decided to undertake an evaluation of the effectiveness of our activities with the following objectives:

(i) so that the group and individual members of the group could review the development which had taken place and how that had affected each individual in his/her work environment;

(ii) to feed back to the Assistant County Personnel Officer (Training and Development) the group's findings on self-development groups as a training method;

(iii) to feed back to the line managers of the group members the work which had been done by the group during the two-year period.

In order to evaluate the effectiveness of the group we started with a brainstorming session to throw out headings under which the evaluation should take place and ideas on the methods we should employ. Members volunteered to write each of the sections of the group's origins, content, methods and development using as a reference document the record of every meeting which took place which was taken on a voluntary basis by one of the group members throughout the life of the group.

During our discussions on evaluation methods we decided to write our own reports of personal development and include one, more detailed, case study which is included to give more depth to the issue of personal development. The person concerned was selected both for his willingness to undertake such a case study and because the group as a whole felt that a really dramatic change had been evident in him in particular. As it is somewhat difficult to identify changes in attitudes and behaviour within oneself, comments of immediate superiors were considered vital to the exercise and we agreed to interview one another's line managers, each group member being responsible for making all the arrangements to interview their colleague's boss and to write up the report afterwards. The format for these interviews was agreed by the group in advance and we sought the permission of our own line managers before our colleagues contacted them.

Another step we took to seek objectivity was to obtain the comments of colleagues in our work group wherever possible and to interview the members who had left the group. In only one instance we were unable to obtain a comment from a member who had left the group. One member then took full responsibility for editing the material submitted, but this was done throughout in consultation with the group. This chapter itself has also been written in discussion with the group as we have been anxious to ensure throughout that our comments are representative of all our opinions and experiences. The evaluation report itself ran to approximately 40 pages and has been used by the County Personnel Officer as information for employees in the authority who are interested in joining a self-development group, but wonder what it is all about.

The following are our individual reports of our personal development, including the case study, supplemented by a summary of our immediate superiors' comments on our development throughout the first and second phases of the group.

Reports of Group Members

Each of the group members participating in the group when the assessment began has written a brief report on the effect of the group.

Keith Cope – County Treasurers Department

I felt that the approach adopted in previous management training courses had been mechanistic, and that because the courses were of short duration they offered no scope for discussing problems in depth. Secondly, I felt that a great deal of the benefit derived from management courses were from the informal discussions that took place with other course members. I was attracted to the idea of a course which had a longer timespan and seemed likely to provide a means of harnessing and structuring the skills and experiences of a group of individuals. I had no specific expectations other than that through sharing problems, anxieties and hopes with trusted colleagues I could move towards being a more effective manager.

I feel that the specific benefits I have obtained from participating in the course are:

(i) an appreciation of the need to consider the underlying issues and pressures that may be influencing people's behaviour and the need to respond to those as well as the surface messages;

(ii) the opportunity to apply skills and ideas obtained from the self-development group to work problems and to share with the group members this experience and to benefit from their advice and, where appropriate, criticism;

(iii) an increased awareness of the importance of assessing priorities;

(iv) more self-awareness of my own strengths and weaknesses.

Sheila Davies – Social Services Department

While I cannot claim anything dramatic, I am aware that there have been changes and benefits for myself, although they are difficult to illustrate.

When I joined the group it was with a sense of curiosity and not much in the way of expectations, although I hoped it would provide 'time out' to think from a busy and pressured work situation. At the beginning I felt that in common with some other Social Services members, I had some knowledge of groups, several years experience of management and an understanding of people both in group and management situations. Consequently in the early weeks I felt that I was not learning much, although I enjoyed the experience and companionship of the group. Just once as I travelled to the evening session did I wonder if I would find it sufficiently rewarding to want to continue but that was my only 'lapse'.

As the group has developed I have got more and more from it and no longer feel in any way in an 'advantaged' position vis-à-vis the other members of the group.

(i) The first and most obvious benefit to me was to find an opportunity to be still and, in a relaxed and accepting environment, think about issues in management and my own responses to them.

(ii) Later in the group's life I experienced tremendous support when discussing problems and pressure in my work situation. While I think I am fortunate in having good support from my line manager and my subordinates at work, the group offers a different level of support – that of 'disinterested' peers.

(iii) I have been aware recently of some changes in my style of management. It is hard to say how much this is due to the group as structural change in the office and a completely new team of subordinates in the last six months have influenced my style. However, I think the group has played a significant part in encouraging me to make necessary changes. I think I am more assertive and confident and more 'my own person'.

(iv) There have been examples of my taking experiences from within the group back into the work situation. This includes training – I have used some of the group exercises in a training forum within the office and attempted others. I have fed back information and ideas from the group discussions when it has been appropriate.

(v) Finally, I have experienced the nearest I have ever got to 'concensus' management within the group. This was particularly rewarding as I was sceptical about the possibility of its existence previously.

Mike Garton – Treasurers Department

Primarily, I have realized that the group and my membership of it has made me into a more mature individual by improving my confidence and awareness. But more deeply than that it has given me the ability to perceive what life generally is all about. I can see where I am going, what motivates me, what my strengths and weaknesses are, and also observe these things in others.

It has also given me the opportunity to share my problems and frustrations, resulting in my being able to put them into perspective. More generally, it has shown me that management in other disciplines have similar problems and frustrations and the group has enabled me to help others as well as myself.

Nevertheless, being a group member has resulted in a change in my personality as I feel I am no longer a placid individual but now more realistic and assertive as well as being more extrovert which is seen as a possible threat by my superiors.

In conclusion, I feel I have found some sort of 'inner peace'.

Barbara Harris – Personnel Department

Expectations on Joining

I saw this opportunity as a way of adding to my management skills – I did not really join to increase my confidence (I was not particularly honest with myself about my lack of confidence at that time).

Progress in the Group

During the first few sessions we were trying to get to know one another. As the group knitted together, I started to pick up bits of self-knowledge to do with how I operated in a group situation. No, I did not like conflict (who does?) and often assumed a placatory role to combat it, but if I was in a secure situation I could express strong opinions, directly questioning others on their motives.

Apart from general group sharing and discussion, we undertook specific exercises. It was during the roleplays that I discovered the value of being a conciliator and learned some hard lessons about adjusting one's role to suit circumstances.

I have also acquired a great deal of knowledge of how other departments operate, their constraints, and an insight into such topics as new technology.

Applications to the Work Situation

The security of the group helped me to take a set-back at work, and thanks to the group I have put the experience to good account.

Generally, I have tackled my job with much more confidence. This has also been due to an honest appraisal by my boss and his commitment to enable me to grow. I have been far more open-minded and gained more 'political' sensitivity – using the informal organization far more than in the past.

Trying to assess the change in oneself objectively is difficult, and a carefully thought out assessment from my closest colleague is probably more accurate:

> 'Calmer overall; more confident; more able to stand back – not so reactive; more aware of defects and can control them; attitude to work – lets go more, not so intense; not so immediately impressed by others – realistic, reserves judgement initially.'

She felt that some of these changes had to be down to the group – the timing was about right. I would add that she and other members of my work group have also contributed to my development. Perhaps the capacity of the group to help us to grow is generally somewhat underrated.

Ann Simpson – Social Services Department

The personal benefits attending the course have been the most productive for myself, in enabling me to perform as a manager in the last two years. The course came at a time when I was experiencing a great deal of personal stress in my life, and it gave me the time and space to disentangle personal emotion and stress from management issues. It made it possible to prioritize and make some realistic goals.

Management

The formulation of the group into a working team was particularly pertinent as I was involved in the formulation of new working teams in Community Homes. It gave me the opportunity to observe and experience the process of trust building, roles, communication and carrying out of tasks. I have transferred a great deal of this learning in a direct sense to my own work.

Dealing with Others

My career has focussed for many years on the skills necessary in dealing with others whether they are adults or children. I would feel that as these skills always need maintenance and refining there has been some improvement, though nothing very dramatic.

In Conclusion

The personal sustaining of myself during particularly the first eighteen months of the group's life was crucial to myself as a person and as a manager. There was some refining in personal performance, particularly around using personal experience to the detriment of thinking through issues, and my ability to analyse management problems and seek solutions. It brought up again the issue of feedback between colleagues and myself and the need for a formalized appraisal system to ensure good person management.

David Pearce – Architects Department

(David was a member of the group up to the commencement of the evaluation and he has continued to keep in contact with the group since he left the authority for a new position. He has also recently been awarded the MBE for his work in Energy Conservation.)

I elected to join a management development group because I was anxious to take advantage of any training that would assist my management development.

In company with the other members of the group who came from the more practical backgrounds of accountancy and building maintenance I found it more difficult to settle into the group activities than the members who, with a Social Services background, were more at home with the concept of analysis and sharing.

In the earlier meetings I was content to listen and limit my involvement to comments on subjects that others introduced. To be useful, however, full involvement is essential.

It is difficult to assess the effect on my attitude to life or on my management skill, and I suppose from the county council viewpoint the fact that I have now changed my employers makes my involvement a failure.

To be constructive, it is interesting to consider my situation within the Architects Department before and during the period when the group was in existence.

I was an engineer responsible for a small team of engineers and architects. I was also just on, or passing, my fiftieth birthday. The management structure within the department is such that all posts senior to mine would be architects or building surveyors and no natural progression was possible from my post. The post was not going to be regraded so there was no financial incentive for me. To counter this I had made efforts to publicize on a national scale the work of the department in my field. Subconsciously I was therefore at a crises point in my career.

Case Study

Andrew Jarvis – Architects Department

Introduction

This is a personal case history setting out the background to my joining the course, the initial impact the course had, the development of my management style and role, other factors which have affected my development and an overall summary of the benefits I think I have obtained.

Background

When I first received details of the self-development course I was attracted to what seemed to be a different approach to management training. I liked the idea of transcending departmental boundaries with a group, and it appeared the lack of pre-ordinated structure would enable me to investigate management problems that directly affected me.

I must admit, however, I found the exploratory meeting at County Hall confusing, and I had serious doubts as to whether I should attend or not.

Early Development

The most noticeable early benefit was the group support. The willingness of the group to discuss my problems and offer impartial advice which was new to me had a tremendous impact.

During the early part of the course I became more aware of a need to clarify in my own mind what I was trying to achieve at work, and how I was going about it. I had up to that time a very task orientated, practical approach to management which had very little regard for human reactions or individual needs. The course members suddenly started me thinking about how people were reacting to my actions and how they expected me to react to theirs.

The very basic awareness came just as I was taking over the leadership role in the Area Office and I realized I had to make it clear to the staff what I expected of them and how I wanted the office to run. I learned to listen to what was being said, to check that others had understood what I was trying to say, and to become more sensitive to how those around me reacted. I began to realize the importance of individual personalities in making a successful team, and trying to work out why some worked and others not.

This probably seemed very strange to the members of my Area team who found themselves being asked all sorts of unexpected questions, but I was very lucky that they were prepared to go along with me and co-operate in my development work.

Development of Management Style and Role

When it was confirmed I would be permanently transferred to the Area Office I found I had been developing a style of management to suit my personality which I had not previously considered. This would not have been possible without the group. I am not criticizing my own colleagues but I do not believe I could have developed these ideas with them. At the same time I was very lucky to have already in existence a team of staff prepared to tolerate my experimenting and a line manager who was prepared to let me get on with it. I could not have reviewed progress or discussed success and failures with these people, however, and the support of the group has been invaluable.

While developing the style of my team I also found myself taking a more positive role in the overall management of the Building Surveyors Division. I became more sensitive to unspoken feelings in meetings and prepared to speak out on issues which I felt strongly about. I began to use my ideas and philosophies in this senior management forum. More time was spent thinking through arguments so that I could make a positive contribution to discussion when the time came, and I found myself building a newer, and I believe, stronger relationship with my line manager through this new found confidence.

One of the biggest successes I have had came as part of my divisional responsibility for training. The Divisional reorganization which followed the Management Services Review resulted in the promotion of several members of staff with high potential but little experience or training in management skills. With the help of the Central Training Unit I developed a course concentrating on the management skills they needed to cope with their day-to-day work. This was most successful, not only in improving their skills, but by also instilling a common sense of identity so that they have now formed a support group of their own.

Other Influences on My Development

It is probable that some of my recent development would have occurred anyway, although I believe I would not have obtained the same level of benefit without the stimulation of the group. Several incidents occurred which had a direct bearing on my performance, and although these would have occurred anyway, I believe my reactions would have been different if I had not been involved with the group.

Summary

I believe this course had a very great effect on my development. It has helped me crystalize my management style, it has given me confidence to stand up for what I believe in, provided impartial support when needed, and in general enabled me to become a far more effective manager. I feel the fact that the group has been meeting regularly for over two years has helped maintain this progress, and I shall wish to carry on with my personal development in some form on completion of the course. The support of the group has been enormous and I feel any individual could benefit from a similar experience, provided they do not start with too many preconceived ideas.

Report of Line Manager

Andrew Jarvis's line manager is John Collins, Chief Building Surveyor, and the following comments were made by him in an interview with Keith Cope, another group member.

Changes in Managerial Behaviour

Andrew generally adopts a questioning approach to solving problems and John has seen this as a useful contribution to the management team. This approach has now been extended to examining his own feelings and actions.

As Andrew's self-confidence has increased he has taken a larger role in management team meetings and his sensitivity and support to his line manager has at times been particularly appreciated. However, this does not mean that Andrew is acquiescent to the line manager's, and other colleagues', opinions; if he does not agree he is prepared to present his views robustly and clearly. Once a decision has been taken Andrew will then strive to ensure it is successfully implemented whatever his own original viewpoint might have been.

Andrew has become increasingly supportive of his staff, involving them more in the running of the office, and drawing his line manager's attention to particularly meritorious work by his subordinates. He always tries to consider the human aspects to problems and thinks through the likely implications of different courses of action. On occasions he can be somewhat oversensitive to personal criticism both of his staff and himself.

Managerial Performance

Andrew has become a more positive and assertive member of the management team. His level of achievement and performance has improved and John would expect Andrew to accomplish successfully any task he might be given, inevitably some with more enthusiasm than others.

Where Andrew believes that he can solve a problem himself he will do so, and would not usually feel it necessary to seek approval or assistance. He does, however, keep his line manager informed on all important matters and there seems to be a high degree of mutual trust between Andrew and his line manager.

Not only does Andrew display a greater willingness now to take decisions, he is also prepared to delegate to a greater degree than previously. These changes are possible due to his greater confidence in his skills as a manager.

Any Other Comments

While there have been no formal meetings between John and Andrew to discuss what was being obtained from the group, John does feel that it has contributed towards Andrew's development. However, the department was radically restructured at the time the SDG started, and it is therefore difficult to identify to what degree the group, the new environment, or the greater work experience have individually contributed to the changes that have occurred.

Marked changes have occurred and Andrew, in John's opinion, has developed considerably during the past two years. He has supported other members of staff wishing to join development groups and feels very positive about their role in staff training.

Reports of Division Team Members

Area Building Surveyor

Since moving to the Central Division Andrew has more confidence, is less ruffled by events and not prone to panic. He is able to argue and defend decisions, even if they are not his own, and speaks clearly and constructively at meetings. He also shows a very competitive nature when challenged by his peers.

Andrew makes it clear that he is the boss and once a decision has been made there is little point in arguing further. He is, however, reluctant on occasions to make decisions, although this may be because it has to be referred to higher management.

Andrew has tried to bring the Central Division together but some staff still doubt his sincerity for their welfare and feel he spends too much of his time in administration. However, I feel his move to Central and his management training have made him more aware and supportive of his staff, and he certainly has the support of the Central Area team.

Senior Clerk

When Andrew first came to Central Area from County Hall he was quite aggressive and therefore we were all ill at ease in his presence. Gradually the barriers were broken down and he began to look at his staff as individuals and as a whole.

After each session of his course, I was aware of him taking stock of the running of the office and his personal approach to staff and working problems. He was more aware of his early morning 'black' moods and did his best to overcome them.

Over the past year in particular, although still being very much the 'Boss', he is available for anyone to approach him and invites staff to air their views and tries very hard to involve staff in the general running of the Department. Management under his guidance are given a fairly free hand, but he is always ready to give advice if and when required.

From my own point of view he has given me the confidence to follow my own instincts in running the administration side of the Department, and this, I am sure, he would not have achieved with me when he first came to Central.

The course, I am sure, contributed a great deal to Andrew's change of attitude in his dealings with staff and his approach to running the Department, all this being on the plus side.

Summary of Interviews with Line Managers

We interviewed one anothers' immediate superiors as part of the evaluation. It is difficult and can possibly be misleading to oversimplify the comments by summarizing them, but broadly speaking they can be grouped as follows:

(i) Personal changes:
   - More assertive, confident and mature
   - A clearer perception of personal objectives
   - A recognition of personal strengths and weaknesses
   - Relief of personal stress.

(ii) Workplace changes:
   - Improved personal work organization
   - Improved communication skills
   - Ability to separate personal and work issues.

Most line managers were unable to identify changes in their group member which they could specifically identify as being a result of the development group. This was partly due to the confidentiality of the group which meant discussion with line managers had been limited.

However, nearly all managers felt there had been changes and if they were not directly connected with the group activities then the group certainly acted as a catalyst.

They all recognized the benefits there had been from the group support of individuals, and although some had felt their work had been questioned more by the group members, this was viewed in a positive way, and there was very little negative comment.

Conclusion of Our Evaluation – Why the Group Worked

(i) We were very highly motivated – all had requested to attend and therefore had a vested interest in the group's success. It is felt that if managers were told to attend this type of course, they may not approach it so positively, or obtain the full benefits which are available, and could form a destructive influence.

(ii) Good early leadership. This was crucial in moulding the group together, creating the right atmosphere for trust and support, so that when the leader left, the group was well established and could continue on its own.

(iii) All the group members were experienced middle managers, although their experiences had been gained in different fields. This meant that everybody felt that they had a contribution to make, and all could benefit from the wide range of experiences available.

(iv) The group members were all prepared to accept the confidentiality and trust which was necessary for group development, and to take risks in raising topics where they were personally vulnerable.

(v) The personalities of individual members seemed to compliment each other – any group would find it difficult to make progress if there was a major clash of personalities between members.

Cost to the Authority of Running the Self-development Group

The cost of running this group for two years can be summarized as follows:

(i) The cost of the professional leader who attended the first eight group sessions.

(ii) The accommodation and travelling costs. Each session up to the end of 1985 was residential, in a County Council owned establishment, or on two occasions at a similar low cost establishment.

(iii) The cost in staff time for the periods when the group members were away from their workplace.

Comparison of a Self-development Group with Other Management Training Methods

Part of the evaluation of the self-development group must be its comparison with other forms of management training. At one end of the spectrum is workplace training by the line manager and at the other end the formal management courses run on the traditional 'lecturer-student' format. The comments on these training methods are based on the experience of the group members.

Workplace Training by Line Manager

This is probably the most common but least recognized method of management training in everyday use. Some line managers have regular supervision sessions with their staff, but because this is part of day-to-day work, and not labelled as training, it often goes unrecognized as such by both parties.

It is probably most effective in the imparting of skills or knowledge where examples can be used to clarify points. There is obviously very little cost to the authority, but success does depend on the commitment and level of expertise of the line manager, particularly in terms of a coacher/trainer, and the environment in which such training takes place. An open and honest relationship is usually vital to any change in attitude or behaviour and this is not always possible between superior and subordinates. Pressures of work can also mean that adequate time is not available for coaching. Having said this, the one-to-one relationship is a very good teacher/student ratio, its only disadvantage being that learning is often limited to one person's experience.

Traditional Management Courses

Such training where there is a professional tutor teaching a group of individuals is the traditional method of imparting management techniques.

While the teacher-student ratio is likely to be greater than with the workplace training, this method has the benefits of a professional tutor, with a greater depth of knowledge of the subject, and hopefully the skills to pass it on effectively. It is more costly than workplace training, in that greater resources are required and the individual is taken away from the workplace, but this does have the advantage also of removing workplace distractions.

There are however some disadvantages which may be important in some circumstances:

(i) The course is rarely tailored to suit individual needs, so for any one person it may be aimed too high or too low in relation to their current level of skill.

(ii) The relationship between teacher and pupil is usually formal, pre-defined by previous experiences, and limited to the subject of the course. It may be possible for a group support system to grow accidentally if the course runs over a number of months, but the course content is not aimed at this and the student may therefore not get required support.

(iii) There is no maintenance of the skills learnt and little feedback on completion of courses, so that after the initial enthusiasm generated by the course has died away a student may revert to his/her original level of skill.

(iv) The passing of information is often one way only, from teacher to student, and the knowledge which is available within the group is sometimes lost.

In our view, management is a set of experimental/practical skills and although the theory is useful as a framework it is not particularly a key element in managerial performance. Theory and techniques alone, without the experience of practical application, are meaningless and no management training is valid without follow-up and feedback.

Self-Development Groups

These courses, less structured than the formal courses, can be tailored by the members of the course to meet their needs. Emphasis must be placed on the development of the group, but apart from that, the areas of work covered will depend on the membership. The lack of structure imposes the need for self-discipline in the group if progress is to be made but this helps build up the trust and support which is required for success. Groups usually aim to develop the individual members by learning from the skills and experiences of other members and how much is learnt will depend on what is available in the group. Outside resources can of course be brought in to enhance group knowledge but this may tend to weaken the group identity if done too regularly.

Managers, by definition, operate in groups, and it is therefore logical that their training will be most effective in the same environment. The mutual support and maintenance of on-going development provided by a group meeting over an extended period is also beneficial, providing the group members are flexible in their approach and are aware of the needs of other group members.

Summary

The group felt that there is no one training method which is more effective than all others; they tend to be complementary. Workplace training and traditional courses are probably most effective for training in, respectively, specific skills and knowledge, and overall theory and techniques. Development groups seem to be most effective where members are aware of the theory, have some experience, and are flexible enough in their approach to be able to benefit from the experience of others. In our view such groups offer the possibility of changing attitudes and developing the individual to the benefit of the authority. They will not suit everybody, nor every situation, but should be considered along with other training methods as an approved system of management training.

DIFFERENCES AT WORK AND SELF-DEVELOPMENT

Part Two contains four chapters which use differences at work as a springboard for self-development activities. All four actually focus upon gender issues and there are clearly many others, notably race, age and disablement, which share the potential of gender both for creating discrimination against minorities at work and for forming a sense of collective and individual identity which provides a powerful motivation for self-development.

Rennie Fritchie and Jane Skinner stress the need for women to develop their own particular ways of working and spell out some of the guidelines for designing the process and content of self-development programmes for women managers. Janet Atkinson writes from the perspective of being a tutor to a women managers' self-development group and describes the stages through which the group went together with some insightful comments on her role.

Jan Hennessey and Martin Hughes describe their guided self-development programmes developed exclusively for women managers and later extended to men. They comment on some of the observed differences between women and men at work in terms of their development needs.

Tom Boydell uses his own biography to launch *Transformations for Men?* which he sees as one of the important paths to be trodden in transforming work organizations. Only when we men and women truly understand and respect ourselves and each other will we be free to celebrate our individuality, our 'manness', or 'womanness' and our 'personness'.

6

Self-denial, Self-worth and Self-development: Beyond Catch 22 for Women Managers

*   *   *

RENNIE FRITCHIE AND JANE SKINNER

MAN   We're agreed that we'll go on a family outing this afternoon. We just
have to choose where we want to go.
I'd like to go to the river and see the boats.
CHILD   *I* don't want to go to the river, *I* want to go to the farm and the
woods.
MAN   (To woman) What do you think? Where do *you* want to go?
WOMAN   Me? Me? What do you mean, where do *I* want to go? I just want
you both to agree, which ever place you can agree on is where I want to
go.

Context

If the feminine concept of 'self' tends to be inclusive and relational and
the masculine concept centred and separate, then 'self-development'
instantaneously has a different meaning for many women than for many
men. In this chapter we set out our views of the background, approach
and content of self-development programmes which will be able to draw
out and enhance the abilities and values of women. We set this in the
context of our observations as trainers and management consultants
concerned with what may be currently happening in many organizations
which are embarking on a self-development programme.

Inclusiveness, respect for differences and willingness to change in
organization 'culture' are prerequisites for 'self-development', particularly
where women are not only part of the movement to improve 'human
resources' but partners in shaping their own development as well as
contributing to the development of others. So we are advocating the need
for 'unselfish development' if women are to feel part of organizational

plans to improve workforce capacities by reliance on 'individual' choices and routes to developing for the future.

From exploring boys' and girls' capacities and attitudes at school, to longitudinal studies on MBA graduates in the USA (AMA 1985), it is now firmly established through a comprehensive range of research into male and female attitudes that in *self* definition of capacities and qualities females consistently 'underrate', while males consistently 'overrate'. Both misperceptions may be damaging to organizations concerned with maximum development of all potential talent. Self-development, if it over-relies on individual choice to opt in, may actually exaggerate what we call the 'King Complex' among men and the 'Cinderella' complex among women.

At present, many self-development programmes are often limited to a subset of a particular workforce – often 'high-flying' managers. The majority of these pre-identified people are almost certainly male, for whom opportunities and resources for self-development with the organization's blessing are open and available. Obviously, these models of self-development cut out of the reckoning most women, who are usually concentrated in the lower echelons of employment.

A second common purpose for introducing a self-developing approach is to restimulate 'plateaued' middle managers who have little immediate prospect of career progression. Once again the majority of such managers are male, as women unfortunately have not reached a middle management plateau but are on or below the bottom rung of the management ladder. We urge that this be *avoided* by organizations who are at the thinking and designing stage in relation to self-development in their organizations and be *reconsidered* by any company operating such an exclusive approach to developing the talents of its workforce.

We therefore suggest that before self-development for individuals reaches a working agenda, self-development for the organization is a necessity. Only then will organizations who have a *wholesome* approach to their own development be able to consider seriously and develop creatively a *holistic* approach which both builds on the similarities of individuals and at the same time values their differences.

It is clear that to write about how to undertake organizational self-development is worthy of a book rather than a part of one chapter. In today's new-wave management writing from Handy to Moss Kanter and Toffler, the *case* for enhancing different healthy cultures within organizations has been made. However, much is still to be done to pioneer practical steps to bring this about.

Inclusivity – a whole workforce approach – is fundamental if women are to have the possibility of developing their qualities. So 'self-development' for women must be far more than just self-development for managers (some of whom may be women) unless this approach is, by its boundaries, to exclude most women at work. If exclusive approaches continue they could constitute a programme variant of 'careers for men and jobs for women', the two-tier workforce – with all its implied and real neglect.

If this is the case in many organizations, it is necessary to look at the reasons behind this reality and what is needed to change it. Organizations traditionally work on their tasks and their processes; when there is a shifting population at the top they rarely go back to first principles and philosophies to rediscover and redefine the self or 'soul' of the organization. This means that 'self-development' for the organization rarely becomes a live working issue until times of extreme crisis.

Yet clarity about core values and purposes is crucial not only for organizational effectiveness but also to ensure that workplace behaviours are not driven by rather shallow 'can do' value sets. The United States Marine Corps has developed a 'can do' management approach which encourages people to agree instantly with enthusiasm to any request or challenge put forward from a senior level. As a marine colonel put it: 'This means that we can agree without thought as to whether it is appropriate or right.' Her view was that it also had the effect of pushing people beyond their capabilities in a less than healthy way and in a manner that engineers personal development to suit the organization rather than the person.

It can be all too common for organizations, who can demand absurd behaviour expectations not linked to any purpose or core mission needs, simply to perpetuate itself partly because those seeking to develop successfully in its midsts 'can do' that which has come to be expected as demonstrations of potential or executive qualities. We suggest that organization 'self/soul' development may help avoid this 'can do' culture with its tendency to an action culture and a likely consequence of clubs and clones in management cadre. It may thus help evolve a 'to be' culture which more readily touches base with key purposes and sees various actions and inactions in terms of these.

Having stated the importance of organizational self-development, as a prerequisite to individually focussed self-development, we move on to set out practical strategies and approaches to this 'second stage' work.

Strategies for Introducing Self-development for Women at Work

Strategic choice is inextricably linked to where a person is in their organizational structure and culture as well as what that organization's existing qualities and preoccupations are. From the overt and overall to the covert and 'domestic' every strategy encounters problems when trying to encourage women to self-develop at work.

However, vital first steps for a manager (who may or may not be a personnel or training specialist) seeking to encourage individuals to develop and self-manage their own development are reflection, analysis and 'self-situating'. Three simple questions clarify this point:

(i) REFLECTION: '*Why* do *I* wish to encourage women to develop their capacities, skills knowledge and awareness as managers?'

(ii) ANALYSIS: '*Where are women* in my place of work and what are their *views and attitudes* and how are those taken into account currently by management?'

and perhaps:

(iii) SELF-SITUATING: 'Am I a self-developer? If so what are the qualities and benefits of self-development that I can share with women to encourage them? If not why do I consider it good for them?'

Central to this first stage of 'inaction' or self-reflection and finding out is thinking about women's current living situation in the workforce. It is common for managers to take women's roles as, for example, support staff, for granted. This 'un-curiosity' about women's views of how work is for them is accompanied by an awareness of how the organization currently 'uses' or ignores the range of women's skills, qualities and abilities, now or in the future.

This first, foundation stage may be carried out quite informally in a small-scale way if that is all that is possible on the part of the change or 'self-development' agent. But it may be the first visible organizational stage of moving towards recognizing, valuing and developing female contributions. So this work could eventually include listening to women's views in an 'organized' way. Some possibilities for this include encouraging groups of women to meet and come forward with ideas for individual development at work as well as sensitively conducted 'surveys' of women's current attitudes and of their priorities for individual development. Of course an organization which has a long history or a deep culture of neglecting or rather simply not seeing women's vital role in their workforce, may encounter some suspicion or detachment if it moves straight to this first step. Demonstrating and explaining the will to act differently and inclusively may be a prerequisite of moving towards a self-development programme to convince women that their hopes and energy are not being wasted by some short-lived managerial fad. One simple way in many workplaces to demonstrate the will to act differently is to include part-time staff much more wholly in the processes, decisions and resource allocation of day-to-day work.

These foundation steps may take a considerable time. They often require the help of outside consultants experienced in working in women's development, and this phase will almost certainly produce some surprises about women's priorities for changes to unlock their potential as employees.

It is simple common sense and therefore wise to hasten slowly at this stage. Rushing to prescribe the framework and parameters of self-development programmes for women from a structural situation of long oversight or neglect may well prove both expensive and ineffective.

As well as these first stages of finding out and listening to women, there is frequently a need to convince colleagues, superiors and subordinates of the need for self-development for women. Arguments against including women in programmes which are expensive range from the Fundamentalist Traditional ('We've never done it before', 'they're happy in their work', 'I've not noticed any demand by women', 'women are just working for the extras – they're not interested in careers') and the Harassed Reluctants ('it is going to stir things up', 'I can't spare my secretary for x days per year'), to the Efficiency and Economy Technocrats ('there are plenty of skilled women – don't waste money on them – we can always recruit more') and Tomorrow's Men ('I believe in women's development wholeheartedly but women here are not at an appropriate level yet').

Strategies for convincing are, we think, almost wholly dependent on the individual or her/his culture. In some organizations the argument about preventing waste of the neglected resource is a powerful one – in others it will cause sexist sniggers. For some female managers the risks of speaking up for other women may be very great in individual career terms ('she is one of those Feminists') while male managers may risk derision and sexist remarks if they are identified with encouraging women at work. But these problems of attempting to marginalize or embarrass change agents into a training standstill are very familiar; the personal and political approaches to overcoming them are the subject of strategy and political philosophy textbooks. It is clearly more important to gain a network of sponsors for the worth of the idea before it becomes a policy matter. In gaining this support the power of facts and views emerging from the reflection and analysis work can be considerable.

Once the groundwork has been done, the go ahead for spending resources on self-development has been given by management, and women have been consulted, then organizing the style and content of development programmes can be organized. We now move to another strategic issue in encouraging self-development for women – that of results.

There are a number of results any organization investing in self-managed development will have in mind. For example, increased technical skills, enhanced motivation and the encouragement of new attitudes and wider knowledge can all be expected to result from a programme of self-development. Certainly these are reasonable results and may well be priorities. We also urge that the vision or organizational purpose for encouraging women's self-development should consciously include discovering and testing different *ways* of work – as envisaged by women. This means that strategies to encourage self-development should have space for encouraging diversity of approach in the workplace. It seems to us this cannot be done in a vacuum or simply by words of encouragement. Encouragement will include considering the ways in which behaviours are valued or devalued. (For example, how are people with management potential identified? Are the qualities looked for masculine qualities in the main? Is this directly linked to job requirements or not – if not how can selection processes and day-to-day working value feminine qualities ...?) It will probably mean re-assessing and rediagnosing how 'talent' is spotted and encouraged. It will be likely to mean everyone in the organization will be touched by the changes necessary to really encourage women's ideas and ways of working.

So self-development and organizational self-development are likely to have to go in partnership if women are to be a part of this progressive approach to 'improvement' in the workplace.

If the process of the strategy for introducing self-development as well as the input is important, it then follows that the *internal process* of self-development programmes is as much a priority as their content. In the following section we explore that process, some possible content and how to facilitate self-development programmes for women.

Designing the Process and Content of Self-development Programmes for Women Managers

Process

The timing of any structured self-development programme must of course fit as conveniently as possible into an organizational timetable. However, two points are worthy of consideration. Today most women still carry the prime responsibility for home management and care for children. Any extension of the working day to allow for group meetings can be a particular difficulty for women at work. Some mixed self-development groups arrange to meet on a regular basis, starting mid-afternoon in order to limit the use of 'work-time'. Often these meetings are just getting into some important issues at a deeper level at the end of the working day. Some continue their formal meetings in an informal way at a local inn well into the evening. Women may reluctantly opt out of the informal part of the work because of personal responsibilities.

The second point also relates to these extra responsibilities. There is likely to be a real interest in continued work on self-development, for example through reading and research, outside the workplace. Women generally have much less totally 'free' personal time than men so this can be a burden rather than a bonus.

Use of computers and other open learning methods can be a real boon to self-development; however, they have to be integrated carefully into the process if they are to be of real help to women. One of the common problems for women managers is the fact of their limited numbers and the real isolation they experience in often being 'one of a kind'! Programmes which rely too heavily on machines rather than people can magnify rather than reduce this very real issue. Women need to be with others in order to recognize that they manage in ways that are similar and also ways that are different – and that it is 'all right to be different'. The message, then, is to allow plenty of 'work-time' for self-development as it is *work*; involve others so that self-development does not become development alone; and 'their way is okay!'

Content

In self-development work it is desirable for individuals and organization people (trainers, managers) to build a joint agenda. It can be useful for individuals to know about the current and future needs of the organization in terms of knowledge, skills, qualities and abilities, as well as to know what the development of these will entail.

However, as we stated earlier, if these needs are not to predetermine wholly the personal development of individuals then they must be balanced by an understanding of the current qualities and abilities of individuals, their personal hopes and aspirations, together with a self-understanding of character, temperament, learning styles and life situation.

Part of self-development is self understanding. One way of achieving this is to use the Career Life Planning Model recently developed by Rennie Fritchie which poses a series of open questions for individuals to work on. If the 'medium is the message' then sometimes just working on the questions has been the answer. This is a deep process and will not be completed quickly; it can be paced, however, to suit the individuals.

There are two fundamental life questions and seven strategy questions. They are as follows.

The Two Fundamental Questions

 (i) *What kind of human being do you want to be?* Describe the kinds of skills, abilities, qualities, disposition, character and understanding you want to have.

 (ii) *What do you want to do with your life?* Think in large as well as small ways of achievements, actions and important issues for you.

The Seven Strategy Questions

 (i) *Where are you?* Describe fully your current life state both personal and career.

 (ii) *How did you get there?* Look back in your life and trace all the elements, happenings and people who influenced your life path.

 (iii) *Where do you want to go?* Using the material from fundamental questions (i) and (ii) begin to describe your real intentions.

 (iv) *How will you get there?* Refer to the information you've gained about your journey in life so far and consider new ways.

 (v) *What will you do when you arrive?* Begin to sketch in your intentions and actions.

 (vi) *Where to next?* Life is a continuous process therefore it is important to begin to look beyond your immediate horizons.

 (vii) *How do you begin?* All this work leads to some clear, concrete first steps. Begin to list them with some timings attached.

   A useful way of starting the self-development process is the self-awareness *'I am' exercise*. This exercise asks people to complete *ten* 'I am' ... statements, and then categorize their statements into *five* different areas. These five areas are:

 (i) *Physical attributes*: bodily characteristics – age, height, weight, etc.

 (ii) *Emotional attributes*: the feelings you possess – shy, happy, cynical, frustrated, etc.

 (iii) *Mental attributes*: your intellectual characteristics – clever, average, dull, analytical, etc.

 (iv) *Roles*: functions you fulfil in relation to others – single, married, profession, rating in a group, etc.

 (v) *Relationship with others*: the characteristic stance you take towards others – closed, open, withdrawn, etc.

Some may find they tend to describe themselves more in one way than another. For example, they may be role conscious:

I am a mother
I am a personnel officer
I am an office manager
I am a student

or aware of emotional traits:

I am often depressed
I am sensitive to criticism
I am optimistic

While a listing of only ten statements cannot be taken too seriously, it is usually an indicator of what is important to them. People are more likely to have listed personal attributes that they have given some thought to, possibly had doubts about, or tried to improve. It is then useful to ask people to put on a plus or a minus beside statements to get some indication of how they view themselves.

For women who have had periods of time out of paid employment it is important in self-development programmes to be able to help them identify the skills, abilities and qualities they've been using in their personal lives and consider which of these are directly transferrable into the workplace. Many women dismiss management of home and their human relations expertise as being nothing very important and believe they have to learn again from scratch. It can be quite a revelation to discover that you are an excellent time manager, work progress chaser, public relations person and all round organizer.

Women tend to adopt the 'hokey-cokey' style of management, that is they put their whole selves into work and take their whole selves home. It is important therefore that self-development includes personal as well as career development and that present situation as well as future life position should be worked on in some depth.

Who Should and Should Not Help with the Self-development Process

Clearly facilitating skills are very important, far more important than training skills, in working with a group of people on self-development. Self-development facilitators should be enablers and not doers. They should be people who can walk beside those who are working on their own development, not experts who know best. They should be people who can move with the process rather than guide or manipulate it. Listening is far more important than talking. We would not say categorically that men should have nothing to do with the self-development process of women, or that all women would be excellent self-development enablers. We would say that, in addition to the skills mentioned above, they must first of all have a very good understanding of what it *means* to be a woman in today's society, and secondly they must have an ability to help women develop their *own ways* of working, rather than helping women to fit into a masculine model of self-development.

We have spent a great deal of time in this chapter talking about why it is important for women to have a particular approach to self-development. We would end by saying that it is not only important for women but also for organizations to be able to nurture and help women to bring, out of their own creativity, their different ways of thinking and doing as well as their different lives, some 'heart' to the organization. These qualities will nurture the soul of the organization which is essential for healthy organization – and self-development.

7

A Women Managers' Self-development Group: An Exploration of the Task and the Process

* * *

JANET ATKINSON

No man can reveal to you aught but that which already lies half asleep in the dawning of your knowledge.
The teacher . . . does not bid you enter the house of his wisdom, but rather leads you to the threshold of your own mind.

The Prophet, Kahlil Gibran

As part of a national project carried out by Sheffield City Polytechnic for the Manpower Services Commission, a small group of eight women, most of them employed within the Planning Department of a northern metropolitan county prior to its abolition, decided to form a self-development group.

Imminent change was a real part of their lives, creating a climate of uncertainty and threat but also prompting them to think creatively about their futures. This chapter describes their journey as a group. Their facilitator reflects on the preparation and discussions that took place beforehand, explores the stages in the life of the group, and describes her own experience and learning about the process.

Pre-meeting

Prior to the start up of the group there were two opportunities for people to come together to hear about the self-development process. For the first, the training department of the organization invited women staff members to an introductory meeting – although the invitation letter was actually addressed to Chief Officers and the Chief Constable! It invited participation from women in management and supervisory roles. Those who came to the meeting had either stumbled on the information and were interested or had been sent by departmental heads who thought it might improve their performance!

This first meeting was addressed by a member of the MSC project team (a man) and was attended by two male members of the training department. The external facilitator was also present, though she played a minor role in the proceedings.

Subsequent feedback described the presence of the two male internal trainers as inhibiting and unhelpful. This was partly a reflection of anxiety and uncertainty about the nature of the self-development process, but was also related to tensions within the organization and the effects of some other previous training which had been experienced as confronting and destructive. The trainers had come as they were interested in this new approach to learning and change and were wanting more information, understanding and clarification from the meeting. This left the participants with a considerable amount of confusion and perception distortion.

The meeting felt large, formal and 'addressed'. No firm conclusions were reached but it was agreed that peopleee should go away, think and then return to a second meeting to make decisions about a possible group. The eight women who attended the second meeting went on to form a group.

Feedback from the first, that is large, meeting highlights important guidelines:

(i) The need to ensure that initial publicity about a self-development group is clear and is directed at the appropriate target group.

(ii) The style of the meeting and the venue should conform to the ethos of a self-development group (e.g. people should not be sat round a formal arrangement of tables in a large committee room!).

(iii) The meeting should be led by the facilitator who will be involved with the group.

(iv) Discussions should take place at an early stage about appropriate representation of the internal training department.

It is important to stress that individual motivation to take part in a self-development group is essential. Being sent by someone who thinks it might sort you out or be good for you can be disastrous! At best the experience will be a waste of time: at worst it could be destructive to the individual and will inevitably hinder the development of the group. It is crucial that anyone deciding to join a group should have a clear commitment to career development or personal change and what that involves – i.e. challenge, risk and readiness to think about issues to do with the self.

For people currently experiencing major personal crisis, recent loss, or ongoing personality distress, a self-development group may not be the right place in which to explore change. It is important to be able to listen and to give to other members of the group, as well as to use the group for one's own needs. This is often very difficult for someone who is caught up emotionally in their own personal upheaval where other forms of support or learning may be more appropriate.

Purpose of the Group

Inviting potential members to an exploratory meeting is a very important part both of the recruitment process and the starting up of a group.

The idea of a self-development group is often new to people; it contains much that feels exciting and worth exploring, but also evokes feelings of anxiety and apprehension about entering a group which is not bound by the safe, but restrictive, approaches of most conventional modes of learning. A preliminary meeting allows people to explore that ambivalence. It is at this stage that it is important to offer some guidelines about the purpose and nature of a self-development group.

At times this attempt at definition feels very elusive. Central to the struggle to define purpose is the relationship between the task and the process. The *task* is about individuals seeking change and growth; about individuals taking responsibility for their own learning and their own development; about seeking change both in behaviour, attitudes, life style or circumstances. For each member it may be about one or more of these issues. The whole notion of working out of members' own issues and needs is difficult to grasp.

The *process* is about understanding how we learn; about how sharing ideas and experiences in a group can enable us to move ahead in our own understanding about ourselves, about others and about issues to do with culture, personality, and organizations, it is about engaging with the task.

Rather than enrolling on a course where other people (i.e. employers or trainers) make decisions about learning needs, members of a self-development group are responsible for making those decisions themselves – both collectively and individually. The group decides what kind of learning experience it wishes to engage in and identifies its own goals and tasks. No one person decides what is relevant or 'best'. Members choose to work on issues, choose the level and pace they wish to work at, stop when *they* feel ready. It is about making choices, but also retaining control.

However, identifying these decisions as a group responsibility also implies a shared commitment to tackle and keep at the task. This entails working together, not allowing people to avoid issues, keeping people at it, etc. . . .

Hence a preliminary meeting offers opportunity for people to hear, ask and decide whether or not a self-development group is for them! It lessens the likelihood of people committing themselves to a group without understanding what this approach to learning is about and then using group time to challenge basic assumptions, thus hindering the group from moving into its formative phase. Time spent seeking to understand and question the nature of the process is an important part of the learning, but time wasted by people not seeking that kind of experience and trying to deny that opportunity to others serves very little creative purpose.

For most people this approach to learning is something new and it is important that they have some idea about the nature of the process beforehand, even though that understanding can only be fully realized as the life of the group unfolds.

The Group

The group that finally came together met approximately monthly on eleven occasions with the facilitator. Sessions lasted some 4–6 hours, either afternoon/early evening or mid-morning/afternoon, and extended into some time for informal interaction and exchange, usually involving food and drink!

Location

The group met on neutral ground, not on departmental territory. This was about being apart from the work situation physically, about inaccessability, about feeling in control and about freedom and space.

In selecting a place to meet consideration needs to be given to comfort, space to work both in pairs and individually, access to facilities for refreshment, etc. Decisions about the right venue and emphasis on feeling comfortable and relaxed in the environment are crucial to the first stage of setting up a group.

Size and Composition of the Group

This is an important issue. Members felt that the size of the group (eight) was exactly right and that size was a critical element in its success. More than ten or less than six would have made a great difference to the way the group worked. Less than six restricts the range of ideas and experience of the group and puts intense pressure on individuals; more than ten means the group often breaks into sub-groups and time and space for individual sharing within the whole group is limited.

Some work was done individually or in pairs, but the group's preference was to stay together. All except one member were from the planning department, although they represented different levels of seniority within the organization. They brought into the group an initial understanding of similar work situations and were often expressing common needs. Although from the same department, most of them did not know each other before joining the group. The other member was a trainer from an outside organization, but she joined the group as a member not a trainer.

The group made some interesting comments about group composition which are substantiated by Tom Douglas in his book *A Decade of Small Group Theory*.[1] He comments that common needs or similarity of experience can lead to:

(i) easier and quicker identification of members with each other;

(ii) fewer difficulties in communication and in the expression and exposure of self to others;

(iii) faster problem-solving and more ability to harness the full power of the group for simultaneous help for members;

(iv) less scapegoating;

(v) reduced friction and enhanced ability of members to define and pursue a group task.

These observations applied very closely to this group, although those same characteristics could also lead to competitiveness, lack of trust, fear, etc.

Although the advantages of common needs and shared understanding were evident and were certainly the experience of the group, members also commented that:

Maybe the group was too homogenous to push issues further, though conversely a more mixed group might not have achieved the same level of intimacy and trust.

Again, Tom Douglas[1] comments that:

Homogenity may eliminate a degree of conflict necessary to produce new ideas and methods and arouse people to maximum effort!

Exactly their experience!

This was a women-only group which gave rise to a mixture of emotions from male colleagues – challenge, confusion and fear. The project report[2] raises the following critical issue:

> It can be argued that real women's development is going to challenge and change the masculine domination of organizations and hence their very nature. . . . Change of this nature must inevitably pose a threat.

Presumably such fear is reflected in comments the women received from male colleagues. For example, before the first meeting:

> What are a group of women going to do all day? Are you taking your knitting? Talking about clothes?

And after the first session, in a leering, sexually laden way:

> Are you well developed then?

Stages in the Life of the Group

Coming Together

Finally we were together as a group, discovering who we were, sharing our stories and exploring the purpose of the group. At this stage people felt very positive and brought certain expectations, hopes and fears. They were seeking information and clarification about the group. There was a feeling of energy and enthusiasm. However, many were still quite anxious about becoming members of a self-development group and what would happen to them.

It seemed important to acknowledge this and to encourage people to share their apprehension, to move slowly into the experience allowing the group time to reflect and assimilate what they were hearing and thinking.

Entry into the group contained a mixture of confusion, excitement and apprehension. This was evident from the approach/avoidance behaviour in the group as described by Garland, Jones and Kolodny in their model for stages in the development of social work groups.[3] Members alternated between enthusiasm for group tasks to apparent apathy, from being willing to take on responsibility to the avoidance of planning or engaging in group tasks. This reflected the ambivalence members struggled with about becoming part of a new group.

It is important to allow and support distance at this stage and to invite trust gently, to facilitate exploration and to offer some initial structure to the group. Although as facilitator you are protected from the emotional trauma of being a member of a developing group, the often intense anxiety you experience before a meeting is an uncomfortable yet seemingly essential part of the creative process.

Although much basic information had been shared at the preliminary meeting, members needed time at the first meeting of the group proper to look at the following:

 (i) *Who we all are:* Each person needs time to talk about themselves, what they bring to the group, details about themselves, etc., sharing as little or as much at this stage as they wish to offer.

(ii) *Defining the task:* Exploring the purposes of the group and reasserting common or different perspectives about self-development.

(iii) *Setting an agenda:* Exploring issues that individuals wish to spend time on either collectively, in pairs or individually.

At this stage some members expressed strongly that they only wished to work on areas that were employment focussed; they had other places to take their personal issues! They were unable to acknowledge that we need to develop an holistic awareness about our lives. It was interesting to observe how attitudes changed as work began and trust and openness developed within the group.

Initial concern to limit the range of acceptable issues may have been a reflection of anxiety about the process and fear of being asked to expose vulnerability:

(iv) *Establishing the ground rules:* This may include discussion and decisions in any of the following areas:

  (a) *Commitment:* Regular attendance at the group is crucial. It must be a priority commitment. It determines how the individual perceives and uses the group experience. It is also related to the needs of the whole group and the role that each member plays within the group: about group identity, purpose and development.

  (b) *Shared responsibility:* For decision-making, achieving a task, responding appropriately to individual members, defining roles within the group.

  (c) *Confidentiality and trust.*

  (d) *Membership:* Is it to be an open or closed group? How long will the group remain together?

  (e) *Practical arrangements:* Shared responsibility for such matters as length and frequency of meetings, venue, refreshments, etc.

(f) *Content:* It was agreed by the group that if a decision had been made to tackle a particular issue in a session, that decision could be open to change if an individual came to the group asking for time to be spent on something crucial or unexpected. It is important to negotiate this at the outset.

(g) *Setting priorities.*

Subjects worked on were identified initially in the early stages of the life of the group, but were added to or modified as the meetings progressed. These included real issues to do with personal aspects of the self, decision-making, action tendencies, learning styles, assertiveness, team skills, job sharing, attitude formation, interpersonal interaction, time management and networking.

The most frequently used methods of learning were discussions, case studies based on personal experiences, brainstorming, questionnaires and exercises. There were also opportunities to practise skills.

Power and Control

After the start up, when usually the trainer is accepted quite warmly, the group begins to look for some structure, some behaviour which conforms to previous expectations of leadership role. When this is not provided, members are often angry or dissatisfied about lack of organization and planning and can send up strong silent messages: the sort of comments can include: 'You'd think she would know'; 'What is she getting paid for?'; 'It's a real cop out'.

One can sometimes sense a strong expression of feeling even though it is often not openly acknowledged. As a trainer one needs to sit tight at this point and not fall into the trap of providing answers and behaving as you feel the group would like you to – although that is easy and a quick way to gain approval. It is important to use this stage of confusion about leadership behaviour as a way to help the group move ahead in its own understanding about self-development.

This can happen even in groups where there has been a very positive response to the idea of the trainer as facilitator, to shared responsibility, etc. Here we reach the point of translating what starts as an intellectual understanding of a concept into real understanding derived from experience. The trainer also has to deal with her own feelings about role and take a similar path in her struggle to understand it.

The following example illustrates this:

Returning home after what felt like a very bad ending to the session I carried a strong sense of responsibility and failure as facilitator to the group.

I suddenly realized that what felt really bad to me actually contained the elements of a crucial learning experience both for me and for the group. It was a real opportunity for us to understand as a group what shared responsibility was about. For me it was about being able to let go.

The session had been about *self-awareness*. How do we know if our own self-image conforms to the image others hold of us? We tackled the task in several ways, but avoided the chance to use the group for feedback. (This was our third meeting and this group had expressed a strong wish to limit agenda issues to work issues!) I offered an exercise to the group to take us further. They did not respond to the idea. This happened twice during the session.

It did feel right to me. Towards the end of the day they returned to the idea and decided to use it – 'Let's have a go!' The group then quickly engaged with the task – but time ran out and we were unable to complete the feedback. People had to go. There was a lot of unfinished business. Feelings had been expressed. People were leaving without completing the task. It felt bad.

Here I felt the analogy of the Angel and the Beast really came to life. My beast retreated and my angel saw the potential for group learning – the importance of timing, of releasing responsibility, of using what felt like chaos creatively.

Issues to do with power and control are crucial for the group and in particular throw up powerful challenges to the trainer. Sometimes it seems as if trainers can release one set of behaviours which are explicitly didactic or authoritarian, but unaware of their own needs for power and control they hang on to a more subtle, but equally powerful, position within the group. This awareness about letting go is not a once-and-for-all-time discovery; it is a struggle that has to take place to a greater or lesser extent within every group, both for the trainer and for individual members.

Intimacy

The central theme in the group now seems to be about closeness: how close members will be able to come to each other emotionally. You can feel the group moving in and backing away from intimacy. The loves and hates of intimate relationships are played out and the group begins to become a place where growth and change take place. The ability of the group to carry out work varies during this period. It is important for the facilitator to reflect this back to the group and confront them on occasions when they fail to undertake agreed tasks, to provide consistent support to the members and to enable them to clarify feelings. At the same time the facilitator must also begin to encourage the group in its ability to take on responsibility for planning and action.

As the group learns to express feelings more freely and openly individuals are establishing a firm base from which they can explore personal need.

Real Creative Work

Members now need to re-order a sense of purpose and priorities. They begin to identify new, important but realistic goals. They have come to a real understanding of what they are into. This feels a halcyon period in the life of the group.

There is no way in which these 'stages' happen in an ordered sequence and there is always some moving back and forward within the group, but there feels to be sufficient form to identify some pattern. The group constantly seems to have to balance itself between undersanding the process and getting on with the task. There will always be a creative tension between these two. As a trainer one is constantly using what is happening in the group to enhance and develop understanding about the process.

People can respond to the same session very differently. When a member has taken up a large chunk of time at one session they often express guilt or concern. Others sometimes admit to feeling a session has not been useful. People have to learn to acknowledge and value the importance of what they have to give as a member of a self-development group. At times members will be using the group directly and will feel that they are learning or receiving something; but membership of the group is as much about giving as receiving. The getting moves around the group. People need to acknowledge that listening and reflecting and offering ideas as a group member are as important to the development of the group as feeling that one is moving ahead in a precise way oneself. Developing an awareness of this seems to be a very significant stage in the life of the group.

Closing Down

The ending of a group should not creep up unnoticed but should be addressed positively and directly. A self-development group can make significant emotional demands on its members and time should be given to acknowledge this. The following description from the project report[2] illustrates this:

> The closing down process was fairly gradual, members taking time to integrate what they had learned from the group into their lives. Any

feelings of dependency on the group were gradually withdrawn and the feeling of sadness that a period of sharing was coming to an end was offset by the anticipation of new beginnings for us all.

The last three sessions focussed both on evaluation and future initiatives. Part of these discussions emphasized the importance of feedback into the organization to encourage it to incorporate a self-development programme into its training. The group was unanimous that other women should have the opportunity to participate in similar programmes.

It is interesting to note that a high proportion of the women felt that decisions about career development and subsequent promotion could be attributed to thinking that had started during their time in the group.

The Role of the Trainer

Understanding the role of the trainer is one of the major struggles encountered by the group and does not come quickly or easily. The style of leadership frequently feels strange and does not conform to previous experience or expectations.

Part of the initial role of the trainer is about leading the way, about answering questions, about clarifying. It is about releasing potential in the group, helping it to identify and use resources. In our group these were many: the one member who was a trainer in her work situation brought many resources, particularly information and exercises that could be used to work on certain issues. Both for me as trainer in the group and for her there were initially some feelings about acknowledging roles and exchanging permission: it did feel strangely uneasy. She was anxious about offering too much too quickly. It was important to clarify roles, to acknowledge her contribution as a very important resource within the group. She wondered how she would experience the group. She became a very valued member – offering a great deal, but receiving as much. At a turning point in her own life she used the group to test out new ideas and rebuild confidence.

This illustrates the importance of the trainer being able to encourage others to play roles in the group – being able to release roles, which are often seen as part of 'the training function'.

As facilitator it is often not the content of what you offer that is the significant part of your role so much as the style of leadership which you adopt. As the group develops your role as facilitator certainly seems to change, and you can see more members playing roles that initially had been attributed to you. I remember being very aware during the sixth session that suddenly it felt different – that people were talking about the group and its work and each other very differently. One member said she thought they could now carry on without me. There was a real feeling of commitment to the process and to the ongoing life of the group. This came after 27 hours of meeting together (not, I add, consecutive hours).

The kinds of behaviour which I predominantly displayed in the early stages were in the following areas: picking up and acknowledging feelings in the group; listening; reflecting back as a way of clarifying what was being said or thought; checking that my perception of a situation was accurate (sometimes doing this by repeating what had been said, but using different words); summarizing and pulling themes together; bringing the group back to an issue if they were unable to stay with it.

At the start of each session I always encouraged the group to reflect on where we had left each other; what decisions we had made; what work we had agreed to do. Members were asked to bring each other up to date with issues and this felt important. It was about remembering what others had said and done and valuing both the contribution and the particular situation of each person in the group.

This style of leadership quickly became accepted as a part of our *modus operandi* and different members adopted different roles within this pattern. Some quickly adopted 'socio-emotional' roles and some 'task area roles'.[4] The longer the group remained together the fewer of these roles were played solely by myself as facilitator. Being honest with the group was a crucial part of this process – being able to share anger and frustration when the group was opting out of its work or its responsibilities. For example, when members returned to a session without having spent time preparing an agreed task, I did raise issues about commitment, pointing out that they would only get something out of the group if they put something in! Very quickly other members took each other to task in this area.

Allowing the group to be silent, to reflect and consider what has happened and been said is very important. There is a significant difference between the silence that is about thinking and reflection and the silence of hostility. The former needs to be acknowledged and respected: the latter needs to be opened up and looked at to enable change and growth to ensue.

Confronting individuals or the group as a whole can result in improved communication or increased understanding; it can be received as a threat, and it can be seen as helpful. Confronting certainly involves some risk taking and it is important to be aware of what you are doing. Feedback is only helpful when received in small amounts, about things that individuals do have the capacity to change. I have always felt it important not to expose vulnerability in another person unless I am able to offer through the group, the support necessary to enable a person to work through it. It seems important not to leave flesh bare without offering support and to be sensitive to vulnerability. As a trainer in a self-development group this is a responsibility I feel I do retain throughout the life of the group. The line between facilitator/member is a very narrow one and as the group develops that line is often very difficult to discern. This is about the only clear area where I personally feel I still carry more responsibility as facilitator than other members of the group carry.

As a trainer one enters a group with a strange mixture of emotions – a combination of excitement and apprehension. Once having completed the initial task of exploring together the self-development group's fundamental purpose and the framework within which it can grow, the group then begins to discover with the trainer what shared responsibility and commitment actually mean in practice.

The rest is unpredictable and by the very nature of the experience has to be so. This is the challenge of it all! To me as a trainer this stage always carries some apprehension. The protection or security of a pre-packaged course or prescribed programme is gone and apart from a very loose framework there is no safety net. One has the confidence from having been on the same journey before, although each route is different; one also knows that for most people the experience becomes a very creative one. The ambivalence is about the uncertainty of it all, knowing that although the experience at the end of the group will be meaningful, before that point is reached the group has to struggle with both the task and the process. T.S. Eliot sums it up for me in the *Four Quartets: East Coker:*[5]

> In order to arrive there,
> To arrive where you are, to get from where you are not,
> You must go by a way wherein there is no ecstasy.
> In order to arrive at what you do not know
> You must go by a way which is the way of ignorance.
> In order to possess what you do not possess
> You must go by the way of dispossession.
> In order to arrive at what you are not
> You must go through the way in which you are not
> And what you do not know is the only thing you know
> And what you own is what you do not own
> And where you are is where you are not.

References

1. Douglas, T. *A Decade of Small Group Theory 1960–1970.* Bookstall Publications, Bristol, UK.
2. Boydell, T., Pedler, M., Hammond, V. *et al.* (1986) *Self-development Groups*

for Women Managers. A report of a project carried out by Sheffield City Polytechnic for the Manpower Services Commission, Sheffield, UK.
3. Garland, Jones, and Kolodny (1965) A model of stages of development in social work groups. In Bernstein, S. (ed.) *Explorations in Group Work.* University School of Social Work, Boston, Mass.
4. Bales, R.E. (1950) *Interaction Process Analysis Reading.* Addison Wesley, Boston, Mass.
5. Reprinted by permission of Faber & Faber from *Collected Poems 1909–1962* by T.S. Eliot.

Other Reading

1. Dickson, Ann (1982) *A Woman in Your Own Right.* Quartet.
2. Harris, Thomas A. (1973) *I'm OK – You're OK.* Pan.
3. Pirsig, Robert (1974) *Zen and the Art of Motor Cycle Maintenance.* Corgi.
4. Storr, Anthony (1960) *The Integrity of the Personality.* Pelican.

8

Guided Self-development for Men and Women Managers

* * *

JAN HENNESSEY AND MARTIN HUGHES
Consultants, Anne Shaw Organization Ltd

We believe that managers can and should take responsibility for exploiting their potential to the full, and this forms the founding principle of one particular programme, which we at the Anne Shaw Organization designed and launched in 1982 and have been running since then to meet evolving need. The course is now well established and growing market demand reflects the success of the model. This demand will be discussed more fully later, but before doing so it is useful to examine a distinctive feature of the programme – and one which is highlighted in the title of this chapter – its 'guidedness'.

The programme we offer provides 'guided' self-development; as such it serves as a 'bridging' model, spanning the alternative approaches of traditional taught training and wholly self-managed group learning experience. The content of the course is divided equally between theoretical input sessions and project work discussions, and this structure enables us as facilitators to adopt a combination of tutorial and counselling roles; at times we lead, at others support, we tell as well as ask, we look in from the outside and also participate from within, we offer ideas and receive them, signpost routes and follow others' roads.

At the conference 'Applying Self-development in Organizations' we shared our experiences in this area, and in particular explored our ideas about applications. The programme is called 'Self-development for Managers' and we examine it here in a number of ways:

  (i)   Introduction to the programme;

  (ii) The evolution of market demand;

  (iii) How the programme has been used by men and women;

  (iv) Outcomes for participants and their organizations;

(v) The programme design: some costs and benefits.

Introduction to the Programme

The programme is aimed at participants holding managerial positions. The main objectives are to increase these managers' abilities to develop their own roles and to equip them to respond constructively to challenge and change.

The programme is a modular one, comprising four workshop sessions totalling nine days, interspersed over a period of about three months during which participants also undertake a specific, self-development, work-related project. Each workshop has a theme. Figure 8.1 illustrates this structure.

Workshop theme	Workshop duration	Project period
1. Understanding the managers' situations and raising self-awareness	3 days	
		1 month
2. Organization and management of projects	2 days	
		1 month
3. Managerial skills and individual effectiveness	2 days	
		1 month
4. Consideration and projection for future development	2 days	

Figure 8.1 Structure of 'self-development for managers'.

Workshop learning activity is divided into two parts. For half of each module we act as 'tutors' outlining theme-related theoretical models, alternative perspectives, techniques and skills. Participants are invited to discuss these, consider their own managerial and personal effectiveness in the context thus provided, to plan and measure their own development using these and any other concepts as appropriate.

For the other half of the workshop sections, our tasks are those of 'facilitators' in relation to the self-development projects which form the continuous learning element in the programme. Participants define and undertake work-related activity that both meets their own requirements and contributes practically to the goals of the organization in which they work. To meet these objectives, projects may be directed towards exploring new ground, strengthening basic skills, extending competence into new areas, solving a particular problem. Although they are 'owned' individually by participants, there is shared, group responsibility for the ways in which they are tackled, and group benefit from the learning experience they provide.

As participants gain understanding and confidence, so our involvement in the project group discussion steps back from being proactively guiding to reactively supporting, as shown in Fig. 8.2. It is this combination of tutorial and facilitative support that constitutes the programme's 'guided' character and gives it a specific profile in the market place. We do not argue that this profile is the only valid one; we have proved, though, that there is a place for an approach which promulgates self-development through an initially more structured and other-directed process.

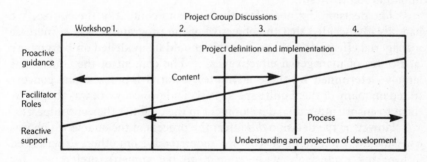

Figure 8.2 Involvement of tutor/facilitators.

Our programme is targetted at participants who need the support of a tutor in the early stages of their self-development and at organizations who seek prepared ground in which to sow the seeds of this approach. This targeting has been validated in terms of market response, and the next section focusses on this.

Evolution of Market Demand

The ASO 'Self-development for Managers' programme was originally designed exclusively for women managers. The design resulted from a research project we undertook in 1980 to explore in what ways our clinets thought we could best meet the training needs of the women they employed. This research identified the following requirements:

(i) special training was required to recognize the specific challenges faced by women;

(ii) potential interest rested mainly with women holding managerial appointments;

(iii) training was required that could take account of the employers' objectives as well as the individual woman's needs.

At the time this market research project was under way, ASO was also working on the design of a project-based programme for managers using the principles of guided self-development described above. This programme fitted in all respects with the training requirements for women identified through our research. After a great deal of thought and discussion with those more knowledgeable than ourselves we decided that women participants would gain most from the course if it was offered on a woman-only basis, and were granted designation under the Sex Discrimination Act to do so.

The decision did not affect the aims and content of the course. We had already decided that the objective of the programme was to increase managerial effectiveness, and that this should be modelled on Burgoyne's 'attributes of managerial effectiveness'.[1] The content of the course was largely determined by these attributes, tutorial input sessions concentrated on many of them quite specifically, and project work was shaped by them to ensure individual development in the qualities they encompass.

However, the decision *did* affect the process of the course which was consciously geared to meet what we understood, from others experienced in working exclusively with women, to be women's preferences for affective, non-competitive, divergent learning. This admittedly stereotypical view shaped the learning vehicles we chose, the style of training input, and the structure and timing of sessions adopted. This was the model we took to the market place with some valued initial sponsorship from the Manpower Services Commission.

For two years the programme ran only on a women-exclusive open basis, attracting management-level participants from a range of private and public organizations. However, in 1984 we were asked by one division of a large multinational chemical company to run an in-house programme for their managers. This division had by then sponsored a total of four women participants on the open programme; these participants had demonstrated significantly enhanced managerial effectiveness and their senior managers sought this for a larger group of managers in the company. This in-house group was comprised exclusively of men for two reasons: first, the unsurprising fact that the vast majority of managers in this, as in most companies, is male, and secondly that the personnel officer concerned favoured the exclusively women's course for moment managers and preferred to continue sponsoring women participants on that rather than the in-house presentation.

This, our first, invitation to run the course for men, both reinforced and led us to question the appropriateness of our model. The fact that the women were proving themselves to be better managers as a result of our guided self-development approach suggested that both content and process met their learning needs, but how would it meet those of men? As far as content was concerned we had no qualms. Burgoyne's model of managerial effectiveness is not gender-specific; we ourselves had used that model with great success more widely than in our self-development work. As far as process was concerned, though, we wondered whether a more stereotypically male approach was required – more cognitive, competitive and convergent perhaps? Mercifully we were saved from this blinkered mistake by the vision of the personnel officer concerned who was determined that we run the course for men in exactly the same way as we ran it for women. We did – and with similar success.

Since then, demand for in-house presentations has grown considerably and these have comprised women-only, men-only and mixed groups of managers. One public authority has recognized the proven value of the women-only presentation, but also the fact that for some potential participants, this exclusivity is a barrier (a barrier that we meet frequently when selling the women-only open programme). This authority offers two versions of the programme, run concurrently, one for a mixed group, the other for women exclusively; women participants are free to choose the version that they feel will best meet their needs.

Another approach to programme presentation is its use by companies to meet group as well as individual needs. Applied in this way, small groups of managers work on their individual self-development projects, but also use the course as a vehicle to implement organizational development of relevance to them all. This application is particularly valuable where there is a need to define and adopt a common managerial approach in a number of structurally, functionally, locationally or stylistically varying organizational units.

A large-scale presentation of the programme involving almost 200 managers was undertaken by a major airline. A cascading approach involved the most senior managers as initial participants who then acted as facilitators to the main body of managers. These participants in turn worked with development groups at the next level down. Our involvement as external consultants was thus initially high but reduced as past participants took increasing responsibility for the programme.

Looking back at the evolution of market demand for our course, we draw obvious satisfaction from its steady growth and the effectiveness this must reflect. We think this applies to both the process and the content of the programme. Particularly exciting is the fact that the flavour of the programme, adopted to meet the needs of women specifically, has been absorbed so successfully by men. Pedler, discussing organizational style in a paper entitled 'Men and Management',[2] argued that 'we need something to balance the awful manliness of our organizations . . . . It demands a conscious celebration of the female and a deliberate attempt to achieve a balance.' We think that our programme is a step in that direction.

As far as content is concerned, we have been interested to see how the course has been used by participants and, particularly, whether women participants have addressed different issues from those addressed by men. Project topics give us the clearest indication of individual concerns and needs; the following section looks at these in more detail.

How the Programme has been used by Men and Women

Introducing the concept of self-development projects to participants, we suggest that they use these to extend existing managerial competence in any of three ways. These are shown diagrammatically in Fig. 8.3.

Choices of projects in these terms are a function of participants' career development needs and their organizations' work objectives. As such they are too situationally and individually specific to be amenable to generalized conclusions.

However, an obviously fundamental objective of all self-development projects is personal growth, the development of skills and enhanced strength *within* existing work competence. It is this aspect in which the needs of men and women are so often identified as being different, and it is therefore in relation to this aspect that we can compare the choices made by them.

Stereotyping male need, we might expect that it would be men who would most commonly address issues concerning:

  (i) lack of sensitivity to subordinates;

 (ii) realization of ambition;

(iii) career recognition and visibility;

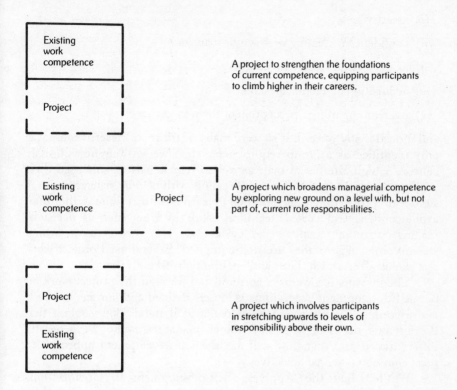

Figure 8.3 **Extending managerial competence.**

(iv) acquisition of 'relational' skills;

(v) competitiveness;

and many did.

However for women these were concerns too. Several needed to develop greater empathy and understanding of their staff. A significant number were strongly ambitious and used their projects to realize higher goals as well as gaining the recognition and visibility they sought. As many women as men focused particularly on the techniques of working relationships, and for a majority of the women participants a desire to compete and win formed the driving thread of their project work.

Perhaps we should not be surprised and/or satisfied about this. Does this not merely mean that women are being forced to adopt 'awful manliness'?

What does the picture look like in reverse? Stereotypically, we might expect that women would be concerned with:

   (i) assertiveness;

  (ii) confidence in dealing with senior managers;

 (iii) anxiety when faced with conflict;

 (iv) acquisition of 'technical' skills;

  (v) overcoming others' perception of them as low level;

and indeed many were. But so were many of the men. Assertiveness was only identified as a group requirement when we ran our first all-male course. A high number of male as well as female participants used their projects to enhance confidence in dealing with senior management. A significant proportion of men needed to learn how to build on rather than avoid conflict, and lacked 'technical' skills in areas such as decision-making, planning, analysis and evaluation – the very areas in which stereotyping suggests they are well-equipped. Several used project work as a vehicle to establish status and credibility in others' eyes.

The information we have accumulated through the project work on our self-development programme is loosely defined and our analysis of it is unrigorous. Nevertheless, the evidence as it stands does suggest that the learning needs of men and women managers cannot be generally differentiated and that they will use the self-development approach to meet common personal objectives.

We felt that the 'Applying Self-development in Organizations Conference' could provide a forum to test this hypothesis in a slightly more measurable way. Our reasoning was that many participants would either have experience of this type of development or be well informed about it, and would thus be able to think personally about its meaning to them within the time constraints of the workshops in the conference. It was for this reason we decided to make project work the focus of our session at the conference.

We spent time in the workshop outlining how we help programme participants to elicit their own self development objectives through the following methods:

   (i) the use of the questionnaire on attributes of effective management to identify self-development needs;[1]

  (ii) a reflective, biographical summary of key development events, discussed in pairs;

 (iii) identification of individual learning styles using Kolb's Learning Styles Inventory;[3]

 (iv) analysis of career and life goals including priorities, time frames and blocks or conflicts;

(v) participants composing a letter written in the third person nominating themselves to undertake the programme and identifying desired outcomes, both individual and organizational;

(vi) visual imagery, through the creation of a collage based on the self now and an ideal or future self, followed by a reflective discussion with other participants;

(vii) repertory grid techniques to give insight into individual construct systems and allowing participants to identify desired changes;

(viii) an exploration of transactional analysis, scripting and sex stereotyping, using the BEM Sex-Role Inventory.[4]

To simplify and short circuit this process, and to enable participants to experience the flavour of a self-development group discussion, we used a simple worksheet in three sections headed:

(i) Identify a situation of significance to you, which you managed less effectively than you would have wished.

(ii) What self-development need does this highlight?

(iii) Suggestions received and from whom.

Participants completed the first two sections individually, and then discussed these for about 45 minutes, in groups of five or six, using the third section to record suggested approaches. Participants valued this exercise as an insight into the nature and process of a self-development group. In addition, some gave a stronger commitment to work on particular issues and to meet or contact each other to review their progress after the conference was over. While the discussions in groups were in progress we recorded the subjects identified for self-development, noting the sex of the participant. In a sample of men and women, the results were as follows:

Subjects/areas identified for self-development

Men (n = 23)	*Women (n = 11)*
Listening and sensitivity	Tolerence
Persuading, influencing, increasing contacts	Gaining influence/self marketing
Assertiveness	Assertiveness – asking for help
Managing life/work/self	Self-management
Communication	Communicating ideas
Career planning	Confidence
Being strategic/politically aware	Presenting ideas strategically/ politically

Delegation   Being less reactive
Time management   Accommodating new culture
Creativity and receptivity
Motivation
Trainers' role directing v.
    nurturing
Taking interpersonal initiatives

It is difficult to treat these results with precision, because some people mentioned more than one area, and in those cases the relative importance of different elements is unknown. However, they do seem to support the empirical evidence of our courses as outlined above.

This is not to say that they will meet development needs in the same way – and we are provided with some illustration of this in the interactive style of the different types of courses we have run. The open women's course is the most 'open' in character; individuals share fully, almost hungrily, from the start, in order to establish understanding and build support for themselves in what are frequently very isolated managerial situations. In-house groups demonstrate more mixed reactions; their common work-language speeds group work but it is balanced by a slight, initial anxiety about openness with people who are in the same organization as themselves. Among these, all-women groups have seemed more quickly to create an atmosphere of ease and trust, but based on our experience, there seems little difference in interactive style between mixed and all-male groups.

These opinions are gut-reactive on our part and not derived scientifically. What we have discovered is that individual participants create the relationship they want within the groups in which they find themselves and, having done so, perceive that grouping as the most 'right way'. To identify more specifically the value of the programmer to participants and their organizations we need to seek the opinions of participants themselves. The next section is devoted to these.

Outcomes for Participants and Their Organizations

Pedler, writing as the external evaluator of our first two programmes,[5] points out that 'on a self development programme it can first be said that any evaluation should involve self-evaluation, in that we can never know another's experience other than through her, or his, communications to us. This is true of all programme evaluation, but especially so here.' He also says: 'Nothing gives the flavour and feel of a programme so much as participants relating their own experience in their own words,' and it is thus both for reasons of integrity and authenticity that this section comprises quotations from participants who have attended the whole range of self-development programmes we have run. These are followed by some views of the outcomes for their employers.

We have not included all the comments provided, but offer a representative sample, grouping these under headings to demonstrate more clearly the nature of participant experience and organizational benefit.

Specification of individual development fell into two categories. The first of these concerned *career development:*

> It taught me to plan my work and personal life together.

> The course helped me to change my career path but not in the ways I thought it could. It helped me in a strange way because I had to justify to the group why I was considering change.

> The main benefit of the course was to enable me to get the job I am doing – it steered me in the right direction, helped me to put together a presentation.

> Immediately after the course I would have said it had a detrimental effect on me. I was very unsettled, rather miserable, because I didn't know which way to go. Now, a year later I have derived a great deal from what we did – I have achieved what I wanted.

> I am enjoying my job much more than I did.

> I have had another look at my career and realized things had not come to an end. I recognized that I had a lot to offer which I had neglected.

> The course gave me the opportunity to take stock of myself and plan my future rather than let myself be moved by the tides.

> What can I say? I have been raving about it ever since! For me it was really incredible; I had come to a crossroads in my career and life and it gave me a tremendous boost to realize I could make things happen for myself.

Personal development was broad-ranging encompassing attitudes and skills:

> I found it thought-provoking and confidence building in terms of knowing where you want to be and enjoying the challenge of going for something you want.

> Confidence was the biggest effect for me; it taught me not to undervalue myself, how to treat more senior managers, caused me to do more advertising about what I do – keeping a higher profile. I have learned to handle stress better and my effectiveness has improved greatly by time management.

The course had a significant effect on the way I thought about myself and it changed my whole outlook.

The course gave me increased self-knowledge and many useful tools to start and continue this process.

I gained an awareness of the breadth of behaviour that people can display and the ability to modify my own style to deal effectively with them.

I had suspected for a while that I was getting certain reactions because of the way I approached people, but I hadn't been able to verbalize this. The course helped me to see how to get the right reaction by approaching things differently. I can now anticipate the result of my actions.

I learned to look to myself to use my resources which I hadn't used before because I didn't know they were there!

I am now able to stand back and think about things before rushing about trying to get everything done.

I am much more creative now – and enquiring.

In meetings I'm a lot more concise and am able to walk in calmly and do what is required.

I can prioritize more effectively, plan my time better and react to aggression and conflict by trying to see things more broadly, identifying other people's needs.

I learned how to handle conflict situations. Now when I get hot under the collar I think of the other person's motivations and that calms me down.

I am trying to fit in more; being more acceptable opens more gateways!

One of my bosses said 'Oh God – you're so aggressive,' and I said 'I'm not aggressive, I'm assertive!'

Participant definitions contribute to our understanding of *the nature of self-development:*

Self-development doesn't stop when you finish the course; I am still growing.

It is difficult to talk about self-development, it affects you so personally.

It's more about feelings than words; I can't give you labels for it – just a feeling that things are working much more smoothly.

The programme was a starting point for me; now it's up to me what I do with it.

Through the course I learned that self-development is optimistic.

I see self-development as a continuing process; once you have the techniques and confidence it is a continuing invisible process which can only be seen by looking back over the years to see how much you have changed. It has had a significant effect on my life.

Turning now to the benefits that employing organizations experienced, we received many comments highlighting *the increased managerial effectiveness of participants*. Summarized here they say that managers who have attended the course are more:

- effective
- courageous
- varied in response
- aware
- assertive
- easier to get on with
- empathetic
- able to prioritize
- responsible
- organized.

Project work benefited organizations directly:

The project work introduced a new perspective to department objectives.

The project was a theoretical one which could not be implemented immediately but gave us a framework for the future.

The project was the design of a training course which was very successful and will be run again in the future.

The course helped the department immensely because the project boosted the work of the team and laid the groundwork for results.

More general value was also identified:

It was a good investment – more satisfied employees who are also more effective.

Our company regularly sends people on the course; this must mean they benefit from it!

Participants become more aware of the two-way commitment between themselves and the organization.

The organization benefited in several ways – from the practical application of the project work, from individual managerial effectiveness, from increased team cohesiveness.

This company is about continuous change and individuals pushing for what they believe in and getting things done. The course equips them to do this.

It is perhaps stating the obvious to point out that organizations considering self-development must weigh the gains of developing managers and people against their needs for control and conformity.

To conclude, a final quotation epitomizes the dimensions of effect of our self-development for managers programme. The manager quoted works for a small part of a very much larger organization in which a formal management structure, tightly constrained resources and diffuse organizational objectives make it very difficult for individuals to effect change. The quotation pays tribute to the commitment of the organization as well as to the development of the individual concerned:

> A work colleague commented the other day that since attending the course, the organization has given me everything that I have asked for!

The Programme Design: Some Costs and Benefits

The ASO self-development programme has proved successful in the market place. This validates its design but does not hide from us the costs as well as the benefits of an approach that sets out to span alternative approaches to management development and in so doing has to accommodate inherent philosophical conflicts. There are four areas in which we have been most aware of these.

The first concerns the fact that we make a commitment in advance regarding the subjects we will cover in the workshops. This approach has clear benefits in terms of our contract with sponsors, but we and our participants pay for this lack of flexibility. This is a conflict we have not resolved and we continue to try to find self-developmental ways of meeting individual needs without disappointing the group expectations we ourselves have shaped through our guiding approach.

The second area relates to the amount of work included in the workshops. We have made a deliberate decision to pack these with content and create pace, to provide participants with a rich learning 'menu' from which to select. This decision is reinforced by our commitment to value for money and time. However, these benefits are not achieved without costs. As a 'learning cycle' process[3] our workshop design is unbalanced, providing extensive opportunities for aquiring data but leaving to the periods between the workshops the opportunities for using the information gathered. While this approach may facilitate transference of learning, it probably inhibits the divergence of thinking and risk-taking which could valuably be encouraged with more time for consideration in the learning group and away from work.

The pace of the workshops leads to a third cost – less opportunity for participants, and tutors, to relax. Feedback confirms that more relaxation would be greatly valued but we have so far reluctantly decided that we cannot release more workshop time for this. In the language of Burgoyne's model[1] it could be said therefore that we place greater value on mental agility than emotional resilience!

Perhaps this bias also contributes to a fourth cost which is specific to us as tutor/facilitators. After working on these programmes for an extended period, we recognize that our approach involves us as 'stepping stones' for the participants as they find their way across the uncharted streams of self-development experience. As they gain understanding and skill, participants leap across alone and with confidence, forgetting – entirely appropriately – that they even needed support. We delight in their self-development, but, being honest, feel at times de-motivated and deprived by the lack of recognition stepping stones attract!

However, this emotional cost is one we own as our own, and its reduction forms an objective for *our* self-development. It is more than outweighed by the benefit we gain from knowing that several participant groups still meet without need for guidance, and that many participants themselves now act as mentors and facilitators for others' learning.

We assure anyone who is considering involvement in self-development training that the return on investment can be very high.

References

1. Pedler, M. Burgoyne, J. and Boydell, T. (1978) *A Manager's Guide to Self-development,* McGraw Hill, Maidenhead, U.K.
2. Pedler, M. (1981) Men and management. In *Management Education & Development* **12** (1). Spring.
3. Kolb, D.A., Rubin, I.M. and McIntyre, J.M. (1971) *The Learning Styles Inventory in Organizational Psychology: an experiential Approach.* Prentice Hall, Englewood Cliffs, NJ.
4. Carney, C.G. and McMahon, S.L. (1977) *Exploring Contemporary Male/ Female Roles – A Facilitator's Guide.* University Associates.
5. Hennessey, J. and Hughes, M. (1984) *Self-development for Women Managers.* A report by the Anne Shaw Organization. Manpower Services Commission, Sheffield, U.K.

9

Transformations for Men

*   *   *

TOM BOYDELL

Transform and Sheffield City Polytechnic

The title of this chapter contains its final question mark because it is intended to pose questions, to raise issues, rather than to provide answers. This whole area is a relatively new one for me – territory that I only began to explore three or four years ago, and that still remains mysterious, intriguing, exciting, challenging, frightening.

This may seem surprising; after all, I am a male human being, and have been for 47 years. Furthermore, I work with managers on various aspects of their development, and the majority of managers are men. So what's new about it?

Well, what's new is my changing consciousness about being a man. This has become a key element in my own development – although I have only become aware of that fact over the past 5 years or so – and has led directly to my current interest in this whole area. So I want to start this chapter with a brief biographical overview of the way in which my own awareness of being male has changed.

I assume that when I was born I was completely unaware of the differences between men and women, or that I was one of these. I also assume that at quite an early age I began to associate certain roles, certain sources of various satisfactions, with my mother and father respectively, and that somewhere along the line I also linked mother with woman, father with man. But when this was, I have no idea; I have no recollection of it whatsoever, which leads me to believe that it was when I was pretty young.

I do remember that when I was about 5 or 6 I discovered, with intense curiosity, that the girl who lived over the road had certain amazing anatomical differences from me. And gradually I must have begun to form a picture around certain differences – physical and social – between boys and girls. I say here 'I must have' because I have very little recollection of any specific learnings; it was all done subtly, unconsciously, and in a way that very much led me to believe that it was 'normal' to be a boy; we males were 'proper' human beings, and therefore girls and women were abnormal. Inferior, weaker, born for certain relatively menial tasks, capable neither of thinking properly nor of driving a car safely, women needed to be protected, looked after, sheltered from the harsh realities of the world. As a man, it was my lot in life – privilege or burden, however I chose to see it – to behave towards these curious and unfortunate creatures with a subtle blend of decorum, gallantry, protection, condescension and violence, the exact proportion of the mixture depending on a number of sometimes interdependent factors, such as their age, class, race, sexual attractiveness, role, and what I felt I was entitled to get from them.

In a way, therefore, I could be said to have become more conscious of being male in that I was now aware that I wasn't female. I didn't know what being a man meant (indeed such a question wouldn't have made any sense to me), because being a man was normal; a man was a normal human being. If pushed, the nearest I would have been able to give in answer to 'what does being a man mean to you?' would have been in terms of not being a women. And indeed, when working with men's development groups now, by far the commonest response to that or similar questions is along those lines. Thus, asked to identify two or three things they like about being men, most reply in terms such as 'I like being able to go into a pub on my own'; 'I'm glad I'm not a woman because it would hold up my promotion at work'. In other words, at this level of consciousness being a man is seen as not being a woman. Furthermore, this is good news. Being a man means I'm not a woman, thank goodness. After all, who wants to be abnormal? There are some exceptions to this, of course, with envy of women for the apparent – and manifestly unfair – easy time they have of life. While the poor man slaves away, the kept woman stays at home with her feet up. Alternatively, women get away with things (again unfairly) because of their ability to burst into tears when the going gets tough, or because they are able to use (yet again unfairly) their sexuality to get what they want.

That's certainly how it was for me for many years. Looking back from where I am now, I would say that my next turning point was in my mid 30s. At that time my colleagues and I were very much influenced by the ideas of Carl Rogers, and became heavily committed to learner-centred strategies of managing learning programmes. In particular, we adopted this approach wholeheartedly on our courses for the training of trainers.

One of the first things I then began to notice was that women participants on these courses tended, as a broad generalization, to take more readily to this style of learning than did the men. They seemed more able to tune into what was happening in the group, into their own – and other peoples' - feelings, needs, issues and concerns. Not only were they able to tune into these, but they tended to respond to them more flexibly, caringly, creatively than did the men, who (again making quite a sweeping generalization) tended to look for structure, for logic, for systematic preplanning, and who wanted to spend less time working on needs and feelings, becoming impatient to 'get on with things'.

I have acknowledged that this is rather a sweeping generalization, but nonetheless I think the analysis stands. However, in the context of this chapter it doesn't actually matter much if it stands or not, since I'm not investigating the respective responses to non-directive learning by women and men (although that looks like rather an interesting area for investigation). No, what I am trying to do is to trace the effect of this on my own development. And since that's how I began to perceive things, then it is the effect of that perception on me (irrespective of whether it was 'right' or 'wrong') that is important.

So I was now in a position of seeing in women certain qualities that, with my enthusiasm for learner-centredness, I was valuing more and more. In addition, I was seeing in men certain other qualities that I had previously taken for granted as being both 'good' and 'male' (e.g. strong desire to get on with the task), but that which now started to become a nuisance. And for some 7 years that process continued and deepened. Course members and students were divided into heroines (usually women, but sometimes men who exhibited these feminine qualities) and villains (usually men but sometimes women with masculine qualities).*

This led me to begin to idolize women (caring, intuitive, sensitive, flexible) and denigrate men, devaluing their potentially positive qualities such as rationality, logic, task-orientation and so on. In fact, I tended to overlook these qualities entirely, and merely concentrated on their apparent lack of feminine ones, twisting this lack into something actually negative. Thus, what I now see as relative difficulty in showing care became *un*caring; difficulty in being sensitive became *in*sensitivity; difficulty in working with intuition became *stupidity*. Towards the end of this period this polarization was accentuated by my coming across that branch of feminism that sees all things male as bad. All men are rapists, thugs, boors. This fitted in well with my own position, which was thus reinforced by the ideas of my idols – women. Of course, there were a few exceptions among men whom I met; these were mostly quite 'feminine' in that they showed care, sensitivity, etc., but I very much considered them as rarities, as abnormal.

---

* Perhaps a note on terminology would be in order. I use *male* as a noun – a boy or man. *Masculine* and *feminine* are adjectives, describing qualities that both males and females possess, although traditionally masculine qualities are associated mainly with men, feminine ones with women. Later I use the term *manness* to describe all that that goes with being a male. A commoner word would be maleness, but there's so much confusion between male as a noun, male as an adjective, and masculine, that I want a word that is both clear in meaning and is deliberately provocative.

But, of course, *I* was a man – one of these beings I was now despising so much. So my consciousness had moved from 'being a man is not being a woman, thank goodness', to 'woe is me, being a man is not being a woman, and is thus being something hateful, despicable'. This had one positive effect, in that I worked hard at trying to get in touch with my feminine self, but nonetheless it was a most unhealthy position to be in, since basically it meant that I was hating much of myself. (There were other consequences, sometimes positive but mostly negative, arising out of idolizing most women and hating most men, but I won't go into those here. Suffice to say that when idols are found to have feet of clay they get knocked off their pedestals; that contrary to alleged male mythology it is idolatry that can lead to blindness; and that in a world of idols the non-idolized get a raw deal.)

As I have already indicated, this phase began gradually and then lasted some 7 years. In contrast, it ended very suddenly. As part of a 'women and men as colleagues' course with which I was involved, I found myself, albeit reluctantly, in a men's group, listening to some quite normal men talking. (By 'normal' here I mean men who, as far as I could tell, were not among the few exceptions to my current rule about the hatefulness of males.) And I suddenly found, to my amazement, that they were really nice people. They *did* have feelings, worries, fears; they *weren't* all machismo; they *did* show support for each other, and for me. In short, I suddenly felt at home with them; I was one of them.

Furthermore, I also noticed that some of the conventionally masculine characteristics displayed by these men were actually quite attractive. In the right time, at the right place, and used in the right way, qualities such as clarity, firmness, strength, objectivity, proactivity, pursuit of goals, are very useful.

This discovery had profound implications for me, for it now seemed that:

(i) most, if indeed not all, men might potentially possess the feminine side that hitherto I had attributed solely to most women and a few exceptional men;

(ii) there are a number of potentially positive and attractive masculine characteristics;

(iii) most, if indeed not all, men – *including myself* – might potentially possess these positive masculine characteristics.

Here, then, is scope indeed for further exploration, both of myself and with other men. But, one might ask, how might we go about it? And why bother? What has this got to do with organizations, with the world of work?

Before looking at reasons why, I would like to examine how we might set about this exploration. In so doing, I will use some ideas about the nature of the transformation process that we use in Transform, ideas that originated from the NPI in Holland (and which in turn have their roots in the work of Rudolf Steiner).

We look on the process of transformation as having three dimensions (see Fig. 9.1) corresponding to the three fundamental human processes of thinking, feeling and willing:

(i) *Thinking:* The dimension of ideas about the real world. Thoughts, ideas, concepts, hypotheses, facts. Hence the two ends, or polar opposites, of this dimension are *ideas* and *reality*.

(ii) *Feeling:* The dimension of feelings about oneself and about others, hence is about relationships with oneself (inner) and with others (outer).

(iii) *Willing:* The dimension concerned with making things happen, causing things to come about, over a period of time. Hence the poles are *past* and *future*.

Transformation may be seen as a process of balancing or synthesizing these poles, of establishing a continuous flow between *ideas* and *reality,* between *inner* and *outer*, and between *past* and *future* (see Fig. 9.2). How to do this will depend on the individual (or the organization) concerned. In the context of being a man, however, we can make some suggestions for transformation strategies.

Let's start, then, with thinking (the ideas–reality dimension). We may ask the basic question:

What is Manness?

Suppose you are heavily involved, out of balance, in the direction of *ideas*. That is, you have come across ideas but have not yet related them to the real world, you haven't grounded them. In this case, it would probably be helpful for you to look more at *reality*. How do all these ideas, concepts, theories, hypotheses, data, etc., relate to and tie in with your own observations and life experiences with men and with yourself as a man? How can you translate these ideas into the reality of your own life as a man? What are these ideas about the nature of manness saying to you about yourself (or your self) as a man?

On the other hand, you may be heavily involved, out of balance, in the direction of *reality*, conscious of your life experience as a man, aware of how other men are, but not yet having made sense or meaning out of your observations. If so, it will probably be fruitful for you to look more at *ideas*. That is, what concepts, theories, hypotheses, data, etc., can you

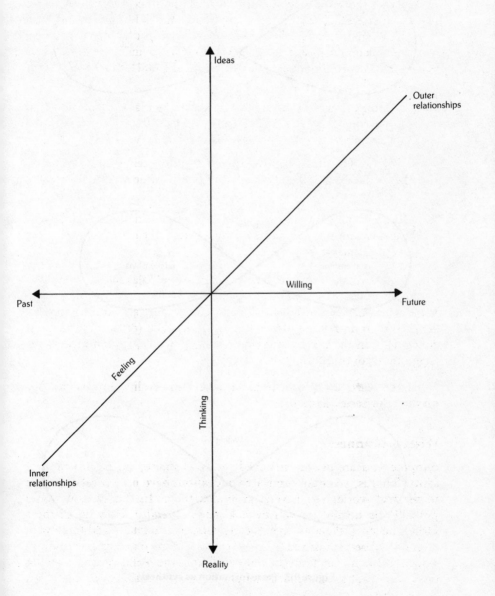

Figure 9.1 Process of transformation.

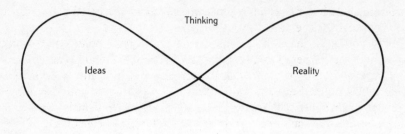

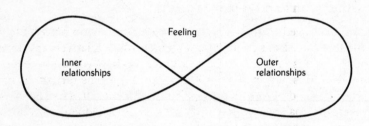

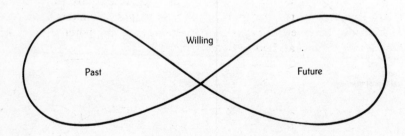

Figure 9.2 Transformation as synthesis.

generate or discover that make sense of your experiences? What are these telling you about the nature of manness?

Of course, it may well be that you are at neither pole – that is, you have not yet gathered many ideas about being a man, you are not particularly aware of your man-based experiences, and you haven't consciously noticed much about other men. In this case you can start to work at both *ideas* and *reality* more or less simultaneously, gathering ideas, becoming aware of experiences, in parallel, and constantly relating the two together.

Now we'll turn to feeling (the inner-outer dimension). We may ask the basic question:

How am I in Relation to my own Manness (inner) and to Other Men and Women (outer)?

Again, you may need to work on one or other pole, or on both more or less simultaneously. Let's assume for a moment that, relatively speaking, your greater need is to work on the *inner* pole, on how you are with your own manness. This will involve exploring what it means for you to be a man, in terms of both your masculine and feminine self. (Applying the same principle of balance between poles, if you have done quite a bit of work on your masculine inner-self, then now is the time to look at your feminine, and vice versa – see Fig. 9.3.) In the first part of this chapter I gave an account of my process so far on this dimension, which gives rise to the tentative model of Fig 9.4 – although this is only my model, and each of us may have to find his own. It's also interesting to see how my most recent move at the *inner* pole was triggered off by my changing relationship to a particular group of men, which in turn altered the way I related to other men. This is a good example of the potential constant flow between *outer* and *inner* and *outer* and . . .

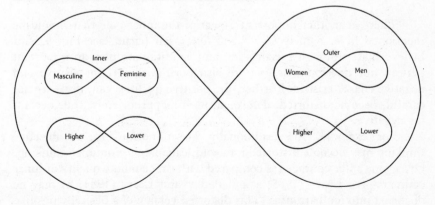

Figure 9.3 Feeling dimension.

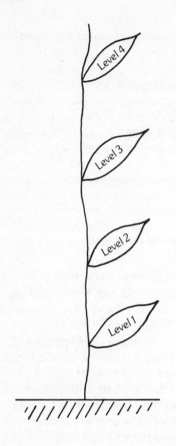

Men and women are adult
persons. Manness and womanness
are different. Personness is
shared

'Man' means 'manness';
higher and lower masculine
and feminine selves

'Man' means 'not woman';
and is normal

There is no difference
between male and
female babies

Figure 9.4 Model of personal development.

There is another important aspect of the inner pole that should be
mentioned here, namely *higher* and *lower* self (again, see Fig. 9.3). I
believe that, although socialization and conditioning play an important
part in our development, we are also born with certain positive and
negative characteristics. Further, the positive qualities can, if we are not
careful, become distorted, deformed, used inappropriately, thus becoming negative.

For example, the traditionally masculine quality of objective
thinking may become distorted into cold, calculating, inhuman thinking.
Or, again, outer courage (as compared with the feminine quality of inner
courage – see Leary (1985) 1 and Pedler and Leary (1984) 2) may be
distorted into foolhardiness. This distorted version of a basically positive
quality is also known as the 'double' of that quality. Much that has been

written and said about the negative aspects of maleness in fact relates to
these doubles of masculinity. Thus, again, aggression is the double of
assertion.

There is, luckily, a potentially positive corollary to this notion of
double. For, just as a good quality can become distorted, so can a
negative one be transformed into something positive. Thus, aggression
can be tamed into assertion, violence into risk-taking.

Naturally, there are also feminine higher and lower selves, or
doubles, to be found in both women and men. Receptivity can become
gullibility; caring may degenerate into smothering. And, again, feminine
doubles can be transformed – subjectivity into intuition, for example.

Part of working on our masculine and feminine inner selves, then,
involves both taming and transforming our doubles, and valuing and
using our positive qualities appropriately – in the right place, at the right
time, in the right manner.

When it comes to the *outer* pole of this dimension, we need to
become more conscious of the nature of our relationships with other men,
and with women. Here too there is scope for much learning. In what ways
do I relate differently to men than to women? What qualities do I bring
or give to those relationships *(inner*? What qualities of relationship do
I look for, seek, attract *(outer)*? How do I think, feel, will *(inner)* and
behave towards women and towards men *(outer)*? In more detail, how do
various aspects of my masculine and feminine higher and lower selves
(inner) interact with the masculine and feminine higher and lower selves
of women and men *(outer)*?

Finally, there is willing (the past-future dimension). We may ask the
basic questions:

Where am I in Becoming the Man I was Born to be?
Why am I Here as a Man?

This, then, is the dimension of development – of taking my next step in
becoming who I was born to be. It is very much the domain of biography
work, linking as it does the *past* with the *future*. How have I become the
man I am now? What events and themes in my life as a man in the *past*
are living in me now, or telling me something about my *future*?
Conversely, if I can see something coming to me in the *future*, can I look
back into the *past* for clues as to what this might mean, or what to do, or
what to avoid? And above all, what does it mean to me to have been born
a man? what is my purpose in life, as a man in these times?

Associated with this process of becoming who I might be is the
crossing of thresholds, with all that that implies. As a man, what or where
is my next threshold? Am I indeed at such a threshold now? What
resources (inner and outer, of course) do I need to cross it?

These, then, are some aspects of the transformation of men as I currently see it. As to the final question – what has it all got to do with organizations – well, to me that's obvious. I want to move towards a world in which, at work and elsewhere, we all of us – men and women – really understand and respect ourselves and each other; where we have tamed our doubles, where we encounter and enjoy our higher selves, where, with equal rights, we will be free to be different, to celebrate our individuality, at once rejoicing in our manness and womanness while at the same time celebrating our personness. That's what I want, and it seems quite clear to me that one part of the process of bringing that about is through the transformation of men.

References

1. Leary, M. (1985) Men and women – what are the differences and does it matter? In Boydell, T. and Hammond, V. (eds) special issue *Men and Women in Organizations. Management Education ad Development* **16** (2).
2. Pedler, M. and Leary, M. (1984) Notes on development. *Management Education and Development* **15** (1).

PART THREE

CAREER DEVELOPMENT AND SELF-DEVELOPMENT

Careers are one of the mainstays which bind individuals and organizations, harnessing individual motivations and collective goals when all is well. This is perhaps the most obvious place to look in work organizations for the application of self-development ideas.

Janice and Malcolm Leary contrast their own careers and look at how decisions and patterns are made. They favour a biographical approach to provide ways of looking at career from a past, present and future perspective.

The other three chapters in this part all concern attempts in three major companies – American Express, Pedigree Petfoods and Esso Chemical – to link self-development with appraisal and career planning. David Miller describes the system developed at American Express for some 600 professional staff and discusses gains, limitations and next steps. Cynthia Roobottom and Tony Winkless used a computer-based repertory grid approach at Pedigree Petfoods which enabled appraiser and appraisee to develop unique criteria for the assesment of performance and for indicating further development needs. Calvin Germain illustrates the use of a career planning workbook at Esso Chemical for integrating self with organization in order to try to meet and match the development needs of both.

10

Transforming your Career

* * *

JANICE AND MALCOLM LEARY

What Does a Career Mean to Me?

Careers are usually seen as a means to an end rather than of interest in themselves. We confess that until recently this tended to be our attitude; careers were either boring or beyond reach. Yet we found that by asking more searching questions and looking back over time at what careers have meant to us, another level of significance was revealed.

The part that careers play in our work life (or life's work as we prefer now to call it) reveals more about ourselves, our values and attitudes than first appears. By looking at all that a career has meant/can mean, we can begin to change our relationship to ourselves and our work. This can form a platform for a fuller transformation of a career involving greater choice and freedom.

We made a beginning along the road to 'transforming' our careers by using a biographical perspective, exploring the question 'What has a career meant to me?' This revealed some minor shocks, deeper insights and a few new discoveries. Thus, at the end of the process, a new relationship with our careers was beginning to form.

From the start we met with a barrier inside us, resisting facing up to this type of question. We had had experience of looking for deeper than superficial meaning in many areas of our lives, but . . . careers, surely not? For one of us it was a case of taking a career for granted, never really seeing it as relevant to explore further. For the other it was a case of hardly daring to attach the label 'career' to a life/work history at all. Careers were something that other people had. No prizes for working out that in the first case we are discussing a white, middle aged, qualified man, in the second an unqualified woman and mother.

Once we began to live a little more with this career question we began to realize how developmental it could all be. Intriguing contrasts between personal and professional experiences emerged. Conventions and theories about careers clashed with our actual biographies.

For Malcolm, a 'qualified male':

149

A career of some kind was expected, even demanded, as a direct outcome of the qualification process: it followed as night follows day. Initial experiences, however, were just as dark. Any views I formed about careers during these fledgling days tended to come from older and wiser work colleagues, one of whom said sagely 'careers are a series of other people's decisions'. A career was something that I fitted into, without a great deal of thought or effort. Once a career path was embarked upon it kept you on the straight and narrow. As long as you kept your nose reasonably clean success and glittering prizes would naturally follow – at least, that's how it seemed to be in the steel industry in the mid 1960s. Whether the career path led in the direction of sales or personnel or production didn't seem to be all that important. I could afford to be quite sanguine and even opportunistic about it. It never crossed my mind that other people might have viewed the presence, absence or opportunity of a career (any career) as being more critical. My colleague's convention of wisdom about careers had an underlying cynicism, which, as a fresh-faced naive graduate apprentice, disturbed me a little – but not too much. It was after all a more realistic approach to careers than some of the more trite slogans I had so far been fed – generally to do with batons and knapsacks, I remember. What gave my colleague's view added authority was that at least he had a career. For all his experience and hard work, I felt rather sorry for him, as he didn't seem to have managed to scramble very far up the ladder of success. It was envisaged that for graduates such as me, things would be very different. I was in great demand, the sky was the limit, it was time for high-flying and fast-tracking. How times have changed!

This somewhat simplistic 'world is my oyster' approach to careers became modified later; it became apparent that I had to be more conscious and deliberate about some aspects of it. Certain external time-scales and patterns needed to be considered in successfully planning my future. One quite well-known aphorism which applied then still sticks in my memory. Indeed, it could still apply in certain fields. This was the three year cycle – the amount of time you were expected to stay in one position before you got stuck, became stale and did irreparable damage to your long-term prospects. Looking back now these rules of thumb about careers were appropriate for me in my 20s – at least they gave me some markers against which to assess myself. That my career and pace of progress did not match any of these patterns didn't strike me as serious or relevent at the time. Perhaps I was less career minded than most. What is more, most of the people I knew didn't fit in exactly either, but this didn't seem to alter the theories.

As training and development work became my professional focus, careers became a subject of general as well as personal interest. Careers were, after all, part of the developmental scene, although I could never somehow take them as seriously as some of my colleagues. Maybe I was looking back to the cautionary words of my first mentor or looking for a new explanation. Career patterns, paths, choices, decisions and transitions became part of my portfolio of interests. I was still mostly non-commital about careers but it did come as something of a shock to hear a group of management trainers (appointed from line management for an indefinite period) describe coming into training as a 'career risk'.

As a consultant working for a variety of clients, with a group of equal colleagues, I often claim that I don't have a career any more – Thank God! There is, no doubt, some sense of release from having to struggle with some of the by-products of having a conventional, i.e. paid, employment career. No more problems of status, position, rewards and authority. But, how true is my claim? Have I merely replaced one kind of career for another? Do I feel the way I do because I find myself in a different set of circumstances? Has my age and growing experience got anything to do with it? These seem to me now as rather self-indulgent questions anyway, born out of a privileged position. I can afford to be blasé about my career.

In contrast, for a woman (in this case Janice), the experiences of a career are different and life/work takes on a very different meaning. The route taken was in some ways very similar to many other women of her generation and the story itself is certainly not a new one. However, when it is examined in the context of career some interesting issues are raised, particularly the difficulty of separating out a part of life called 'career' from the rest:

During my time at school I was told in no uncertain terms that 'It doesn't matter if you fail, you are only a girl after all. You'll probably get married.' Being trusted and gullible I believed that this was my place in society. Although it didn't 'feel' right it was the same route that many of my peer group were taking. When I left school I was 'lucky' to become employed by a sweet manufacturer – 'in an office as well'. I was on my way and in a most respectable sphere of activity. My ambition then was to become head of a small section from starting as office junior. I moved up the ladder naturally as women left (usually they were having babies) by stepping into their shoes. The recommended life path also involved getting 'a good catch to look after me before I was too old, and thus avoid getting left on the shelf'.

While all this pressure was being exerted I had a vague feeling of not quite being in the right place, not doing the right thing, not fulfilling my potential in some way. This feeling has never really left me. I followed what was expected of me despite the feelings. Married at 20, I gave up outside employment, had my first child at 22, the second child at 24, third at 28.

After raising my family and going through many formative experiences, I can now see that certain strong elements and qualities were being developed within me during these years, that later searched for an outlet outside of the cramped environment of the home. I became involved in many more external activities with different people who began to make use of my abilities and talents. I was amazed to find I was being recognized as being 'good at' certain surprising things. Organizing, leading, initiating, teaching and understanding human beings. I was able to adapt what I had learned to a variety of different circumstances. My experiences I had gained along the way could be used by others and were recognized by others as being valuable. My activities began to involve new learning, aquiring a wider range of skills, more formal training and education. This again awakened in me new aspirations and motivations. A few more closed doors began to open. This 38 year old began to 'take off'.

This kind of relatively unstructured 'career' patterning does have its disadvantages. There were many fixed pictures around about what a proper career path should look like – mine did not match any of these. A career break is taken to raise a family yet is this an integral part of a broader view of a career? Part of the whole picture of a career/life-work?

To some it would also seem that my career has been a rather chequered and tattered mixture of accidents and opportunisms. Perhaps this serves to highlight how different from the neat conventionality real careers can be – and often are.

During a recent session on Careers and Biography we asked 30 or so participants to map out this 'real' career path – including highs and lows, ups and downs, accidents and planned moves. As a framework for doing this we provided seven-year time-spans (a flipchart for each) starting from 0–7, 7–14, and so on. The participant career 'biographers' were invited to illustrate what a career had meant to them during these seven-year periods of time, and see how their views had changed. We also asked them to think of attitudes they had now towards their career in the future, as well as examining past and current views. We strongly encouraged them to use a form of expression which came closest to their feelings at the time. So we had a huge variety of different anecdotes, quotations, mini-stories, verses, pictures, etc. These individual contributions when displayed together covered quite a span of time, gave a living and rich picture of careers in terms of how they had been and were being experienced inwardly, as well as illustrating graphically the outer features. This inner dimension often contrasted sharply with the outer form and substance, the outer form being determined largely perhaps by external circumstances and pressures. How a career (involving changes, thresholds, decision points, etc.) is experienced inwardly needs to be understood much more if a fuller picture of what careers are all about is to be built up. The tableau of careers built up through the above exercise showed a rich and somewhat confusing patterning of inner and outer, ups and downs, highs and lows, ins and outs. If seen in purely conventional 'outside' terms career patterns could be all over the place. However, seen within a wider context and in terms of personal ambitions, orientations and challenges, every twist and turn, each movement however made, made its own sense and had significance for each 'owner'.

Career Patterns

Over the course of a particular career certain characteristic features may stand out, such as repeated changes at regular intervals, periods of stagnation or consolidation followed by quick movement, adjustments made to external circumstances. Yet even when the outer pattern is clear, we may still be left with residual doubts and questions as we search for a different level of meaning and significance of past changes. Why did we really make that career decision? What caused that specific change of direction, at that time? What may appear to be merely a 'good idea at the time' can in retrospect seem a stroke of sheer genius; what was a well thought out move at the time now appears to be no more than a crazy whim.

It may be difficult without hindsight to sense any discernible route which the overall career is taking from among the many twisted turns, yet somehow we sense an underlying purpose. Spectacular outer changes are interspersed with long periods where nothing particular is happening – 'aimless meanderings' as one colleague described them. When this is happening who is steering the ship? What combination of factors is playing into the determination of a career path, and what influence have they? Am I having a career or is my career having me? Is my career determined by my conscious choices, other peoples' precipitate decisions, or is the whole thing a combination of coincidence and sheer accident? These questions can take some answering. Having some generalized examples of familiar career structures and patterns against which to compare and contrast our own can help us to think more clearly and more deeply, as long as these set patterns are not used as templates that we feel somehow obliged to fit into.

Some attempts have been made to describe a number of these more familiar career patterns. The following commonly used categorization includes a description of the four different types (based on Driver (1987)[1]):

(i) *The drifter*. Moving from job to job at random. Shopping around to see what suits. Not building up a 'track record' in any particular field. Little solid experience to offer.

   Flexibility is acquired which can be useful in times of rapid change.

(ii) *Life's work*. Choosing a direction early and continuing in a chosen field throughout working life. Usually involves a professional commitment, qualifications, etc.

   Can be fixing and limiting and difficult to change. Can also be very rewarding both economically and personally.

(iii) *Snakes and ladders.* A more traditional view of careers often evident in large organizations. Involves climbing up the rungs of career ladders. Some take you to the 'top', others are dead ends. Sometimes it is possible to cross from one ladder to another (e.g. changing from one function to another) but this is difficult.

The snakes represent the demotions, redundancies, shifts into backwaters and other mishaps which can befall ladder climbers.

This approach requires political astuteness and a preparedness to adapt to the needs and interests of the organization. It can have a narrowing effect, limiting personal development, but the rewards can be high if you get to the 'top'.

(iv) *Reflexive.* The focus of attention here is more on the person, developing skills and interests to be made available for a wider variety of possible career purposes. This can develop flexibility in times of change. It involves a degree of self-management and opportunism.

Against this generalized background the following more specific discoveries were made recently by a group examining their career patterns:

(i) In their early stages careers can be seen almost exclusively in terms of a job or task to be performed and the role to be played: 'I want to be a footballer, nurse, an engineer.' Later (sometimes much later) the quality of the person behind the role becames more important: 'No matter what I do I want to use my athleticism, I want to use my caring qualities, my ability to organize things. etc.'

(ii) In mid-life and often mid-career, extra energy seems suddenly to become available. Roles can change, positions are altered and there is an urge to move on. There is an urgent need to see around the corner – 'What comes next?' If no alternatives can be found or the options are closed off there is a strong sense of being denied and blocked.

(iii) In mid-career comes the realization that the good news about careers is only one side of the picture. There is a price to pay and this comes in terms of restriction of opportunities, no time or room for yourself (or others), stress and heavy emotional demands to keep up. The post-career period is seen as a time to make up for these sacrifices.

(iv) Retirement was seen ahead by many as a positive time to do things that they had no time for at the present, e.g. hobbies, relaxation, time for yourself, travel, a catching up time.

(v) Different attitudes to careers emerged at different ages. What careers mean in our 20s can be vastly different in our 40s. These attitudes seem to be influenced partly by societal conditioning, but are also reinforced by our own inner questions and development needs as we move through different age phases.

(vi) Conventions and cultural norms about careers affected peoples' perceptions of themselves and their careers. Paths which began in the 1950s and 60s were influenced strongly by concepts of: 'What do I want to be when I grow up?' Later a more functional and instrumental question emerged: 'What job would you like to do?' Now perhaps the most urgent question becomes: 'Is there a place for me at all?'

Careers are obviously influenced at a deeper level by more than the requirements of an organization, a profession or society as a whole. There is more to having a career than the ordering and forming of work around people into particular shapes, according to certain convenient criteria. Within a career real questions of individual development and transformation are raised. Yet there is rarely any encouragement actively to work through these 'personal' issues within the rather limiting confines of existing thinking and attitudes about careers. This requires a more expanded paradigm within which to look at career, one which enables the full individual to be able to place themselves within a career context, including all their questions, doubts and uncertainties, struggles and strivings – as well as their abilities, capacities, skills and achievements.

A more expansive way of assessing and working with careers is needed if a career is to become all that it could be to ourselves and the world of work.

Career and Self-development

There are encouraging signs that more developmental views on careers and their place in our working lives are emerging. Changing perceptions of careers and the place they have in our lives gives expression to residual inner and personal concerns about careers as well as indicating more academic concerns. Any study of careers reflects the working times in which we live. The choice of issues focussed on reveals the breadth and scope of conventional thinking. The following summary of the main shifts which have affected and influenced our perspective on careers over the last 30–40 years highlight this change in mood and emphasis.

In the 1950s

Careers seen only in terms of job, tasks performed.

The days of pure *'career development'*. Careers seen in isolation, very closely related to the demands of the job, task and role. The professional and organizational view of careers into which the individual fitted (and gained) or fell outside (and lost out).

In the 1960s

Life surroundings within which a career is carried out are deemed to be 'influential'.

A new emphasis comes in, i.e. *career/life planning*. How the rest of your life (i.e. home, family, outside interests, values) affects your career becomes an important influence on your career choices (note the direction of the interest, from the career towards the rest of you). This may involve you adjusting your life to take account of the requirements of your career, taking more care that your career is not adversely affected by what you get up to in the rest of your life.

In the 1970s and 1980s

Concern for the balance of life: how career affects other aspects of life, and vice versa.

The emphasis shifts again. Concerns for life and careers are almost reversed. It now becomes *life/career development*. Typical questions which have become legitimate are now:

(i) How does your career fit into the rest of your life?

(ii) What are your priorities and how does a career fit in with these?

(iii) What sacrifices does a career call for?

(iv) What price has to be paid for the benefits of a career and is the price to high?

(v) How does my career significantly affect others in my life?

(vi) What are the consequences and implications for them as well as for me of making a particular career decision?

    (vii) Most specifically, what have been (and are likely to be) the consequences for me of having chosen a particular career path?

    (viii) Has the way my career proceeded formed some of my ways of thinking, behaving and how I approach people and problems?

    (ix) Has it meant certain 'deformations' have crept in?

    (x) Has developing certain strengths and capacities in a particular direction also meant that I have become just a little one-sided in my views, opinions and ways of doing things?

Towards the 1990s

Perhaps the beginnings of an even more integrated, holistic approach to work, individuals, careers and their place in our lives? Narrower concepts of careers are slowly becoming more open, fluid and flexible. A career can be a path of development (or part of an overall route to development).

There is evidence of strong moves away from seeing careers in a narrow sense, i.e. as the unquestioned focus of attention and source of satisfaction from life. Careers have to earn this right. They need to be viewed within the context of *a person's whole biography* and against a *fuller image of the person* to escape from the straightjacket of convention, accepted practice and oppressive adherence to strict rules and norms. Liberation from the prison of a career which is experienced as a trap or a rut (however fur-lined) can only come through the free response of individuals to life/career choices out of raised consciousness about options and consequences. This greater freedom comes about firstly through encouraging career decisions to be made out of greater understanding and awareness of ourselves and our circumstances – against which the real and full effects of career decisions can then be judged. Then a career can be allowed to influence our 'life'/work but it does not take over or dominate to the exclusion of all other aspects of work, home, family, interests, health and hygiene. Too often we have allowed careers to become the masters of our fate rather than the servants of our destiny. Careers have somehow been allowed to take over – but these situations can be transformed. Setting them within a broader biographical context is one step in this direction which we can all take.

Looking at Careers with a Biographical Perspective

It is not the intention here to describe in fullest detail the methods and techniques used in biography work. This is adequately done in a number of places elsewhere – for example Boydell and Pedler (1985).[2] The biography process as described here specifically shows how individuals can begin to relate better to themselves and to their major life interests and challenges, many of which are wrapped up in a career. A biographical perspective takes in the past, present and future. It attempts to make links between the varying elements which make up any life and career patterns, uncovering many of the internal workings as well as highlighting the course and structure of external happenings. Thinking about and working on our career in this way can provide:

   (i) an overview of a career so far – i.e. the past;

  (ii) a 'stocktaking' of questions and issues regarding a career which are coming our way in the present;

 (iii) a platform for making conscious, purposeful decisions about our career in the future.

   Working with a career in terms of *the past* involves examining:

   (i) *Events.* Highlight key events which stand out, using this picture to reveal the cycles, patterns and rhythms linking up various career decision points. This shows, in relief, significant changes in direction, turning points and blockages.

  (ii) *Periods.* Between the key events may be periods of time where nothing spectacular happened but which nevertheless represent important contributions to a career portfolio. Often during periods when nothing much is going on externally as far as our career is concerned there are considerable inner changes taking place. Often a period of consolidation is beneficial after a hectic time, and certain qualities (from a career) can emerge over a *period* of time. These periods are characterized, and with key events provide a background against which careers can be assessed.

 (iii) *Themes.* These are concerned with the underlying trends in a career. Themes can be:

      (a) recurring patterns of thoughts, teachings and behaviour;

      (b) constant features of a person and their life reflected in the career pattern;

      (c) a personal characteristic which emerges from time to time as a career preference or criterion for making career decisions;

(d) a tendency for certain things to happen (or not to happen) within a career which says something about the person as well as the career;

(e) particular aspects of the person making themselves visible in different ways consistently throughout the career.

All the above elements can work their way into the fabric of a career, giving it its particular shape, form and colour. The career we have represents one focus of the total biographical story written by us out of whatever raw material we have at our disposal.

Looking at the past in this way can alter substantially the way we see ourselves and our career. The following comments have been made by those who have worked on their career biographies in the ways described:

I can now see the whole picture rather than the bits and pieces.

Working with my biography/career highlighted significant features which I have never noticed before.

What happened surrounding the key events in my career was often more important than the events themselves.

Taking Stock of the Present

This involves facing and confronting career questions and the issues of current concern. Some methods used here include:

(i) *Building up an overall picture of your life,* imagining you are someone else describing your career, particularly concentrating on unfinished business, sensing what has currently to be faced up to, what decisions and choices need now to be made, what work remains to be done.

(ii) *Identifying the major themes* in your career and considering what you want to happen to them:
   – Do they fall away?
   – Are they to be replaced by new themes?
   – Which do you wish to continue with and why?
   – Do they need strenthening?

(iii) *People in your consciousness,* looking at current relationships with individuals and/or groups:
   – What is the nature of these relationships which your particular career involves you in?
   – What is the quality of these relationships?

– Are they satisfactory or do you wish to change them?
– How did they get like that?
– How has your career influenced the relationships?
– Have these relationships been the consequence of having a particular career?

A particularly challenging step to take is to become more aware of the questions which others are asking you as a consequence of having a particular career. These questions posed by others may not have been asked directly. They may have been whispers rather than shouts but nevertheless they can constitute important elements to take into consideration in managing a career in the fullest sense. Too often they are considerations which are left out in the rush to take immediate advantage of every opportunity which comes up.

Moving to the Future

Often career counselling concentrates almost exclusively on helping people look to the future. Without an underpinning in terms of what has happened in the past, and what this means for the present, careers advice can often appear to be left hanging in the air – unconnected and without any continuity or purpose behind it. Career planning in this atmosphere then becomes a very unsatisfying activity, a hit-and-miss affair.

Future orientated approaches taken from biography work build on the basis of work done in looking at the past and present. This can prove particularly helpful in showing a wider range of options in terms of employment patterns and forms, e.g. job sharing, self-employment, part-time working. Broader future directions can be sensed before moving to make hasty specific decisions, a range of options and alternatives can be pictured and considered more deeply. The moral consequences for self and others can be formulated before 'leaping off'. After realizing that maybe previous career decisions had not fully taken account of the needs of others, one participant's retirement options were hastily re-examined.

Looking at a career within the broader biographical context shows the futile one-sidedness of artificially separating a career from other life and personal issues and concerns. We cannot do this without either denying ourselves or placing unreal boundaries and constraints around us.

The biographical process is best used, not as a strict linear progression from past, present and future, but as a constantly flowing stream, illustrating clearly the underlying dynamic, organic and forma- tive processes constantly at work in shaping a career:

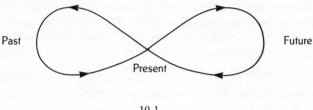

Past

Present

Future

10.1.

These basic 'biographical' forces of conception, formation, birth, maturation, metamorphosis, decline, breakdown, death and rebirth are reflected in the cycles and patterns of a career. If these forces are better understood and consciously worked with, in response to, and in conjunction with, external opportunities and challenges, an individual can go some way to determining a self-directed career process to replace an externally determined career path. A career evolves in cycles. As some elements arise others die away, to be replaced by more significant features, more appropriate to our phase of development and maturity. What was right for us at one time on our career path is not meaningful at later stages. We constantly outlive and outgrow aspects of our career; as long as we allow them to fall away naturally, to be replaced by more relevant features, the overall career pattern remains a developmental focus in our lives.

Often these cyclical elements are hidden beneath the paraphernalia of imposed patterns, conventional wisdom about 'right' careers and other people's expectations.

The overall pattern will contain a number of crossover points, crossroads and thresholds associated with major career changes. These breaking points involve leaving things behind as well as moving on. Between the endings and new beginnings may be crises and turbulant times. Each of these stages will have distinct features to learn our way through.

(i) *Making endings.* Through changes of role, redundancy, being replaced, moved, demoted or even promoted. Involves breaking away from unconscious dependencies, tying up loose ends, dealing with unfinished business, coping with a sense of loss. Deliberately *opting out – saying no to things;* also leaving behind people, organizations, relationships, places. Breaking with physical habits, established routines and prescribed roles and relationships.

(ii) *Managing transitions.* Can mean managing, coping with changes, meeting thresholds, taking steps into the unknown, facing risks and uncertainty. Leads (hopefully) to:

(iii) *Taking initiatives.* Concerned with making new beginnings, taking promotion, starting a new job, joining a new organization, forming new relationships, making choices. Involves inner preparation for new tasks, consciously stepping into new situations. Deliberately *opting in – saying yes.*

This basic cycle of endings, transitions and new beginnings can be repeated many times throughout a career:

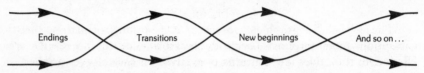

Endings   Transitions   New beginnings   And so on...

These cycles can be managed better if we prepare for them – by raising the consciousness with which we experience them. Endings are often badly dealt with or left to take care of themselves; with transitions it's often a case of holding our breath; and in taking initiatives we are frozen rigid by apprehension or overcome by recklessness. There must be a better way of handling these issues which, after all, are natural enough consequences of being a career person.

Careers and the Total Person

In order to appreciate fully the impact a career makes on us as individuals we must consider its relationship with all other key aspects of our make-up. A full developmental perspective on the individual also considers how these various aspects fit together, as well as examining the parts themselves in detail.

The parts in question are those different elements which make up the total personality, i.e. the character, the temperament, our particular orientations, attitudes and basic outlooks on life, brought together by our individuality. All these elements of the personality will be affected by, and be brought into play through, the particular way in which our career proceeds. Career decisions and events give rise to inner questions such as:

(i) What does my career do *for* me as well as *to* me?

(ii) Which elements of my personality are enhanced by a career, which are held back?

(iii) How am I empowered or disabled by my career?

(iv) How do changes in one area of my personality affect the rest?

If demands placed upon us by our career run against the grain of our developing personality at one time, they will be met by inner resistance and lead to distortion. If we are required to undergo many changes as a consequence of our career this may clash with our basic need for stability. Career requirements at a particular time call for the stengthening of particular qualities and this may not coincide with our personal reasons. We can only adjust ourselves so much to meet career requirements before the strain shows.

Careers for All?

Careers have the potential to provide development opportunities for all. No longer can they be considered as the privileged preserve of the fortunate few. A career used to be almost exclusively restricted to those who were in full-time paid employment of a professional nature. Such careers are still viewed by many as the only 'proper' careers, but the field is increasingly opening and widening to include a variety of possibilities for many more people. The concept of a career now quite legitimately encompasses part-paid or even non-paid work, voluntary work, self-employment, education, sabbaticals and a whole range of life/work experiences gained in the home and in the community in general.

For those who have felt 'left out', denied the opportunities which careers open up for others, this is encouraging news. But for careers to fulfil this potential they have to be better managed from the outside and transformed from the outside and transformed from the inside. What does this involve?

Outer Forms of a Career

Having a career can be extremely influential in shaping our habits and routines, our ways of operating and behaving. These career influences often form themselves into particular outer patterns which we somehow find ourselves fitting. Each career has its own rituals, routines and set ways of doing things, normally more visible to those on the outside than to those who are inside the career structure. Being part of a career group develops boundaries between the things which are 'done' and 'not done'. The way attitudes to self and others become formed and hardened are only visible to those on the outside.

Inner Qualities

The inner effects of a career may be less visible but are nonetheless important in helping to make us the way we are. Our attitude to ourselves, our life and career can be moulded and shaped into certain inner stances and orientations giving rise to a particular colouring of attitude. In examining the qualities which managers brought to their work a recent study[3] identified a range of such inner orientations and qualities:

(i) *adhering* – sticking to existing, 'standard' rules and procedures;

(ii) *adapting* – responding to circumstances by modifying rules etc., controlling things and people;

(iii) *relating* – being sensitive and aware, in tune with what is happening, relating to norms and conventions;

(iv) *experiencing* – being prepared to learn from experiences and developing your own way of doing things;

(v) *experimenting/striving* – deliberately setting out to discover more, improve things;

(vi) *connecting* – making links, understanding on a broader basis, looking at consequences and implications;

(vii) *integrating* – a sense of life-task, the needs of the times, making a contribution to something significant.

As well as affecting the way we are, these various orientations also provide different possibilities for development of ourselves through a career, provided we can consciously face up to the challenges, care for our own position and questions, and summon the courage to live with the consequences and implications of our choices.

The more we put into a career the more we will get out of it, and the medium of a career can thus be used for our developmental purposes. Whether this potential is realized depends to a degree on our attitudes – whether we are likely to bring out the best in ourselves through our career, or we allow it to impose its worst excesses upon us.

Careers on the Lighter Side

A career can provide unique opportunities as a vehicle for certain kinds of personal development and individual transformation – opportunities that are unlikely to be presented elsewhere. In this sense a carer is hard to replace.

The contributions a career can make to our overall development can include:

(i) Opening up opportunities for individuals to try new things, do things differently, take on new challenges and overcome difficulties and barriers. The very substance, in fact, of development.

(ii) Chances to work with others on meaningful tasks, become more social, work as a group. Reciprocal support for development. Making conscious sacrifices for others.

(iii) An outlet for natural abilities and 'God-given gifts'.

(iv) Overcoming disabilities, ensuring disabilities do not become handicaps.

(v) Coping with crises, moving through transitions, experience of significant thresholds. Learning from wider experiences. Incorporating learning into future activities.

(vi) Giving back valuable skills and capacities for the benefit of others.

(vii) Making a contribution to something worthwhile.

(viii) Fulfilling a sense of purpose, vocation and destiny. Carrying out tasks you were meant to be doing.

Careers on the Darker Side

It is only too easy, unfortunately, to dwell on the more negative effects a career can have on those fortunate enough to have one. Often careers only present a distorted and deformed version of what they are capable of, a cruel caricature for some of what they have in fact meant to others.

The strongest pressure is to fit people up for careers which are conveniently structured and formed for the benefit of an organization, profession or society as a whole. The individual involved is left out of the calculations, human needs are neglected or ignored. We either become innocent victims of this pressure or collude with it, the immediate rewards blinding us to its real effects on us.

The first vital steps towards making more moral career choices for ourselves and others involves becoming more conscious of the major vital influences careers can have on our development. Once we are more conscious, we can make real choices, claiming back our careers and life work from those who have sought to capture them to serve their own narrow purposes, or opening up new developmental channels for those who have so far been denied the possibility of a career.

References

1. Driver, M.J. (1987) Career concepts and career management in organizations. In Cooper, C. (ed.) *Behavioural Problems in Organizations*. Prentice Hall Inc., New Jersey.
2. Boydell, T. and Pedler, M. (1985) *Managing Yourself*. Fontana.

11

Linking Self-development to Assessment at American Express

* * *

DAVID MILLER

Director – Personnel Services, Regional HQ,
American Express (Europe) Ltd

While I was head of personnel for the regional headquarters division of American Express in Europe I was heavily involved in the resourcing and development of a large number of professional staff, particularly in the area of systems development and enhancement. Some years ago in a previous incarnation as a management development advisor I had had a considerable involvement with appraisal schemes and it became clear as I drew on this experience that for a range of business and career development reasons the existing appraisal process was not meeting the needs of either the business or the individual.

We set out therefore to look at the needs of our staff and to design a new appraisal process which would meet those needs. This process led us eventually to implement the *American Express TRS Professional Staff Appraisal and Development Guide** (referred to from now on as the *Guide*).

This chapter describes a number of the features of this design, development and implementation process. In particular it describes:

(i) the business environment;

(ii) its guiding design principles;

(iii) the design process itself; and

(iv) lastly its implementation and evaluation.

When describing the evolution, planning and implementation of any programme it is usually interesting to reflect back on the business and

---

* Extracts from which are reproduced with the kind permission of American Express.

strategic human resource drives which led to its creation. Within American Express there were probably three major catalysts for change in the way in which we appraised and undertook career planning for our information systems professionals.

The first factor that was important to us was that there had been a tremendous growth in the size of American Express's business in Europe. We had almost doubled our pre-tax profits in three years. This growth had taken place in an arena of fierce competition where the issues of marketing, pricing, productivity and particularly quality and customer service were and are vital to the success of the business. This had led American Express to expand its data processing capacity in order that we could increase productivity and continue to provide a high level of quality and customer service to our customers. This was paralleled by the introduction of a whole range of new or improved services; for example we designed, planned and implemented an automated teller machine network right across Europe, from Barcelona to Stavanger.

Secondly, this growth in the range and size of the DP functions had led us to employ a large number of professional systems, communications and operations staff. When we developed the *Guide* they numbered just over 300. They were faced with an increasingly complex organization and diversity of career opportunities which were often radically different from those five or ten years ago. What was also clear is that this rate of change was unlikely to diminish. Issues of skill flexibility, job training, role changes, different and more demanding expectations were not going simply to go away. These changes were naturally manifesting themselves in, for example, increased demands for counselling, for requests for more appropriate appraisal programmes and an emerging lack of clarity about careers as people tried to make sense out of the change process.

Lastly we felt in the human resource function that, while we had a successful appraisal scheme which had run well for a number of years, we needed to give people more help in clarifying career issues. We also felt we could achieve that through giving them some simple, pragmatic, analytical tools and by linking those tools to a mechanism which allowed management to give good, strong, constructive feedback and coaching to each individual.

Guiding Principles

Before we designed our *Guide* we developed a number of principles which were to act as design parameters. It would, however, be less than honest of me if I didn't point out that some of these became firmed up during the process and were initially rather hazy!

(i) We wanted to enshrine in the *Guide* a number of American Express values, but particularly those of quality, customer service and respect for the individual which we believe differentiates us both in the market place and in our whole approach to employee relations.

(ii) We wanted to make the issues as simple and clear as possible. This is not to say that the outcomes might not be complex and difficult to implement but we didn't see our role as making the process complicated and confusing in its content. In line with this the *Guide* had to be simple to use. From a practical point of view someone had to be able to pick the *Guide* up and very quickly understand how to use it. We believed that there was almost a direct correlation between its simplicity (and length) and the likelihood the *Guide* would be used. It is now used at least annually by over 300 people, so this factor proved to be vital.

(iii) Because it was designed inside American Express we wanted to ensure, as far as is possible, that none of the outcomes could be construed by the employee as a *'promise'*, in other words *'I have reached this decision, it is now American Express's duty to implement it.'* We did this by first encouraging employees at every stage to question the conclusions they had reached, for example *'check it with other people ... What evidence do you have to support that conclusion?'* and so on. Secondly, before they submit their action plans we remind them to think through how they would approach their manager (see Fig. 11.1).

Look over the action plan you have prepared. Ask the following questions:

- How is your Manager likely to respond to it?
- What are the areas of possible disagreement?
- What evidence might you use to support your position and overcome anticipated objections?
- How will your plan contribute to the effectiveness of your department?
- What compromise would you be prepared to make?

When you feel comfortable that your plan reflects the best possible combination regarding the meeting of your own needs, interests and goals and those of the Company, and you feel you can support your belief, then you are ready for the appraisal session with your Manager.

Figure 11.1 Issues to consider prior to submission of action plans.

This may appear to be confrontational in approach but it was crucial to us that the employee as well as the organization attempted to bridge the gap between the employee's expectations and the organizations ability to meet those expectations through providing particular career opportunities.

The Design Process

Once we had established the guiding principles we set out to evaluate far more clearly what the employees' views were, and through a series of pilot sessions to test those views and amend them accordingly. With the help of John Burgoyne of the Lancaster School of Management we set out to do this. The market research phase was probably the most interesting because although we had a great deal of data from attitude surveys we had never really asked our people what type of appraisal and development schemes would be helpful to them. Not surprisingly many had difficulty in pinpointing exact processes that might be useful but a number of consistent themes came through the research. In particular they wanted a far greater input into the career planning process.

> I have a clear idea of where I want to go but I'm not sure how the Company can help me. (Systems Analyst)

They clearly understood the role of a manager in an appraisal but nevertheless saw scope for a greater involvement in the appraisal process. Another clear trend was they wanted a programme which was more forward looking and didn't concentrate solely on appraisal against pre-set goals. Lastly they wanted a single, simple and high-quality product to use.

After that I set off on a tortuous route of writing, piloting and rewriting. A thick skin seems to be an essential element in this line of work! In particular John Burgoyne was invaluable as a resource outside the organization to bounce my ideas off and to provide ideas which were to prove crucial in overcoming a number of hurdles. The feedback, as might be expected, seemed to be saying consistently 'make it simpler', 'this is ambiguous' 'cut it down' and 'less referring back'. This led to a drastic pruning of the *Guide* over two or three pilot runs to about 50% of its original size. I will talk later of the implementation process which was of course crucial to its successful introduction but before that it is necessary to describe the *Guide*.

The *Guide*

The *Guide* consists of two sections:

 (i) a self analysis section;

(ii) an appraisal section.

These are both contained within a slim booklet and are linked by an action planning form which must be completed by the employee.

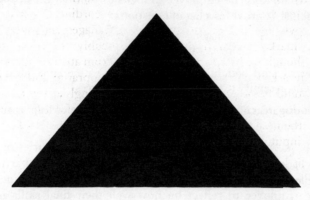

Figure 11.2 Self-analysis section of the Guide.

Self-analysis Section

This is held together by the proposition that essentially a career move within a single organization is the bringing together in one place at one time of three factors (see Fig. 11.2). Therefore career development is seen as a continuous process of reviewing these three factors. The factors are quite clearly interdependent. To take an extreme example an overseas appointment is only possible for the family man or woman if their family is happy to live outside the UK. In the terms of our model the skills and career openings may be there, but the motivation and aptitudes are clearly not aligned. The *Guide* asks the employee to examine one factor at a time. It stresses continuously that people need to be honest and realistic. They must continuously use the boss, peers and where appropriate, subordinates to check data. The idea is neither to elevate or depress people's expectations but to get them to undertake sensible, pragmatic career planning. We see career planning as a practical task-orientated exercise.

Skills, Knowledge and Experience

We eventually used a simple five-step spreadsheet approach which examines the employees skills and the skills which are missing or underdeveloped. It encourages the employee to begin to develop an inventory of skills and a plan for training and development in order to meet the skills shortfalls. The section is prefaced by a list of prompt questions which asks the employee to focus on a wider set of issues than technical skills. It provides a list of questions:

> How good am I at managing my own stress, dealing with emotional situations, coping and living with uncertainty?

> How creative am I both in terms of coming up with original ideas myself and in being receptive to new ideas from other sources?

> Are there any areas of technical, legal or professional knowledge that I need for the future?

These questions were set to try to push the boundaries of people's thinking a little further. It tries to get away from a focus on particular job related skills and to think more laterally about some of these issues. Lastly it asks the employee to reflect on how well their final skills inventory matches their existing career aspirations.

We had a number of staff who started Open University Management programmes after going through this process. It made them focus on a wider range of skills and raised a number of concerns in their own minds about their leadership experience and management in general. It also raised a number of enquiries about business school education which were later pursued.

Motivations and Aspirations

This section rests on the premise that, in general terms, an individual will do well in a job when their preferences, values, style and attitudes are compatible with those required by the position. We wanted employees to think through a wide set of issues when considering career options. At a very basic level, for example, is the amount of travelling, or the extra hours required to work, or working on shifts compatible with their home life? Is it also compatible with their expectations of what constitutes commitment to American Express? In other words they need to think through what are the likely parameters that they are going to set. It may well be at times management's job to try and persuade people to extend these boundaries!

> My family don't understand why I need to work late and this is causing friction at home. (John B. Programmer)

We found that a Work Preferences Inventory (as shown in Fig. 11.4) was very useful in terms of creating a rigorous structure which could be followed and thought through by the employee.

Opportunities

Finally the *Guide* asks the employee to consider what type of opportunities there are likely to be available in the organization. It asks only that people should try and project forward two to four years. The Company and the industry is simply changing too fast to allow anything more. This pace of change is of course exaggerated in DP. For example, what will the effect be of the next generation programming languages on programming careers? There is a great deal of debate as to whether there will actually be a job called programmer in five or ten years' time.

> By working through the process she was very sure about what she wanted. We had a long and sometimes heated debate about how Amex could meet her needs and how she could reach the position she wanted. (Project Manager)

It is an important part of the 'reality checking' that people focus on real jobs in the organization and not on jobs which they believe should exist (although the latter can be useful at times).

You will tend to do well in jobs when your own preferences, values, style and attitudes are compatible with the needs of the position and the company. Below is a questionnaire which will help you describe your own personal characteristics.

This section of the guide focuses on "what you want to do" rather than what you are capable of doing.

As you move through a career you will be making critical decisions, for example:
- The type of environment you feel happiest in
- The balance you want between your work life and your home life
- How much autonomy you want

Work Preferences, Values, Styles and Attitudes.

Consider each of the following characteristics of job situations, indicating the degree to which each is important or desirable to you. Circle the number which best reflects your current personal preferences, using the following scale:

1) Very important or desirable characteristic:
   You would be very disappointed, dissatisfied, or unable to work effectively if this did not characterize your job; this is a central source of job satisfaction for you.
2) Rather desirable:
   You would like this characteristic to be present, but you could work effectively without it.
3) Neutral:
   You would be neither pleased nor displeased with this characteristic; it is not important, one way or the other.
4) Rather undesirable:
   If this were present in your job, it would disturb or irritate you somewhat, but you could manage to work around it; you would not be satisfied.
5) Very undesirable:
   You would have great difficulty tolerating a job with this characteristic; it would probably make you want to change jobs.

Circle appropriate number		Job Characteristics
1 2 3 4 5	A	Autonomy: personal freedom to set your own work schedule, select your own projects, follow your own interests.
1 2 3 4 5	B	Security: stable long-range career path, predictable income and retirement.
1 2 3 4 5	C	Affiliation: teamwork, close, personal relationships with colleagues, social satisfaction through work, frequent interpersonal interactions.
1 2 3 4 5	D	Financial rewards: outstanding income and benefits, material success.
1 2 3 4 5	E	Variety: absence of routine, frequent changes in task demand, many different activities.
1 2 3 4 5	F	Recognition: status, visibility, reputation, titles, awards.
1 2 3 4 5	G	Creativity: demands for innovative solutions to problems, inventiveness, novelty.
1 2 3 4 5	H	Productivity: demands for high levels of concrete outputs, challenging short-term goals.

1 2 3 4 5	I	Managerial influence: control over others, significant impact on events, responsibility for significant leadership.
1 2 3 4 5	J	Clarity: well-defined rules, regulations, and procedures, clearly measurable output goals.
1 2 3 4 5	K	Technical specialisation: need to exercise sophisticated technical and analytical skills.
1 2 3 4 5	L	Advancement: opportunity for promotion, path to higher levels of responsibility.
1 2 3 4 5	M	Self-development: learning opportunities, challenging assignments, personal and professional growth.
1 2 3 4 5	N	Other:
1 2 3 4 5	O	Other:

Figure 11.3 Work preferences inventory.

Action Plan

Lastly this is brought together in an action plan which asks the employee to summarize the outcomes of their deliberations on a single sheet for discussion with their Manager at appraisal. It forms part of the documentation employee files. This can be a difficult exercise for employees (as well as managers) as occasionally the 'self-analysis' may well lead an employee to decide that his or her future lies outside American Express. Should they share this information, or are they likely to share it with their Manager? We recognize that for some people this might be a little too honest!

So the action plan is likely to be a description of what the employees want to say rather than always the exact reality. Our hopes (which are often substantiated) are that this process will alert us to the employee's career intentions even if this is not good news to us. If we know about a problem we have an opportunity to tackle it.

I have been unhappy about the type of projects I have worked on. They're not developing my career. (Analyst)

Appraisal Section

We made a number of substantial changes to the appraisal form both to improve it in its own right and to dovetail it with the self-analysis sections. In particular we:

(i) Replaced the management by objectives section with a section which allowed for commentary and a rating against particular project targets. It had proved extremely difficult to set meaningful, business related targets for a Cobol programmer every January. They are required to be too flexible, and to move from project to project depending on particular and often short-term business needs.

(ii) It builds in a skills inventory approach which asks the manager to comment against certain prescribed skill areas as well as describing some which are particular to a job rather than being generic DP skills.

(iii) Lastly there is a much larger focus on career needs and development. The Manager is mandated to obtain agreement from the appraisee on a career and training programme. We are currently waiting to hear of a session which beats the current record of 12 hours. (Well, we do say appraisal is a serious and important process, and some of our systems managers are setting out to prove this!)

So we have an appraisal and self-analysis package which is slim, simple to use and had been successfully piloted. Of tremendous importance to this process was that our purchasing department had helped us turn the document into a glossy, well designed, nice to hold package. Managers felt it was a well produced Company product and this made it far easier to sell and implement. Probably one of the lessons from this whole exercise to us was that Human Resource products should be produced to the highest quality. Perhaps in the past we had focussed on content to the detriment of quality of presentation.

Implementation

Looking back at the implementation phase we probably had a significant advantage in so far as that the appraisal process was well established. It was (and still is) 'part of the way we do things around here'. The majority of Managers had attended appraisal training, and some had attended counselling training, so we had a strong basis of skills. We also had senior management support for the project which was very overt and vocal. This of course gave the *Guide* the degree of line management ownership which is crucial to most Human Resource programmes.

We decided to utilize the normal communication channels to 'sell' the *Guide* to people. So we proceeded with both management and staff presentations. This was supported by a video which we made in-house but utilized professional actors. This not only made the presentations more bearable for the audience, but also gave a very strong and, most importantly, consistent message.

Evaluation and Next Steps

At the time of writing we are currently two years into the scheme and some six hundred staff have been appraised. The initial pilot reaction has continued with the majority of staff getting real benefit from the programme – it certainly has maintained its relevance.

> I feel the Company is really focussing on my needs and what I do. (Systems Programmer)

With the benefit of hindsight there are undoubtedly areas which needed improvement, one of which we are currently revisiting.

(i) Our training of managers was probably inadequate. In a small number of cases we needed to train managers in the use of the *Guide*.

> Thank you for your action plan – now let's get on with the appraisal. (Project Manager to Analyst)

This was dealt with through strong directional counselling! We had tended to assume that because we had trained our managers and supervisors in appraisal interviewing that this would be a simple transition. I definitely underrated the pressures this type of system can put on a manager. It raised a whole host of issues which probably previously had lain dormant. Some of our managers responded well, others less well to this pressure.

(ii) The skills inventory in the appraisal needed greater analysis. It seemed obvious at the time what the skills were but we should have checked them more thoroughly as we are currently trying to revise the list. We recently have become much more attuned to the needs for defining skills criteria for each level of job in the organization and we will eventually feed that approach back into the *Guide*.

(iii) Lastly we were unprepared for the amount of attention that the *Guide* would draw to career counselling. We in Human Resources were slow to react to the new demands for more sophisticated career counselling. We originally had to use an external counsellor as we brought our own skills up to date and up to scratch. This is undoubtedly an area where we will become stretched in the future. People now seek and expect to find an internal resource which will help them think through their career issues.

But these are all handicaps to be overcome and we continue to grapple with them. The real success of the *Guide* lies in three areas:

It's simple.
It's relevant.
It means something to the individual.

Last year I spent three hours on it – this year twenty minutes

or vice-versa is a typical reaction. These three factors added to its business relevance means that we will continue to work with and improve the *Guide*.

12

Self-appraisal – A Route to Self-development

* * *

CYNTHIA ROOBOTTOM AND TONY WINKLESS

Background

Pedigree Petfoods, part of the Mars Group of companies, is a highly successful company, marketing a well-known range of prepared petfoods. The company has a strong and unusual culture based on principles laid down by the founders, Frank Mars, and perpetuated by the Mars family who are the current owners. These principles seek to encourage an open, egalitarian approach. The workforce is highly paid and there are no unions – each member of the company is referred to as an 'associate'. Personnel policies are designed to reinforce these principles, and the current emphasis is on the need to encourage a high degree of responsibility and a flexible approach to rapid change. The concepts of self-development fit well into this climate, and it is for this reason that we sought to support the introduction of these and related concepts by developing a new approach to appraising performance.

The company has a long history of appraisal based originally on the need to encourage and motivate people to achieve a performance above their average. This led to the development of appraisal systems to the point when in recent times several different systems could be found operating in the seven divisions of the company. While the company still views performance improvement as crucial to its continued success, technological and staffing levels have also brought about a need to change the overall system of development and the corresponding appraisal methods. For example the increased levels of skills needed in the manufacturing process: whereas in the early days many operators would be employed in working directly on the essentially physical process of taking the raw materials (meat, offal, cereals, etc.) and producing the finished product, this is now done by a smaller, but more highly skilled, group of people controlling an automated process via a series of linked computers. Thus the need has developed for a more flexible, skilled and proactive work force, in fewer numbers.

As a means of monitoring the attitudes of associates in relation to their work and company policies and practices, a periodic attitude survey is carried out. The most recent of these showed that there was a disparity between managers and non-managers. Of particular note were responses to items in the survey which referred to the taking of initiative in learning new skills, seeing value in having opportunities to talk over problems, and finding work interesting and enjoyable. In most such items managers gave a more favourable response overall compared with other associates. This contrasted with the company's espoused egalitarian aims of individual responsibility and mutuality.

As a consequence to these findings, it was decided to implement a programme to develop the behaviour valued by the company in all its associates, termed 'responsible behaviour'. This had three sub-themes:

(i) *productivity* – the need continually to seek improvements in output per person employed;

(ii) *shared responsibility* – the need continually to bring about an optimum balance between the contributions of the associate (time, commitment, willingness) and the company (resources and know-ledge);

(iii) *continuous learning* – the need to be continually flexible and responsive to technological and environmental changes.

In this way the development project described here was seen as part of the company's efforts to maintain its growth and market standing through these themes.

As an indication of other initiatives linked to this project the company has established the following supportive schemes:

(i) A *Continuous Learning Information Centre* (CLIC) where associates are given the opportunity in the company and in their own time to use learning resources such as books, video packages and programmed instruction texts.

(ii) *Financial support* for any form of further education or training outside the company in the associate's time. The rationale for this is that learning of any form may encourage flexibility in response to change.

Participants

Sixty-five associates were involved in the development of the project. The associates were employed in two divisions of the company: Administration and Personnel, and Research and Development. The project was eventually to involve everyone, managers and non-managers.

There were three reasons for choosing these two divisions for initial development work:

(i) It was considered that the designers of the scheme (Administration and Personnel) should form part of the 'guinea pigs' in order to gain first-hand experience of their own ideas in practice.

(ii) Both divisions were the furthest advanced in the company in terms of their self-development philosophies and practices.

(iii) Both divisions were very committed to the practice of appraisal.

Early Stages of Development

We first introduced the system in embryo form into the Administration and Personnel Division by means of a workshop to explore, discuss and develop the system. The contents in outline were as follows:

(i) introduction to the new system of self-assessment as a basis for appraisal;

(ii) establishing relevant managerial measurement criteria;

(iii) team objectives setting.

An important outcome of this session showed that, although the participants viewed the overall system as being both interesting and valuable, there were considerable problems over establishing agreed managerial criteria such as 'leadership', 'delegation', 'creativity', 'communications'. Sub-groups attempted to design a range of possible approaches, but few felt satisfied. This reinforced earlier and similar experiences in the company when attempts were made to establish identical 'across the board' criteria. The facts of life here are that we look out at our worlds in different ways, and making judgements about people at work are no exception to this.

For these reasons it was decided to explore in a more individual and useful way the extent to which managers agreed and differed in their perceptions and judgements of managerial behaviour. This was done through the use of a repertory grid approach employing computer-based analysis and feedback using the NIPPER system.[1,2]

The NIPPER system is based on the Personal Construct Theory and Repertory Grid technique developed by Kelly.[3] Underlying Kelly's work is the basic assumption that we each have our own individual ways of seeing and interpreting the world through our own personal, conceptual frameworks. These individual frameworks originate from our previous experiences of the world. In this way, we have our own particular set of spectacles (rose-tinted or otherwise!) through which we perceive the objects around us. What we view though is subject to change as a result of new experiences in relation to our own values and personal judgements. This obviously implies that, faced with the same situation, two people may view and respond to that situation differently.

It is these differences in perception that led us to examine managerial criteria in a more open and explorative way. For, if a manager views his/her subordinates in different ways from other managers, the likelihood is that externally imposed criteria of subordinate behaviour may prove inappropriate and confusing in the appraisal process. So this work was based on the individual viewpoints of the managers, and explored those viewpoints in relationship to how judgements were made about their subordinates.

The method,[4] which is summarized here, involved four main steps, as shown in Fig. 12.1. Ten managers from a range of disciplines participated in the experiment. Behavioural criteria were obtained by employing the tryadic method, which is a semi-structured way of helping people arrive at similarities and differences (in this case their subordinates). Typically most managers produced a first list of around 60 criteria, subsequently reduced to between 30 to 40 criteria after deleting identical words.

Each manager was then asked to rate his subordinates on a 'lowness-highness' scale for each criteria. This was then followed by computer processing. The computer output was then used as the basis for helping the manager in a non-directive way to establish patterns of meaning in terms of (i) similarities in criteria, (ii) similarities between subordinates, and (iii) patterns of ratings for each subordinate. Here are two examples.

Manager 'A'

This manager concentrated on his criteria similarities and was helped to construct his own 'families' or 'domains' of criteria similarities suggested by the clustering of criteria given in the computer output. For most people the domains from the original list of criteria are typically between two and five. In the case of this manager he constructed three domains from his list of 30 criteria.

The first stage involved working on the clustering generated from his full list of criteria. As can be seen from Fig. 12.2, he first established 8 initial clusters labelled by him as 'contributing', 'defending', 'influencing' and so on. Having done this, he brought the clusterings together to form three overall domains: 'the Prime Minister', 'the Maker of New Ways' and 'the Expert Consultant'.

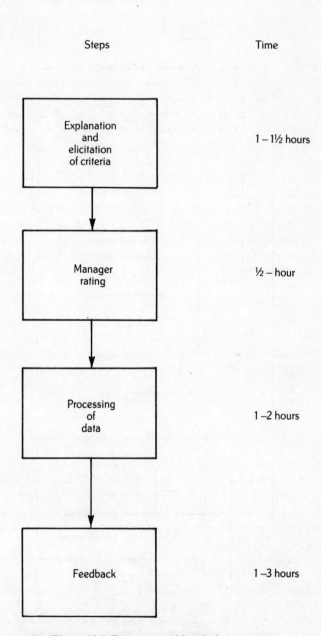

Steps   Time

Explanation
and
elicitation
of criteria   1 – 1½ hours

Manager
rating   ½ – hour

Processing
of
data   1 – 2 hours

Feedback   1 – 3 hours

Figure 12.1 Repertory grid technique.

Stage One: Criteria Similarities

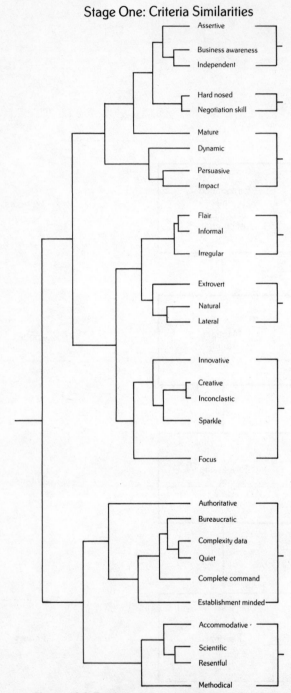

Figure 12.2 Explanation and elicitation of criteria.

Stage Two

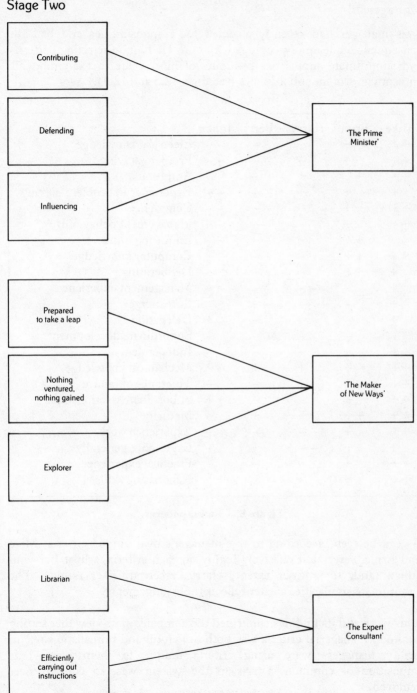

Manager 'B'

This manager had recently changed his responsibilities and had, in consequence, a team of people new to him. He found the rating patterns and subordinate similarities printouts of most value in examining his current views of his subordinates (see Figs. 12.3 and 12.4).

Mike	Ernie	Harry	Bert	Julian	
+ +	+	+	– –	– –	Electrical knowledge
+ +	+	–	– –	– –	Problem-solving
+ +	+ +	+	–	– –	Ambitious
+ +	+	+	–	– –	Experience in problem-solving
+ +	+	–	– –	– –	Confidence
+ +	+	–	– –	– –	Management behaviour
+	+ +	–	– –	– –	Enquiring mind
+	+ +	–	– –	– –	Computer knowledge
+	+ +	–	–	–	Deliberating
+	–	– –	– –	– –	Management experience
+	–	–	– –	–	Bureaucracy
+	–	–	–	+	Delegation
+ +	–	–	–	–	Subordinate development
+ +	+	– –	–	–	Independent
+ +	+	+	+	+	Mechanical knowledge
+ +	+	+	–	–	Tolerance of failure
+ +	+	–	–	+	Subordinate relationships
+ +	+ +	–	+	–	Maturity
+ +	+	– –	–	–	Experience work
+	+ +	– –	+	–	Experience generally
+ +	+	–	–	–	Practical experience
+ +	+	– –	+ +	+ +	Negotiating skills

Figure 12.3 Rating patterns.

As can be seen, according to this manager's own unique criteria, Mike and Ernie were rated relatively highly on each criteria, whilst Bert and Julian (and, to a lesser extent, Harry) received lesser ratings. The subordinate similarities cluster reflects these judgements.

This work and its findings confirmed the company in its view that setting common managerial criteria was both unhelpful and unrealistic since in reality managers were using criteria unique to themselves. This imposition of common criteria in the system was, in consequence, removed.

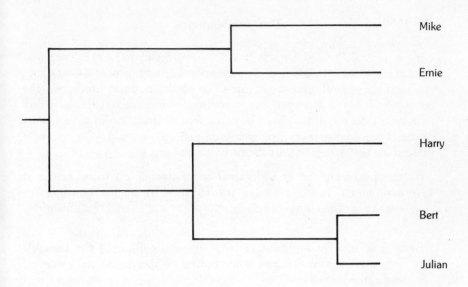

(It should be noted that some care needs to be taken in interpreting the ratings, since each scale represents the distribution of scores about the mean for each scale. That is to say, the ratings represent the relationship between subordinates' scores on a paticular scale, not according to an overall standard applied throughout.)

Figure 12.4 Subordinate similarities.

However, in recognition of the differing perceptions of what constituted good managerial performance the company then introduced into the project the notion of the 'word contract' between manager and associate. This attempts to allow, flexibly, the appraiser and appraisee to agree between them a form of words that summarizes for them the year's activity. This subjective language enables the pair to establish wording which is readily understood by the appraisee and his or her manager.

Second-stage Development

Following on from the earlier work in Administration and Personnel we developed supportive training materials and events, and then introduced them into the Research and Development Division. These materials and events are described under the following headings.

The 'Job Manager'

This aspect of the project was based on our belief and experience that learning and development are necessarily ongoing processes, and not confined to one-off events. In order to assist in these processes, the concept of the 'Job Manager' was introduced – an attractive, high-quality personal folder stimulated in its development by the prevailing popularity of the 'Time Manager' as a personalized management aid. The rationale underlying this aspect of the scheme was based on:

(i) a requirement for an individual and personal aid to be kept and maintained by the associate (rather than by his/her manager) to emphasize the notion of self-development and shared responsibility;

(ii) a basis for the associate to focus on and collate all the valuable information and material contributing to the individual's desired and agreed results;

(iii) a means for reducing time and stress frequently associated with more conventional appraisal and development schemes;

(iv) a ready means for recording information at times when the associate felt it relevant, rather than at pre-arranged meetings.

It was also considered that to have a prestigious folder with its own 'house-style' would reflect the importance the company placed on the process and would increase 'marketability' and acceptance by associates. To reinforce this, other aspects of training and development within the company planned to carry the same house-style in the design of course literature and handouts.

The 'Job Manager' has the following sections:

(i) *Performance Review and Personal Learning Plan.* For the preparation and completion of forms for annual and continuing performance review, personal plans and objectives.

(ii) *Job Development and Personal Development.* For collecting information found valuable in the associate's development, e.g. course handouts, articles, notes, extracts from journals.

(iii) *Career Planning.* For recording notes from feedback sessions, career counselling interviews, curriculm vitae, etc.

(iv) *Projects.* For any other important material, such as information about project-based learning.

Appraisal Workshops

Experience gained from the initial work with Administration and Personnel indicated that several people found the process of self-analysis difficult to carry out. For example, some participants diverted to discussing 'the system' in mechanistic terms rather than looking at their own performance and learning needs. To help in focussing attention on the 'self', a self-administered questionnaire was developed and built in to the 'Job Manager'. The overall aim was to stimulate maximum consideration, before making a plan to action, by means of 'Guiding Questions' under the headings:

Stage One: Analysis of achievement in last year.

Stage Two: Significant achievements and strengths not part of original objectives in last year.

Stage Three: Significant learning points during last year.

Stage Four: Things I intend to learn next year.

Stage Five: Agreed personal learning plan.

With these guiding questions established, together with the learning gained from the original workshop, a series of six workshops was set up as the basis for the introduction of the system to the Research and Development Division. The contents of the workshop were as follows:

(i) introduction to the Job Manager, its purpose and layout;

(ii) a description and rationale of the new system;

(iii) a reminder of the concept of objectives-based appraisal;

(iv) the guiding questions;

(v) performance review and personal learning plan.

Most of the time spent in the workshops was devoted to taking each stage of the Guiding Questions in turn. Participants worked on an individual basis, followed by a plenary session to discuss the process and its outcomes. During the plenary session the questions posed by the tutors were designed to evaluate both the usefulness of the documentation in the process and the lessons learned within the process by the participant in terms of achievements, satisfaction with the year's work and objective setting process for the future.

The majority of the participants found this process extremely valuable. It enabled them to look at their year's work and their learning in a new light. It also gave them an opportunity to transfer their analysis onto the self-appraisal documentation in the 'Job Manager' quite simply.

Some participants found the most difficult process was in deciding on the things they intended to learn in the next year. This was, in part, due to the fact that they were enabled to recognize that the learning from their experience in the past year was often accidental or unplanned. As one participant put it:

> How can I specify what I intend to learn next year when this analysis tells me that what I learned could only be seen in retrospect – and what's more the learning happened quite accidentally.

(This significant learning experience is discussed later in the chapter and highlights the importance of allowing people to learn from mistakes and disappointments, rather than defending or rationalising them to meet perceived organizational acceptability.)

To help in responding to the question 'What am I trying to learn next year' a model was developed[5] to help participants identify the skills that they might need to handle learning experiences encountered in the future:

Areas of management performance	*Skills that may need development*
Managing task	Time management, planning and organization, delegating, problem analysis, creativity, innovation, initiative, setting objectives/goals.
Managing people	Assertiveness, openness, listening, empathizing, counselling, coaching, confronting, awareness of style, personality, influencing, negotiation, collaboration, training.
Managing self	Self-awareness, self-analysis, stress management, time management, relaxing, learning, setting goals, support systems, networking, keeping fit, affirmation, visualization.
Managing career	Career counselling, goal setting, personality, values, visibility, politics, mentors, impact, presentation, ambition.

This model was adopted for all subsequent sessions and participants found the model useful in a variety of ways. For example, one manager felt that, while he was comfortable about the task elements of his job and his ability to persuade and collaborate with others, he seemed to be making little progress towards his goal of promotion. He therefore decided to pursue the development areas of managing his career. Another manager felt that his problem stemmed from feelings of stress and tiredness under pressure. Subsequently he investigated ways in which he could improve his time management and practice techniques of relaxation.

The training event proved to be a useful way of introducing the system into the Research and Development Division. Most participants expressed the view that they were comfortable and satisfied with the system. They also felt confident about introducing and developing the system with their associates, the technicians.

As a result of this work, the company considered that the system had been developed to a stage where it could be introduced to other parts of the company.

Key Learning Points

Previous sections have described how the project was refined and developed through acting on feedback and other data. The purpose of this section is to summarize our key learning points from the project.

The Use of Management Criteria

The original intention was to include in the system a set of management criteria as one means of enabling appraiser and appraisee to analyse performance. Experience in the early stages of the project and our use of the repertory grid/NIPPER application demonstrated that this intention was both unhelpful and unrealistic since people use their own unique mental constructions of what they consider is of importance. This work thus proved useful in helping the manager to recognize the managerial behaviours which were valued in reality and could form the basis for a learning contract. This aspect of the project also highlighted the value of the repertory grid approach in establishing the 'real criteria' used in other activities such as the analysis of training needs, selection, assessment centres.

Design and Presentation of Material

The value of investing in high-quality material in the form of the Job Manager aid was clearly demonstrated in helping in the 'marketing' of the system. The system was enhanced in terms of its credibility in the eyes of users coupled with the feeling that the company placed great importance on the new system. This can be set in the context of a company which in turn has, as a high priority objective, the production and marketing of attractive and high-quality products.

Resistance to Change

Whenever new systems are introduced there is some degree of likelihood that resistance to change will be encountered. Coupled with this was a recognition by the company that cultural differences between the various divisions needed to be taken into account.

With this in mind, we introduced the system by adopting a careful 'selling-in' stance rather than imposing it. At all times there was openness to discussion and debate about how the system could best be developed and used. Earlier sections illustrate this characteristic.

Objections stemmed from a number of feelings and fears evident in similar programmes which call for changes in attitudes and procedures. For example, there were concerns about how the information generated in the system might be used, or whether it might take away the right to manage. These issues were confronted and discussed on an individual basis by the implementers as the development progressed. Where in the past the relationship between associate and manager had been one of trust, the concerns were easily resolved. On the other hand, where the relationship had been less trusting the discussions sometimes led to an improved understanding between both parties. In some cases, people were unclear about what was meant by self-development and how it related to work. The training events were particularly useful in providing a forum to explain and resolve such issues.

The Nature of Learning

Two features about the nature of learning were particularly noticeable in this project:

(i) *The random and unplanned nature of learning for people.* This proved to give difficulties in predicting learning in activities such as 'Things I intend to learn next year'. Many people, in reviewing their learning in the previous year, found that their learning was often accidental, due to making mistakes or the result of painful experiences such as failing to get a promotion. Most of these people would not have chosen that sort of learning, but nevertheless, in retrospect, they recognized the importance and value of such events in their development. The aids developed for, and as a consequence of, the learning review aspects of the project proved valuable in both reviewing key aspects of the past year and in providing a 'recognition framework' for the year ahead.

(ii) *The value of prior self-development experience.* It was clear from the development work that those who had previously experienced and valued the self-development approach reacted more positively to the underlying philosophy and practices of the new system. In the Research and Development Division, for example, all managers had attended a series of workshops, overviews and training sessions in assertiveness, self-development, appraisal, coaching and counselling. We felt this helped considerably in supporting the subsequent technicians' training in such events as a five-day modular programme in assertiveness and self-development. This training had taken place during the two years running up to the introduction of the new system and was designed to encourage and support attempts to share responsibility. The company considers that this groundwork contributed significantly to the success of the new system.

Flexibility

The key learning points set out above all incorporate a common theme – the need to be flexible. The company's wish to generate a sense of shared responsibility requires an acceptance of individual differences in experience, values and perception – and the need for all to seek a balance in achieving both individual and company objectives. This project has helped the company to evolve a system which is not imposed (a strong temptation at times), but open to debate, discussion and negotiation.

Summary

In summary, it might be best to quote directly from the Company's Training and Development Manager, Avery Duff:

> The ideas developed in this project have become fundamental to our developing Personnel Strategy at Pedigree.

We are committed to enabling people to develop their latent potential. This enables us to create the most interesting and varied jobs possible and in doing so demands maximum flexibility from our associates in what and how they learn and develop.

The shared responsibility of the Company and its associates is to utilize its resources as effectively as possible. People have been shown to develop more effectively when they understand that such growth is an ongoing process. It is not necessarily synonymous with promotion of the individual in status terms but certainly in terms of personal growth.

The project has enabled us to establish a culture of 'learning' that we believe greatly enhances out business efficiency.

We wish to acknowledge the support of the MSC in this project and also the contribution of Independent Consultants, Rosemary Harris and Bill Evans.

References

1. Boot, R.L. (1979) *The Management Learning Project: Final Report of the Director*. MSC, Sheffield, UK.
2. Boxer, P.J. (1986) *Micro-NIPPER – A Computer Assisted Technique For Reflective Analysis*. Boxer Research Ltd and HPS Software Developments Ltd, London, UK.
3. Kelly, G.A. (1955) *The Psychology of Personal Constructs,* Vols I and II. Norton, New York, USA.
4. Winkless, T. (1985) *Development Project: Pedigree Petfoods/Manpower Services Commission*. MSC, Sheffield, UK. (July)
5. Roobottom, C. (1985) *Success Criteria: Is There a Magic Ingredient?* Unpublished essay, MA in Management Learning, University of Lancaster, UK. (November)

13

Integrated Career Planning

* * *

CALVIN GERMAIN

This chapter gives an account of self-development in an organizational context. Starting with the first 'career development' project in the late seventies, it deals with the growth and implementation of ideas, concepts and tools consistent with the notion of self-responsibility for career and personal development.

While self-development promises the release of untapped sources of motivation to learn, of dealing with complex development needs economically and of ensuring relevance of learning[1], organizations, on the other hand, may tend to see the dangers of self-development as loss of organizational control, and development becoming selfish or self-indulgent and relevant to personal needs rather than legitimate organizational ones.

The kind of statements often heard in response to the idea of self-development include:

Will this raise the expectations of our people?

Thinking about careers and one's own development is something you do in your own time.

Will people leave if we encourage and help them to think about their lives and careers?

Where do these kind of statements come from? Perhaps they in some way reflect underlying assumptions about the people we have in our organizations:

(i) that our people do not have the interests of the company at heart;

(ii) that if people are getting what they need from work then by definition the company is not getting what it needs.

Indeed, the possible effects of self-development on a company or part of a company seem quite risky at the outset, especially in organizations where the message has been that 'We will look after you' and the employees in turn have offered loyalty throughout a whole 'career'. However, with fewer and fewer companies able to give the total career promise, we have to look for new ways of handling the careers of our people. In addition we have to embrace the notion of self-responsibility for careers and personal development within our organizations[2].

The following assumptions are offered as an alternative and a starting point from which to view self-development in organizations in a more positive light:

(i) Future success depends on our organization's ability to match the needs of the individuals within it with its own needs.

(ii) That if people are getting what they need from work then the organization is more likely to get what it needs.

(iii) The days of promising a 'career for life' are fast departing.

(iv) The responsibility for career and self-development lies 80% with the individual and 20% with the organization.

If the above is true, or seems to have some relevance to the position we find ourselves in approaching the year 2000, the next question is: 'How do we enable individuals to take responsibility for their own development without falling foul of the negative possibilities mentioned earlier?'

Careers and Self-development

Our work on careers and career development began in the late seventies. The Management Team of the then Esso Chemical Technology Centre at Abingdon were asking such questions as:

(i) What skills will we need in our organization in the year 2000?

(ii) How do we better manage the careers of our people and base our decisions on real information?

(iii) What skills and potential do we already have in our organization?

So our starting point was in the areas of skills and careers management. Self-development was an issue we addressed later when considering the question of responsibility.

The early work was centred on defining for ourselves what 'career' meant to us and the people in the organization. As one might expect the concept of career conjured up a picture of vertical movement through the organization for most people. This rather narrow perception of career was most apparent at a level in the organization where we met people who saw themselves as having jobs, not careers. This self-perception was based almost totally on the element of upward mobility, or lack of it. However, there were a number of people who were very clear about what role their work played in their lives and did not see their job as being central. All of this of course may not appear as earth shattering and new, but it did lead us into considering the wider aspects of career management.

First, we noticed that, although we had extremely sophisticated career management systems, there was not a strong integration between these systems and others such as business planning, training and appraisal. It was clear from the outset that if we were to embark on work that would begin to answer our earlier questions we would need to build in:

(i) a broader concept of career than already existed in the organization;

(ii) concepts and tools that better integrated systems and issues related to the development of people within our business.

The process created to satisfy the initial criteria is shown in Fig. 13.1. The title given to the work reflects the approach taken to the concept of career, i.e. a partnership approach to career development. It was at this stage that we began to address the question of self-responsibility for career and personal development. Clearly, if we were to encourage individuals to think about their futures in terms of career and their own development we were in danger of creating the wrong impression about who would be responsible for actions resulting from the work.

It was thought unlikely that the organization could ever provide all that was necessary for each individual's career and development needs even with its high level of commitment in these areas. The real concern was, will we raise expectations to a level that we have no hope of fulfilling? The next essential ingredient for our process was therefore to build in the notion that individuals had to take a high level of responsibility for their career and development needs that they identified for themselves. Hence the *partnership approach.*

The process described in Fig. 13.1 begins to describe the kind of activities involved in the first project. As a sequential flow it looks quite straightforward. However, some steps were carried out as parallel activities and the following description should serve to provide a more complete picture.

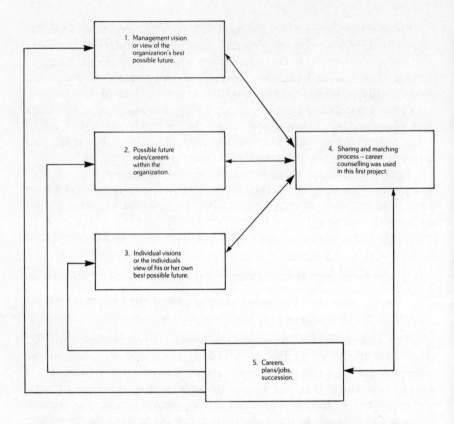

Figure 13.1 Partnerships approach to career development.

Step One

The first step involved the management group in discussing the best possible future for the Technology Centre and producing a statement of the mission for the site. This, together with a description of the career development initiative, was given to employees by the site manager at a meeting attended by the whole site.

Following this meeting the work began to develop a self-administered Workbook for use in Step Three. This was done by first collecting data from a cross-section of employees and then establishing a pilot group to help with overall design. The Workbook became a central part of the project and is described in Fig. 13.2. (Through the years since the first project the Guide has been developed by using it in different environments and testing it with three to four hundred people. However, its importance, although central, is only overshadowed by the processes which it supports . . . See conclusions to this chapter for an explanation.)

THE WORKBOOK
A Guide to Career Planning and Personal Development
The guide as used seven years ago was a workbook that people could work through on their own. It offered help in thinking through related issues about career and development, and led to a number of personal career scenarios and a personal development plan covering the 'how' as well as the 'what' of work related learning. It deals with personal and organizational issues, the past, present and future, as well as career formation.

The individual is required to go through eleven steps and build up a picture on a summary sheet culminating in a set of maybe three career scenarios and a personal development plan. The eleven steps in the original guide were:

1. *Rational skills tester*
Some 'warm-up' reasoning tests intended to emphasize the relevance of rational as well as inter-personal skills.

2. *Your skills and your job*
The user looks at own skills and current job demands. Unutilized skills are noted as one source of ideas about future jobs. Skills demanded but not possessed are noted as likely development needs.

3. *Your life and your work*
Is concerned with clarifying what the user wants out of life and the part work should play in this. It also looks at the future and encourages thought about how personal priorities may change over time.

4. *The world in which you live and work*
This turns the user's attention to the organization and the world of work, both present and future, and invites a consideration of how things may change with technical, economic, political and social developments.

5. *Exploring career options*
This completes the stages mainly to do with career, giving the user the opportunity to map out some possible future career options.

6. *How do you solve problems?*
Gives a way of looking at problem-solving habits and skills in general.

---

7. *What can you learn that will help you in the future?*
This step simply takes the user through the process of deducing from the career section things that it would be useful for them to learn if you are to follow those career paths.

8. *What should you be planning to learn?*
Helps with the choice of the most important of the various possible learning goals.

9. *How do you learn best?*
Begins the process of helping users plan how to learn by helping them review learning habits, styles and skills.

10. *How do you keep up to date?*
Provides a check on how users keep up to date with the technical content of their work.

11. *Opportunities and resources for learning*
Turns the user's attention to the opportunities and resources needed to pursue the envisaged learning, and encourages the user to consider everything around as a source of learning.

Figure 13.2 Project Workbook.

Step Two

Attempting to predict the kind of roles and jobs which may be required in twenty years' time is not a task to be taken lightly, and involves a great deal of soul searching as well as an appraisal of what business we are in. In this case we were able to identify certain trends but were less successful in predicting actual jobs.

At first sight this apparent inability to predict the future is predictable. However, the very fact that we did consider the future led to a far better understanding of how to handle Step Four in the process, i.e. the bringing together of individual and organizational needs. It was clear that managers would not be able to make commitments about future jobs; rather Step Four would be about identifying trends, possible directions and individual development plans.

Step Three

From the outset it was assumed that individuals would need help when considering their future and making their own development plans. (This proved to be the case then, and over the past seven years I have confirmed time after time that approximately 5% of the population are capable of developing themselves. The other 95% need help from other people.)

The self-administered Workbook was the vehicle chosen in this case, and as mentioned earlier its design was based on data collected from the organization and subsequently tested by a pilot group before being launched. A brief description of the book is given later.

Step Four

This step represented the bringing together of organizational and individual needs. It was preceded by a number of activities aimed at making the counselling/coaching interviews successful for the organization and the individual.

The managers themselves were the first to use the Workbook with help from the designers. This was followed by individual counselling interviews with the site manager. (One significant event took place shortly after the introduction when a manager who was determined to stay in his present job until retirement saw the process as not applicable to him. Later he commented that even if he did stay in the same job, in ten years' time the job would be very different to the one he had now. The major issue for this person became how to keep his job bearing in mind the inevitable changes there would be.)

Following the interviews, the managers were trained in coaching and counselling. As part of this process the managers took responsibility for deciding how to progress. A number of important design decisions were taken at this time:

 (i) that the counselling interviews would be separate from the normal annual appraisal (since one was less essentially a retrospective activity and one was forward-looking);

 (ii) that individuals would need to go through the whole process three or four times on their careers (this was based on the work done by Dalton, Thompson and Price on career stages);

(iii) the managers also chose the first people to participate, and asked for feedback on the success of the activity following the first thirty or so interviews.

Step Five

Although the organization had some of the most advanced planning tools available to it, there was still a need to design ways of transferring

information from the interviews into these systems. While the details of
the exact format may not be of interest here, suffice to say that interview
summaries agreed by both parties were carried forward to the normal
career planning process and for incorporation in the training plans.

Overall Design

The steps described above are simply a way of communicating a process
which was quite long and involved. It may also seem at first sight that the
process was plucked from thin air. The major influence over the design of
the process was from the work of Ed Schein.[3] His notion of a career as a
continuous matching process of individual needs with those of the
organization was central to the flow. This gave us the broader definition
we needed. Taking this and linking it to self-development gave us the
ability to step outside the view of career as purely a vertical movement in
an organization.

In other words, it does not matter if a person wishes to have a career
consisting of one job, there is still room for personal development. Recent
history also suggests that, in a state of continual change, it will become
increasingly difficult simply to keep up with changes as they affect our
jobs.

Feedback

We mentioned earlier that, following the introduction of career counselling, information would be collected regarding the apparent benefits of
such an intervention. Accordingly, the first thirty people to experience
the process were interviewed, in addition to the managers who carried out
the interviews. Some feedback was related to improving the design of the
Workbook, but the following summary gives an overview of the benefits
as seen by those involved.

There were three main areas of benefit:

(i) *Organizational.* The consistent feedback from managers was that
the counselling had given them real data to feed into their career
planning activities. They expected fewer surprises in the form of
individuals refusing career moves since they were now more aware
of the individual needs.

Individuals had also generated ideas for future trends as they
related to their work and began to think about redesigning their jobs
to meet future needs.

There was not a great increase in the demand for formal

training courses but a willingness to look for alternative appropriate ways of learning.

(ii) *Relationships*. Most managers reported that the counselling activity had been of great benefit to their relationships with subordinates.

In addition, the question of external counsellors was raised in the context of certain interviews, from the point of view that there are occasions when an external person would have been more appropriate.

(iii) *Individual*. The majority of people who had worked through the Workbook and had a counselling interview with their boss reported that it was a very positive experience. They were most positive about the Workbook activity, saying without exception that this was the first time in their lives they had thought in such depth about their lives and careers.

Interestingly, the people who were least positive about the experience were those who reported the most difficulty completing the Workbook. They also happened to be people in their mid-forties and reported that this was one of the most difficult things they had ever done.

Finally, the most common suggestion for improving the process was that people working on the Workbook should be able to do so in a group environment. The thought was that this would make the process easier and more fun.

Self-responsibility

Since the first project at Abingdon, the concepts, tools and early insights gained have been applied and tested in a number of different organizational settings, as shown in Fig. 13.3.

- In the planning design and growth of a green fields organization.
- In the support of organizations in a run down situation.
- In the development of new career development systems within existing organizations.
- In whole organization change programmes.
- In one-to-one career counselling situations.
- In the development of a new guide or self-administered Workbook based on the seven years' experience.
- In self-management programmes and the introduction of support groups and mentoring networks.

Figure 13.3 Subsequent applications of the project.

A number of common themes have been identified over the past seven years, the most important of which, we believe, is the issue of self-responsibility. It is clear that self-responsibility and career development cannot take place unless individuals take responsibility for themselves, and begin to make conscious choices.

In our experience the issue of self-responsibility is the single biggest hurdle for both the organization and the individual. Most commonly it is an unwillingness to believe that one can have an effect on one's own future which blocks the process of self-development. We mentioned earlier that most people need help with self-development and it appears to be in this area of learned helplessness or powerlessness that the help is most often sought.

From the organization's point of view the blocks to self-development seem to be embodied in the following questions, usually put forward as reasons for not embarking on the path of career and self-development.

Will we raise the expectations of our people by asking and helping them to consider their future careers?

Won't the self-development process simply encourage people to leave the organization?

These appear to be realistic fears in the minds of many senior managers, probably based on an assumption that people are totally dependent on the organization, therefore any expectation about development will be an expectation that the company will do something rather than the individual. Some organizations have in the past, fostered this assumption with promises of careers for life and by encouraging a paternal approach. Linking this with the trend towards flatter organizations, which normally means fewer promotional opportunities, we begin to see the reasoning behind the second question.[4]

Richard A. Richards begins to provide some clues for us and sums up the dilemma as:

Organizations must encourage people to take on work that is meaningful for them, not merely a 'better position'. For many people the decision to climb the ladder is the only decision they make, and, frequently, that decision is not made in a wholly self-responsible or even conscious way. It is rather 'what everyone is supposed to do'. When organizations encourage a 'climb the ladder' attitude, they rob themselves of the energy that arises from people exploring the consequences of important life choices, and they become not 'arenas for self-expression' but dull and dangerous arenas for manipulation, secrecy and deceit. In such arenas the only self-responsible act may be escape.

He also offers a model for understanding self-responsibility in an organizational context which we have found useful over the past few

years. The model is summarized in Fig. 13.4 and suggests that
self-responsibility has two main components:

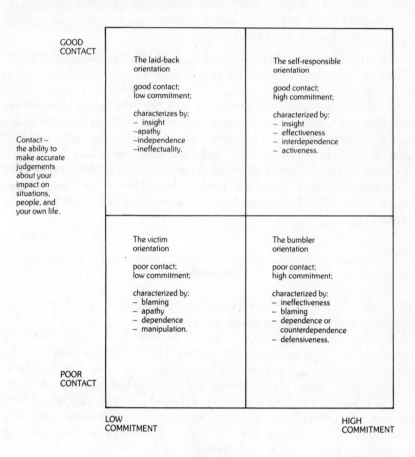

Figure 13.4 A model for understanding self-responsibility.

(i) *Contact.* Contact involves perception and describes the ability to
     make accurate judgements about our contribution to situations and
     our impact on others. It is a willingness to understand and fully
     accept that we cause our own feelings, thoughts, beliefs, perceptions
     and actions.

(ii) *Commitment*. Commitment is the behaviour dimension of self-responsibility. It describes a way of behaving, a way of acting and reacting. It is the ability to pursue some personal standard of excellence, to hold high aspirations and act on them. To express oneself through choice and action.

In its simplest terms, then, self-responsibility can be thought of as the ability to judge one's impact on oneself and the world, and to express oneself through committed action.

Finally, our work has continued over the past seven years in the direction of finding ways in which to reshape our understanding of what a career means, and to help organizations to develop new ways of integrating their career activities with the changes necessary for growth. We have developed ways of viewing organizations which support the matching processes discussed earlier. In addition, an independent organization called Integrated Career Planning has been founded by the author.

Conclusions

The main conclusion of the work over an eight year period is that for most people, personal or self-development is a process on which we embark rarely alone. Most people need help, and this may be one reason why the Workbook has been so central to the work. However, more than this, the importance of such roles as coach, mentor and counsellor has been highlighted in whatever environment the work has been carried out.

In Esso Chemical the work has progressed to a corporate level where we now run programmes, or career management workshops, using the Workbook as supporting material. The workshops are followed by participants finding their own mentors within the organization. This work is also supported, where necessary, by outside counsellors.

We have seen here and in other organizations that career planning and development are essential elements of any change programme aimed at creating long-term impact. To be long-term in nature, significant changes must be reflected in individual careers. Without this element, change programmes can be short-lived affairs, sometimes called 'flavour of the month', or fail to even get off the ground.

Integrated career planning is an approach to the development of management processes and systems with particular emphasis on careers and learning within organizations. To date our work has been solely in connection with organizational change programmes and should be viewed in this context, rather than as one-off courses or workshops.

Our work has covered people in both senior and junior positions in organizations. In one organization the phrase 'Be all you can be' applies equally to all levels in the heirarchy, not just the managers.

Finally, it would not be appropriate to tell stories of individuals worked with over the past few years in this chapter. However, we have learned never to be surprised at how resourceful people can be when they are committed to their own development . . .

The site where all this work started some eight years ago now has a new site manager. In a recent conversation he told the author that he had gone through an interesting process to find himself in the job. In the early eighties he had been given a copy of the Workbook at an international meeting by the then site manager who was keen to communicate the work he was sponsoring. On the way home, a nine hour plane ride, he decided to look at the Workbook. A few days later he had completed his initial work on the Workbook and there followed meetings with his boss. He decided then that the one job he really wanted was the Abingdon Site Manager's job. Later, when the possibility of the job was mentioned he made sure it was his.

Earlier in the chapter we mentioned that some three to four hundred people had experienced the processes developed. Not all of them are as dramatic and clear as this brief story, but we will go on wishing for such surprises and no doubt we will find them.

References

1. Germain, C. and Burgoyne, J.G. (1984) Self-development and career planning: an exercise in mutual benefit. *Personnel Management*. April. pp. 21–23.
2. Dunn, J. (1986) Funnel vision. *The Engineer*. December.
3. Schein, E. (1977) *CAREER Dynamics*. Addison Wesley, Massachusetts, USA.
4. Richards, R.A.(1984) A vision of a self-responsible system. Unpublished paper.

PART FOUR

SELF-DEVELOPMENT AND THE ORGANIZATION

In 1957 Chris Argyris produced his *Personality and Organization* subtitled 'The Conflict between the System and the Individual' and thereby set up the subsequent agenda for applied behavioural science and for much management development since. In this book the idea of self-development has been presented as a modest contribution towards resolving this central dilemma in work organizations. In this final part the four chapters continue the organizational themes raised elsewhere, and take the organization rather than the individual as their primary focus.

Simon Cooper describes the ASSET programme in Texaco – a company-wide 'library' of resources and contacts costing a mere £15,000 per year to maintain. Simon touches upon the benefits of this system to a widespread organization and mentions some of the mistakes and pitfalls to be found.

Tony Winkless contributes a thought-provoking chapter on self-development for self-employment and indicates how training for small business should reflect the specific motivations, strengths and weaknesses of the entrepreneur – something which much current provision ignores in favour of a standard approach.

Peter Martin's evaluation of a series of management self-development groups concludes that such groups can be viewed as an organizational development intervention, but that if this approach is to be followed, situations need to be chosen with some care.

Mike Pedler and John Burgoyne envision the 'learning company' as the next frontier in management education and development. The learning company is one which facilitates the learning and development of all its members while simultaneously transforming itself.

14

Self-development in Texaco

* * *

SIMON COOPER

Towards the end of 1982 Texaco decided to rationalize its staff and activities within the UK via a voluntary separation programme. One of the groups to be affected was that of corporate training primarily in management and management related skills. The Company had always had a strong commitment to training, and this it did not want to lose. So the problem I was faced with as the only experienced trainer within the Personnel Group was: 'How could a reduced training staff and budget continue to provide a similar, or perhaps even better, level of service to the employees of Texaco Ltd?'

I embarked upon a specific study of alternative training methods for the first three months of 1983. My research looked at all aspects of training as well as evaluating the effectiveness of these methods. The vital ingredient in assessing the effectiveness of training is the individual her or himself; do they *want* to learn? If a person can be motivated to develop themselves the results will be significantly better.

The conclusion of my study was that we should supplement our traditional management training courses with a comprehensive self-development programme. If there were not enough trainers to do all that was needed, why not encourage employees to do some of their training themselves.

After the initial 3 months' research it took another 3–4 months for the nature of the scheme really to take shape. It was then launched by the Chairman in October 1983 to some 1,600 employees. The success of the initial introduction could be measured in part by the number of people who made use of it – almost a quarter of the staff within the first three months.

The design of the programme went hand in hand with the consideration of how to market the concept. Self-development is a radical departure from the classroom approach, and it was necessary to explain the philosophy of self-development as well as change people's attitudes towards the shift in responsibility for training from being company-driven to being down to the individual's own motivation.

The Resource

Before we were able to offer a scheme to our employees it was essential that we had sufficient material to offer that would genuinely help people's learning process. The base from which we started was an outdated management library, and certain films and videos that we used on training conferences. Before the launch of the scheme we were able to acquire certain self-teach packs, update the management library and purchase more relevant videos to provide a comprehensive coverage.

This resource has now grown to over 1,000 items consisting of books, audio tapes, videos, films and computer programmes. The materials were divided into 26 categories on the following subjects:

Leadership	Written communication
Delegation	Verbal communication
People management	Stress management
Productivity	Flexibility
Accountability	Interpersonal skills
Teamwork	Time management
Administration	Business knowledge
Planning	Technical knowledge
Control	Computer aptitude
Decision – making	Keyboard skills
Organization	Numeracy
Creativity	Financial management
Initiative	General management

These subjects are based on those discussed on a job performance inventory contained within the human resource appraisal programme. The scheme has more recently been widened to include specific self-development material in three additional areas:

Producing and exploration
Refinery training
Health and safety

We realized from the outset that if this initiative was to work it was imperative that it was administered efficiently. It was an obvious opportunity to use computer technology. We were able to design customized software on our mainframe computer utilizing the existing personnel database. To this we added a coded list of all resources within the scheme.

The programme enabled us to record the identity of the borrower, the category and type of resource borrowed, and the length of the waiting list (if any) for that item. Upon receipt of a request the computer checks the availability of the item. If the resource is already on loan, the computer will suggest alternatives from the same category which are then passed back to the employee. If an item has a waiting list of more than two people we made a decision to purchase a further copy whenever feasible.

The standard loan period is four weeks, and every week the computer generates a list of resources that are overdue beyond the four week limit. It also issues a reminder to the employee that the normal period has lapsed. If someone else is waiting the request is made for immediate return. It there is no waiting list an additional two weeks' grace is given.

Marketing the Idea

Once we were certain that we had the basis of an excellent idea we realized that we needed effectively to 'sell' the idea to capture people's attention, and indeed to set them thinking of their own self-development. This second point was critical, for on a limited sample of employees questioned only one out of eleven was consciously doing anything himself to develop his skills.

So, in order to market the concept effectively, we designed a range of material in order to get our message across. The initial task began with the creation of a name for the scheme. After brainstorming many ideas we came up with an instant winner which turned out to be an acronym which had just the right image for the programme. The name was ASSET, which represented *A*cquire *S*kills by *S*elf-*E*ducation at *T*exaco. This perhaps was a little contrived, but when we combined it in a logo, by forming a plus-sign with the word ASSET both horizontally and vertically, it really did give the scheme its own identity:

A
S
A S S E T
E
T

We felt that we needed to raise questions in people's minds about what they were doing to help themselves. With this as an objective we developed a 25 point questionnaire. This was solely for the use of the individual, and not intended to be returned to the training group. The questions were related to a number of technical or management skills and abilities, and asked for an honest reply under three separate headings:

(i) What skills do I possess now?

(ii) What skills do I feel I ought to possess now?

(iii) What skills do I feel I should have in five years' time?

Considerable care had to be taken to pitch the questionnaire so that it left the employee feeling neither totally inadequate nor beyond the need for self-improvement. The employees were encouraged to use what they learnt about themselves to decide where they needed to concentrate their self-development efforts.

Accompanying the questionnaire was an explanatory booklet entitled *Self-Development at Texaco*. This booklet was written in a very basic format, using a question and answer technique to address any possible issues that the users might raise. Some of the areas covered were:

(i) Why should I bother?

(ii) How will it work?

(iii) What do I get out of it?

(iv) What's wrong with courses?

(v) What does Texaco get out of it?

(vi) How do I get started?

The major investment on the launch was the production of a signalized loose-leaf directory entitled the *ASSET Handbook of Resources*. This book was divided into the categories already mentioned, and each resource within the scheme, whether it be book, film, video, audio tape or computer programme, had a full descriptive paragraph explaining exactly what it was all about. This way employees could decide in advance precisely what style of material they required. The reason for the loose-leaf book was because we knew that the resource would grow, and we have been able to update everybody's *Handbook of Resources* by sending out new pages giving details of the new resources we have acquired. To make it easy for people to get started straight away we sent them a card with the 'starter pack' addressed to the training group stating which resource they wished to borrow.

During the months of planning prior to the launch of the scheme we ensured that we kept management and the executive briefed as to our aims. This proved to be important because, to accompany the release of the launch material, questionnaire, introductory booklet and the *Handbook of Resources,* the Chairman and Chief Executive wrote an accompanying letter, pledging his support, praising the initiative and urging employees to take advantage of this new scheme.

As we were expecting staff to devote their own time to acquiring these new skills we made a conscious decision to send the launch package to their home address. This had the effect of differentiating the scheme from the normal communications received at the office, or through the internal mail.

We were extremely encouraged by the initial response. Over the first three months from the beginning of October 1983 to the end of December 1983 we handled just over 380 enquiries, which represents nearly 25% of the total intended audience. By the end of 1986 this figure had increased to some 1,100 different users, which equates to nearly 70% of the white collar staff. Many of these have become 'regulars' coming back time and time again.

Interest has covered the whole spectrum of subject areas. However, the most popular categories have been:

(i) Computers;

(ii) Financial management;

(iii) Time management;

(iv) Communication skills.

Also specific items have proved very popular, such as the book *In Search of Excellence* by Waterman and Peters, and *The One Minute Manager.*

Publicizing the Scheme

We were very anxious that the initial interest shown in the scheme did not wane, so it was important that we maintained the interest in the ASSET programme. This we have achieved through a number of ways: first, by regular features in the company magazine, by describing new resources or by featuring users and their favourable reactions; secondly, by using posters on the notice-boards highlighting some aspect of the scheme (perhaps the chance of taking a computer home with you, and utilizing technology to help you learn); also by holding exhibitions to give staff the opportunity to come and review the resources. These are carried out at lunch-time, and have been known to attract over 120 people – including the Chairman!

Computer-based Training

One aspect of the scheme that has been disappointing is our experience in the area of computer-based training. Right from the beginning of the scheme we forecast that this would be the shape of things to come.

At that time in 1983 there was very little material on the market, so we decided to produce our own programmes based on the highly portable Commodore 64. We purchased 10 of these machines, together with tape decks, and proceeded to develop programmes on the following subjects:

  (i) Planning;

 (ii) Organizing;

(iii) Creativity;

 (iv) Control;

  (v) Time management;

 (vi) Financial management.

These programmes are highly interactive, and take some 1 ½ to 2 hours to complete.

However, after a great deal of effort and expense we found that the usage of these programmes did not justify the cost, and rather than complete our target of some 14 programmes we decided to call a halt at 6. We found that despite changing attitudes there were not enough people willing to use this new technology in their homes.

In the last 12–18 months there is now a far greater availability of generic software, and we have already added some programmes to the ASSET scheme which are compatible to the IMB PC which staff can utilize in their workplace.

An option we are currently considering is to provide a CBT station within the Training Group, so that staff can book an appointment and come and interact with an IBM PC to acquire the knowledge or skills they need.

Educational Assistance

For many years in Texaco there had been a scheme in operation whereby employees could obtain financial assistance with studies, if the subject area was pertinent to their job. However, this scheme was never really publicized, and was only used by a handful of staff.

We saw the opportunity to bring this scheme under the ASSET

banner, thereby giving it a far higher profile. There are now details about the scheme in the *Handbook of Resources,* and a contact point if anyone needs any guidance as to whether they quality for assistance. Advice is also given as to the best material or courses that are available. We currently have several people taking additional professional qualifications and Open University degree courses.

A major initiative we have taken over the last two years is to encourage staff to take the Open University short courses. In 1985/6 we sponsored 40 employees on these courses, and in 1986/7 another 38 are involved. The quality of the material we have found to be excellent, and the feedback from those participating has been very encouraging. The subjects involved are:

(i)   The Effective Manager;

(ii) Personnel Interviewing and Selection;

(iii) Marketing in Action;

(iv) The Planning and Management of Change;

(v)   Accounting and Finance for Managers.

These courses cost between £300 and £500 each and involve the student in up to 10 hours work per week over a 6 month period. There are tutor marked assignments during that period, and they culminate in an examination. Passes in the individual subject areas qualify for credits which contribute towards the Open University Diploma of Management.

This type of learning is consistent with the philosophy of ASSET and certainly provides an extremely cost effective method of training.

Appraisal Programme

The Training Group within Texaco is part of the Human Resource Department with Personnel. Apart from career development the other main responsibility of the Department is that of the annual appraisal programme.

Since the introduction of the ASSET scheme the appraisal programme has been redesigned to incorporate self-development thinking. The first change was to make the scheme more 'appraisee driven'. This means that the employee has the first input in assessing how they feel they have actually performed in the preceding year, and they then rate themself on a 1–20 scale in each of the 26 categories mentioned earlier. The appraiser then adds his/her view on the individual's performance.

Following this assessment the two parties then meet and discuss any fundamental differences in their perceptions of how the appraisee is performing. Where shortcomings or improvement needs are identified and agreed, the appraiser completes a rating under that specific category that indicates that training is required. When the form is received within the Human Resource Department the various information is stored on the mainframe personnel computer records.

As the categories within ASSET relate directly to those on the appraisal form, it is now possible for the computer to generate a memo to the appraiser, acknowledging the form and highlighting certain areas, one of which would be the training needs. In this respect it highlights the area of training need and responds with a full listing of all materials within the ASSET resource that apply to that particular area. The appraiser can then discuss this with the appraisee and send off a formal request for the material that they feel best suits the need.

This does give the Appraisal scheme more credibility in that it highlights the fact that the forms are reviewed, and that the Human Resource Department does follow up on the stated training needs. Another benefit of the scheme is that the manager or supervisor can get much more specific in targeting the actual training received. Before the ASSET scheme the only option was to send the individual on a training course, of which only part may have been relevant. Now the exact training requirement can be met through the self-development route.

Evaluation

Obviously it is impossible to check on every user's understanding of an ASSET item used. However, we do ask that a reaction form is completed to help us in monitoring the nature of the material. There are five areas that the user is asked to rate on a 1–10 basis. These are:

(i) Relevance of material;

(ii) Insight;

(iii) Technical calibre;

(iv) Usefulness to you;

(v) Practicality in general.

There is also a space for any comments they may wish to make. This enables us to delete any material that constantly gets poor ratings and to recommend other items which are highly praised.

Conclusion

As with all types of management training the exact results and benefits of this scheme in improving the quality of management within the Company are extremely difficult to assess. Nonetheless, it is quite clear that a large number of staff within Texaco have now begun to take significantly more responsibility for their own development. This fact alone can only be to the benefit of both the Company and the employees themselves.

At Texaco the commitment to self-development has certainly broadened the areas that the Training Group has historically been involved in. It will never replace the need for traditional 'conference type' training, but it certainly is an extremely cost-effective method, both in terms of human and financial resources, of improving the quality and scope of the training given.

15

Self-development and Motivations
for Self-employment

* * *

TONY WINKLESS

The impetus for the work and ideas I am describing here stems from the rapidly rising growth of self-employment in the UK. Estimates vary as to how many people are pursuing paid work in this way, but around 2 million seems a likely figure at present.

To assist in this growth the Manpower Services Commission introduced their Enterprise Allowance Scheme (EAS) which pays the would-be entrepreneur £40 a week for a year as a contribution towards the running of the business. At the time of writing, to qualify for this scheme people have to be unemployed for at least 8 weeks, be in receipt of state benefit, have £1,000 to invest in the business (which must be a new one) and be prepared to work full-time on its development. No comprehensive viability checks are made by the MSC to establish the likelihood of success, either in terms of assessing the individual or the business plan.

As part of the development of its repertoire of supportive programmes for small businesses, the MSC asked us to design and pilot some programmes for EAS people. These would include an initial diagnostic and action-planning element, followed by a series of supportive workshops run along the lines of an action-learning group.

To meet these points, the programmes provided a residential 'start-up' of three days' duration, followed by group meetings on a fortnightly basis over periods of between three and six months. The start-up element concentrated on group sharing, guided self and business assessment and goal setting. The purpose of the follow-up meetings was to give participants the opportunity to work on issues that were important to them at the time. A further feature was that, if requested by the group, a subject-matter expert could be introduced, although the essential point here is that the content was determined by the participants and not by the tutor/facilitators. In practice we found little need for the latter provision.

That is, we found that most needs could be met within the resources of the group.

At the same time as the EAS programmes were underway, we had been running workshops for unemployed managers and professional people which had also included the opportunity for looking at and developing alternatives to conventional employment. What follows here is based on the experience of working with both these groups, which had included around 200 people in all.

It is not my intention here to discuss the traditionally prescribed needs of the self-employed such as bookkeeping, VAT returns, market research techniques and the like. These are, as they say, written on the walls of every technical college in the land. To be sure, such needs do have to be addressed – and, as appropriate, they were addressed and developed by the participants with the help of their facilitators as required during the programmes.

What I consider to be of equal importance is to take account of one of the less mechanistic elements of the needs in helping people develop alternatives to conventional employment – the underlying forces of motivation and the blocks and springs to development which may arise from these forces. For I believe that we may be in danger of assuming that there is a some sort of homogeneous motivation in the pursuit of self-employment. I would argue that training programme designs which assume this, and in consequence fail to give participants the space and opportunity to take account of their differences in motivation, may give rise to failure for many people.

The people who joined the programmes (a 25:75 split, women to men) came from a variety of former paid work backgrounds. Most were, however, 'PER registrable', that is of a supervisory, managerial or technical background. Some chose to do some form of continuation of their previous career, while others had decided to do something different. Some examples of their business ventures are engineering design, video production, catering, occupational psychology, retail craft sales and interior design.

The participants were all, of course, previously unemployed but, as experience of working with them grew, it became noticeable that the reasons for their taking up self-employment differed considerably. And as they differed so did the ways in which they responded to the programme in terms of their needs.

The following is a tentative classification of motivation which, as with all such approaches, inevitably contains overlaps, omissions and oversimplification. However, it should be said that this classification has been presented by me to several groups of self-employed people who have contributed their ideas and experiences to it – and found it salient, and comforting to know that they were not on their own.

The Reluctants

These people, and they were in the majority, had taken the self-employed route because they had failed to secure regular, conventional employment. That is to say, self-employment was not their primary aim after leaving their previous paid work. The common theme here was, as more than one participant put it: 'If employers don't want me, I'll have to create my own work'.

It is worth noting that in some research I recently carried out on the impact of unemployment for managers,[1] the highest correlation between increasing lengths of unemployment and a variety of factors was one concerned with the likelihood of taking up self-employment. That is, when all else had failed self-employment seemed the only answer. In consequence, the needs of these people often presented themselves as recrimination and bitterness at being rejected by a world they had known for a long time and to which they would have preferred to return. Coupled with this tended to go annoyance or frustration at not having the ingredients or features of conventional employment such as security, regular income, imposed time structure, working colleagues. Other research into the impact of unemployment emphasizes such potential deprivation effects – see, for example, Jahoda[2] and Warr.[3]

Thus the needs in this case may be to do with helping people work through what is often a form of grieving, and to adapt to the demands of a new form of paid work which for many is clearly alien and sometimes distasteful.

Much has been written about such phased reactions to unemployment, although it should be said that not everybody reacts in a similar way. For example, in the research I mentioned above with unemployed managers, I found that, *overall*, levels of anxiety dropped in the first six months of unemployment, contrary to other studies which propose that mental health deteriorates following job loss.[4] Among the reasons I proposed for this was a sense of happy release – perhaps from what Fromm[5] suggests as the manager experiencing, maybe unconsciously, the feeling of being a prisoner of his or her employment.

The Romantics

Typically these people have some burning interest, hobby or unrequited job interest to which they wish to devote their efforts (and often dwindling savings). Painting, photography, an invention, sailing holidays, health foods are some examples. These people were in love with their product or service – and, like many lovers, are blissfully unaware that others (in particular their potential customers) might not share their passion.

Part of the motivating force here may be something akin to Robertson's[6] notion of changing societal values in terms of his 'SHE' scenario of a new world of paid work ('sane, humane and ecological'). What Robertson proposes is that such aspects as an emphasis on qualitative values, human development, intuitive and empathetic goals, may take greater priority over the more traditional 'HE' ('hyper-expansionist') ways of working. Some might of course suggest that Robertson is himself a Romantic, particularly in the light of the continued emphasis on growth, increased productivity and the like in 'the economy', but there are clearly others who are showing signs of wishing to break away from this régime.

Thus the needs of many of these people are not a lack of will (of which they have a lot), but may have more to do with the need to develop a keen eye in the direction of the market place – even if it is one that they may prefer to be different in its expressed values.

The Freedom-Seekers (or the Boss-less)

For many, self-employment holds the promise of no boss, no imposed schedules, no more 9–5 rituals – 'The best boss I know is me' is a frequent comment. Often these comments come from people who have suffered involuntary (and painful) termination of their previous job and who in consequence do not wish to repeat the experience. As one ex-manager put it: 'On Christmas Eve with the company car having to be handed back straight away, security keys handed in . . . I felt that I had committed a crime'.

While these people are often full of energy and determination to succeed, they can often be surprised to find that they have swapped one boss for several – in the guise this time of customers and clients! The more satisfied of these people perhaps are those whose service or product is in sufficient demand for them to choose their clients or customers.

The Portfolio People

These seem to be an emerging and growing group of people. These people do not want to be wedded to one form of paid work, but prefer the variety of two, three or more. There is perhaps a mainstream activity (maybe 75%) which serves as the breadwinner, with other pieces of work which may be paid or unpaid.

The notion of a portfolio approach was first proposed by Handy[7] as one response to growing levels of unemployment:' . . . a mixture of job work, marginal work and gift work . . .'. However, while Handy seems to imply that people may be reacting in a reluctant way to their unemployed plight and, as he puts it, ' . . . end up . . .' with this approach, our experience is that several participants have taken a portfolio approach in a more proactive and joyous way. For example, one disenchanted social services worker voluntarily quit his job in, for him, the over-indulgent South and took on a smallholding in the rural East Midlands, to which he added part-time lecturing and unpaid youth work.

A strong need here is to give recognition that this approach is an emerging way of life – that it is 'OK' to proceed in this way. For such are the powerful socializing forces of conventional employment (which most people in mid-life have experienced for many years) that a feeling of being a social misfit or outcast is sometimes experienced. Especially when the question 'What do you do?' is asked. Tinker, Tailor *and* Candlestick-Maker, ma'm!

The Supplementers

Typically these are people who have sufficient income and capital to live reasonably well but who have a need to supplement their income and/or want to put their experience and energies to some useful purpose. Ex-members of HM Forces, other public service officers or those with large early retirement packages from industry form most in this classification – with a clearly growing number of women 'returners'. With a guaranteed, steady and often indexed-linked financial backing, the need to generate an income is not high on the agenda of most of these people. The overriding characteristics here are the need to do something useful, to keep up social contacts and to 'exercise the mind'. So, with financial targets relatively low, the intrinsic nature of what they do is high, as is their wish to keep their working hours moderate. As people who are self-employed will know, these needs can sometimes produce the conflict of how to be good at what you do while keeping demand down to a level which is manageable and tolerable (or the conflict of not really working hard enough to be successful because of insufficient 'hunger').

The Marketeers

These people, and they were in the minority, had a very clear understanding of the market place and were alert to its opportunities and threats. They had a clear plan, a well-researched market and a well-targeted product or service – the darlings of their bank managers. They may well, of course, have been in the minority simply because they and many of their like-minded colleagues felt they had no need of a 'training course'. In terms of building and maintaining a financially viable business, however, these people proved to be the most successful.

Of the marketeers that we did see it sometimes happened that they discovered they had ignored their own intrinsic needs for what they did in the quest for conventional success in terms of the 'bottom line' of profitability. A case of 'What does it profit man . . .'?

Development Needs

What then can usefully be said about this classification of motivations for self-employment? At one level it is clear that these people, whatever their motivation, were taking steps to create alternatives to conventional employment. Robertson[6] gave one lead on the future of work alternatives in his motion of 'OWNWORK', which he describes as ' . . .activity which is purposeful and important, and which people organize and control for themselves. It may be either paid or unpaid.'

What, I believe, is important here is that by examining some of these underlying motivations, there may be useful pointers to the development needs of people in building, what is for them, a viable way of life. In many ways these people are, I believe, pioneers in creating what is inevitably needed to help build a new paid work scene – a new 'Sign of the Times' (to borrow part of Thomas Carlyle's title for his commentary on the early stages of industrialization).

What became clear during the progress of the programmes was that participants' enterprises grew, or sometimes failed to grow, in differing ways. As mentioned earlier, the design of the programmes gave people opportunities over three to six months to raise issues which were important to them at the time. Throughout each programme records were kept of the issues raised by the participants. At a summary level of analysis we found that the highest frequency of issues could be described as being in the area of marketing and selling, followed by finance. This would, of course, cause little surprise for most observers and practitioners involved in business development. A quick glance through most courses for the self-employed would show these subject areas as having the majority of the timetable devoted to them. However, while it is true to report that many of the issues raised under these headings were due to lack of knowledge or skills, a dominant theme was also a reluctance or block to implementing what was already known to be needed to be done by the participants.

For example, take the Romantic who, locked into his passion of developing his product, refused for weeks to accept why his major potential client had turned down his product when there were serious ethical objections. Or the Reluctant who struggled with the uncomfortable fact that he had to sell to customers when, for all of his working life, that was something done at a safe distance by the Sales Department. Or the Supplementer, comfortably away from the DHSS queues, who dithered over introducing a unique service to the local community. And therein, of course, lies the trap for those who think that we can 'teach' our way into self-employment success through imposed training structures.

As a summary Table 15.1 sets out some possible indicators of strengths and weaknesses of 'motivation positions', and outlines some key areas of development needs (although, as I stated earlier, there are bound to be overlaps, omissions and oversimplification).

Table 15.1 Summary of motivation classification.

Category	Strengths	Weaknesses	Development needs
The Reluctants	'Hunger'	General negative attitude Backward looking Reactive	To complete the grieving period To reorientate and positively manage their transition into a different environment
The Romantics	High drive Total involvement	Market place myopia	To develop a balance between market and passion for product
The Freedom-Seekers	High drive	Rebellion against perceived imposed control	To recognize and accept customer demands and sensitivities
The Portfolio People	Flexibility Versatility	Oversensitivity to role identity	To find self-assurance against the orthodox views of working life

| The Supplementers | Capital | Lack of need to earn money | To develop a more dynamic approach to business transactions in balance with time commitment |
| The Marketeers | Market awareness Proactivity Enthusiasm | 'Bottom-line' fixation. | To keep an eye on their intrinsic needs To manage the balance of time |

A Question of Appropriate Design?

What we found was that experiences such as these needed time and opportunity to explore and resolve – such things are unlikely to be addressed in the 'short/sharp' seminar. It is interesting, and perhaps sad, to see that in much national provision for self-employed people little or no reference or allowance is made for the 'self' side of training for self-employment. Here we see the usual catalogue of logical things that a self-employed person needs to know – bookkeeping, basic accounting, taxation, financial control and so on. Of course, they do need to know about such things, but if these subjects are not timely, or are blocked by fears, emotions and previous personal history, it will not be surprising to find that the success figures after two years' self-employment (which I believe to be a reasonable period for assessing viability) may not be as pleasing as the government would like to see. The issue here, at least in part, is the old dilemma of numbers and costs. And this is understandable, if not forgiveable.

At the very least it needs to be recognized that, as in the case of the impact of unemployment where there is no homogeneous reaction, there is also no homogeneous motivation to self-employment. Standardized content and standardized presentations look orderly, but people are not so conveniently ordered into one box. Carpet bombing may look spectacular, but as a method it is not well known for reaching the strategic targets.

These thoughts on design are not in my experience exclusive to self-employed people. Similar experiences have come from self-development[8] and action-learning programmes run for the MSC and a variety of organizations over the last several years. These programmes, which have been run for a corresponding variety of people (NHS managers, doctors, personnel and training specialists, managers in industry), have a common underpinning or philosophy which evolved through insights gained with working with people on their own personal and career development.

The following four points outline the basic elements of this approach:

(i) Opportunity for significant development often requires support over a period of time – short 'hyped-up' training events are limited in their effectiveness.

(ii) Salient and timely experiences with opportunities for reflection and experiment are important – we can't 'teach' anyone to do anything. We might just be able to help them learn (and only then when they want to).

(iii) Learning can often be enhanced in a community of like-minded people – too many tutors assume that only they have the answers.

(iv) The ability and willingness to work on personal development in a holistic way is likely to bring about useful changes, sooner rather than later – the experiences of life are not contained in water-tight compartments.

References

1. Winkless,T. (1986) Aspects of the psychological impact of unemployment: a comparative review and study of unemployed managers in Lincolnshire. Unpublished thesis, University of Lancaster.
2. Jahoda,M. (1979) The impact of unemployment in the 1930s and 1970s. *Bulletin of The British Psychological Society* **32**, pp.309–314.
3. Warr,P.B. (1984) What's new in unemployment. *Personnel Management*, pp.18–20. (August)
4. Jackson,P.R. and Warr,P.B. (1984) Unemployment and psychological ill-health: the moderating tole of duration and age. *Psychological Medicine* **14**, pp.605–614.
5. Fromm,E. (1957) *The Art of Loving*. Unwin Paperbacks.
6. Robertson,J. (1985) *Future Work*. Gower, Aldershot, UK.
7. Handy,C. (1984) *The Future of Work*. Basil Blackwell, Oxford.
8. Winkless,T. and Boydell,T.H. (1981) Self-development groups. In Boydell,T.H. and Pedler,M.(eds) *Management Self-Development: Concepts and Practices*. Gower, Aldershot, UK.

16

Evaluating the Individual and Organizational Effects of Manager Self-development Groups

* * *

PETER MARTIN

Introduction

In May 1985 I was asked to evaluate a number of manager self-development groups (MSDGs) that were, and some of which still are, operating in a large local authority. I had long been interested in a self-determined approach to learning. This interest had been initially stimulated by reading Carl Rogers' book *Freedom to Learn*[1] back in the 1970s. Rogerian ideas have subsequently influenced my own efforts to help managers to learn. Self-development seems to me to rest largely on the assumptions and values of humanistic psychology. I saw the project as an opportunity to explore the possible benefits of this approach to manager development.

At the time of starting this project I was doing a course concerned with organization development, and I became interested in learning to what extent the introduction of self-development groups into an organization could be regarded as and used as an organization development intervention.

Background to the Project

The project was sponsored by the Central Training Department and the Training Section of the Social Services Department of the local authority. The Council through the initiative of internal training staff had, since September 1982, started up a total of eight MSDGs. The groups commenced at various times between September 1982 and March 1985, when the three most recent groups commenced. Six of the eight groups were still in existence in May 1985 at the start of the project. A total of 65 members of staff had attended the groups. Some had attended more than one group. The majority of group participants (approximately 50) were drawn from the Social Services Department. The benefits of group membership had not been formally evaluated.

Why an Evaluation Project?

The internal trainers who had initiated the self-development programme seemed convinced of the benefits of MSDGs, having themselves been members of groups. However, they needed to convince their bosses, some sceptical line managers and relevant council committees of the benefits of this approach to manager development. There had apparently been a mixture of favourable and unfavourable (informal) comments from line managers about the impact of the groups on the organization and on individuals. The trainers felt that the groups had been affecting aspects of the organization culture. They felt that some line managers found this to be threatening and uncomfortable. Some line managers did not think that this form of development could produce more effective managers. In addition, there were different kinds of groups – mixed sex, male only, female only, mixed department and single department groups. There had been adverse comments about, for example, single sex groups, particularly women's groups. There was therefore some uncertainty about the best way of organizing the groups in the future, if the programme was to be continued.

Objectives of the Project

After discussion with the sponsoring trainers and other interested parties the objectives of the study were agreed to be:

(i)   to investigate the impact of MSDGs on group members and to estimate their consequent value to participants;

(ii) to investigate the impact of MSDGs on the Authority (as represented by the line manager of the participants) and to estimate their consequent value to the Authority (or parts thereof);

(iii) to generate recommendations regarding the future role and usage of MSDGs within the overall management and organizational development effort in the Authority.

Method of Conducting the Study

At the start of the project I was concerned about how to conduct the study and read as much as I could about approaches to evaluation research. I became interested in an approach to evaluation called 'utilization-focussed evaluation' (Patton, 1978 2). I particularly liked this methodology because it is participative (the emphasis is on involving interested parties at each stage of the evaluation process) and it is results-orientated (the assumption being that involvement by key persons will hopefully lead to increased likelihood of the results of the study being acted upon in the organization).

The steps in the process (modified slightly to fit the situation) are:

  (i) Sponsor/evaluator identifies a group of people in the organization who are interested in the project and/or who need to make decisions about the subject matter of the project.

 (ii) Evaluator generates a list of questions with this group of people about the programme which is to be evaluated.

(iii) Evaluator agrees with this group the means for collecting relevant data.

(iv) Evaluator collects the data.

 (v) Evaluator analyses the data.

(vi) Evaluator in conjunction with the group interprets the data and generates conclusions and recommendations.

(vii) Evaluator writes the evaluation report to include the results of (vi) above.

(viii) Sponsor/evaluator disseminates the report to members of the group, participants in the research and other interested parties.

(ix) Group takes action upon the recommendations.

I followed the process of utilization-focussed evaluation as described above fairly closely in carrying out the project. Step (i) is the identification of interested parties in the organization. For this I used, in conjunction with the sponsors, a multiple stakeholder framework. Stakeholders were defined as a person or group of persons who had an investment (e.g. of money, time, effort, credibility, etc.) in the outcome of a MSDG or in the MSDG programme. The main stakeholders in the MSDG programme seemed to me to be the sponsors (the internal trainers), the participants in the groups, the group facilitators (internal and external), the line managers of participants and any senior managers who initially supported the programme. The issue of identifying stakeholders in this situation was complicated by the fact that, in some cases, particular individuals in the organization played more than one stakeholder role. Also, it could be argued that other important stakeholders should have been included, for example, the staff of MSDG participants. However, personal time and resources dictated that the boundaries be limited to the above stakeholders. These included the key people who would be making future decisions about the MSDG programme.

A project steering group containing representatives of the above stakeholders (except the group facilitators) was selected by the sponsors. I worked with this group to brainstorm a list of questions that they particularly wanted answering in relation to the project objectives. The means of collecting the data was also agreed with the group. The methods were:

(i) questionnaires to all members of staff who had participated in a group;

(ii) interviews with a sample of line managers of group participants and questionnaires to the remainder;

(iii) interviews with external and internal facilitators and internal trainers;

(iv) group interviews with MSDGs that were currently operating.

It was agreed that the sample of line managers to be interviewed be selected to include managers who, it was thought, had positive attitudes towards MSDGs and some who had negative attitudes. The sample also had to represent the six different departments who had staff participating in MSDGs.

The next stage of the process, data collection, was not easy. It proved difficult for various reasons to get the co-operation of line managers and MSDG participants to take part in the study. The response rates reflect some of these difficulties. Data was collected by questionnaire and interview from 64% (= 25 respondents) of the total population of line managers of participants. Questionnaires were returned by 54% of MSDG participants (= 35 respondents). Three of the six ongoing groups would not permit a group interview. One of these groups would not agree to completing individual questionnaires either. One group which had finished did not return any individual questionnaires.

The analysis of the data was a complex task. Most of the data was qualitative, subjective data. Therefore there were problems of summation, classification and generalization. To help overcome some of these problems the data was classified according to a scheme devised by Bunker[3] to classify individual learnings of t-group participants. The

Bunker classifications (shown later in Tables 16.1 and 16.2 on pages 238–40) in general appeared to fit the majority of the data collected in this project. The scheme, with modifications, was therefore used as a means of summarizing the large volume of qualitative data for reporting purposes. Classifying data in this way is not entirely satisfactory. Much of the richness of the data contained in individual statements is lost. Some of the data could fit into more than one classificatory heading. However, the benefit of the scheme, apart from its compactness, is that it allows for analysis and summary against more detailed headings than had been used in previous evaluation studies of MSDGs (see Pedler *et al.*[4]). In these studies outcomes tend to be classified by broad headings such as personal, inter-personal, group and organizational areas of learning.

Research Findings

The research findings are examined in the following text by reference to the descriptive model developed during the research given in Fig. 16.1 (see next page). The model contains the primary factors which seem to have a bearing on the effectiveness of MSDGs. Some of the factors in three areas of the model will be explored in greater detail with a discussion of some findings.

Individual/Group Factors Relating to the Organization of the MSDG Programme

The results showed that the respondents were generally in agreement with the way the groups were being run in the organization. They tended to favour:

   (i) mixed department groups;

  (ii) mixed sex groups (although there was substantial support for using single sex groups, particularly from women's group members);

 (iii) equal status group;

 (iv) meetings taking place both inside and outside working hours;

  (v) a separate centre away from the place of work;

 (vi) one day long meetings;

 (vii) monthly meetings;

(viii) a group size of between six and ten members;

 (ix) external facilitators (at least initially).

	Individual/Group factors	Environment factors	Outcomes
Selection of participants	(i) Group membership: – Needs – Sex – Abilities – Level – Expectations – Values – Department – Motivation (ii) Facilitator style (iii) Meeting situation: – Time – Frequency – Place – Length (iv) Group characteristics – Size – Compatability – Interaction of Members – Structure and process (v) The task (vi) Resources available	(i) Senior management support for programme (ii) Line manager support for individuals (iii) Climate/culture of organization (iv) Management development context (v) Trainer's role	Individual/ manager development Department/ organization development

Figure 16.1 Manager self-development groups: model of factors influencing effectiveness of groups.

The model contains the primary factors which seem to have a bearing on the effectiveness of MSDGs. Some of the factors in three areas of the model will be explored in greater detail with a discussion of some findings.

In general, each group was unique and tended to support the current way its particular group was organized. As one would expect from groups of this nature, the group task, structure and process was contingent on the wishes of the membership. One area of particular controversy was the length of group life. The Central Training Department had found it necessary to institute a policy whereby a group would be supported for a year initially (in terms of central funding and time release for participants). Thereafter if participants wanted the group to continue in work time then they had to negotiate their attendance with their individual line managers. This policy seemed to be generally acceptable.

The following aspects of the organization of the programme needed to be improved or reconsidered:

(i) *Marketing of MSDG programme.* The process of marketing and explaining the programme in the organization could be improved.

(ii) *Process of nomination.* Procedure for the nomination and recruitment of group members needed to be agreed, as did any criteria for attendance.

(iii) *Contracting.* The initial clarification of the possible goals and process of MSDGs with line managers of participants needed to be improved. The implications of group membership needed to be spelt out and line managers made aware of their roles (see next section).

(iv) *Evaluation of MSDGs.* Some line managers and some participants felt that there could and should be a more systematic ongoing evaluation of the groups. The results of this could be fed back to line managers and others. Several suggestions were made as to how this might happen (one group in fact did its own evaluation and circulated a report to interested parties).

(v) *Level of group operation.* Some respondents felt that the opportunity to join groups should be more widely available to other managers (at senior or junior level) and for professional staff.

Factors Relating to the Environmental Context

Transfer of training has long been recognized as a problem in the training literature. Although in this case the MSDGs were run in the organization, similar difficulties regarding the transfer and use of learning were identified. Learning outcomes seemed to be mediated by the organizational context in which the groups operated and in which individual members worked. Five seemingly significant factors were identified. These are discussed hereunder.

Role of Line Managers in Supporting MSDG Participants

Over half of the participants mentioned lack of support or hostility towards the programme by their line managers. Suggestions from respondents regarding the role of the line manager in supporting their staff were as follows:

Before the start of the group:

   (i) Identify developmental needs/learning objectives/priorities in conjunction with participants.

  (ii) Recognize, be aware of, and understand the MSDG opportunity.

During attendance on MSDG programme:

 (iii) Facilitate the attendance of participants at MSDG meetings.

  (iv) Offer help, support and encouragement.

   (v) Monitor learning achievement and facilitate its use.

  (vi) Give feedback on job performance.

After the programme:

 (vii) Conduct joint evaluation of the programme.

(viii) Draw up action plans with participants.

Management Development (MD) Content

It seemed to me that some significant comments were made concerning MD strategy and systems in the organization. By implication the following elements of an MD system were mentioned as being desirable for a MSDG programme (and perhaps for any development programme):

   (i) Organizational strategy for training linked to organization and departmental objectives. Strategy to be instituted via departmental training plans and training structure. Other points which also have relevance to this section are mentioned in the section concerned with the organization of MSDGs.

  (ii) A means of identifying individual learning objectives (e.g. via appraisal/development interviews).

 (iii) Career planning system(s).

  (iv) Complementary and integrated management development activities.

(v) Ongoing evaluation of all development activities for comparative purposes.

Support of Senior Management

Some respondents expressed disappointment that senior management did not appear to find MSDGs suitable for their own development needs. There was also some uncertainty regarding the degree of support for the groups by the senior management. No formal statements of support by senior management had been made.

Developmental Climate

The concept of a developmental climate or culture is a slippery concept to define although attempts have been made (see Temporal[5]) to operational-ize the concept. The concept is applicable to an organization in total and to individual departments. In the main respondents seemed to be referring to their departmental climate when they spoke about this concept. Mention was made of the difficulty of a MSDG programme operating in a bureaucratic culture but it was felt that there was scope for MSDGs to operate effectively in this climate and that indeed they may help to minimize bureaucracy. Other respondents felt negative about the current climate in their department. Their comments indicated that in some cases the climate was not developmental. The climate of a department is heavily influenced by senior management style and attitudes and therefore earlier remarks concerning this are very relevant here.

Role of Internal Trainers

One important aspect of the role of internal trainers is that of change agent or catalyst – to initiate the idea of self-development. Internal trainers also have to get involved in administration, organization and co-ordination of the groups. Evaluation of learning needs to be done to help justify the allocation of training resources to self-development rather than, or as well as, alternative development modes. Trainers could encourage line managers to carry out their staff development role (see above). They can influence the creation of a developmental climate in the organization. They also need to be involved in the development of training plans and strategies that take into account self-development approaches. Some members of the Social Services Training section also carried out the role of internal group facilitator.

Outcomes of MSDG Membership

Individual Outcomes

Participants were asked: 'What changes (if any) would you reasonably attribute to attendance on the MSDG programme? Mention any changes you have observed in yourself, particularly in the following areas (i) personal change (ii) change in managerial behaviour/performance.' Line managers at interview were asked similar questions concerning any changes they had observed in their member(s) of staff.

Individual effects were classified as already stated, by a modified version of Bunker's analytical scheme[3] given here in Table 16.1 and later in Table 16.2. These outcomes are divided into inner and outer effects. Table 16.3 then shows any individual effects mentioned, that could not be fitted into Bunker's classification scheme.

Table 16.1 Personal changes.

(a) *Overt behavioural changes:*	P*	LM**	Total
1. Improved communication			
(i) Sending (e.g. gives increased feedback)	12	4	= 16
(ii) Receiving (e.g. better listening)	9	–	= 9
2. Improved relational facility (e.g. better conflict handling)	10	11	= 21
3. Increased risk taking/more assertive (e.g. more proactive)	12	4	= 16
4. Increased interdependence (e.g. more co-operative)	6	8	= 14
5. Increased functional flexibility (e.g. contributes better in groups)	7	3	= 10
6. Increased self-control (e.g. less aggressive)	0	2	= 2

(b) *Changes in insight and attitudes:*	P	LM	Total
1. Increased awareness of human behaviour (e.g. more aware of the nature of conflict)	9	5	= 14

	P	LM		Total
2. Increased sensitivity to group behaviour (e.g. more aware of hidden agendas)	3	2	=	5
3. Increased sensitivity to others' feelings (e.g. more sympathetic)				
4. Increased acceptance of other people (e.g. more tolerant)	12	2	=	14
5. Increased tolerance of new information (e.g. more open-minded)	3	0	=	3
6. Increased self-confidence	16	6	=	22
7. Increased emotional resilience (e.g. more relaxed, less stressed)	7	3	=	10
8. Insight into self (e.g. more reflective)	20	9	=	29
9. Insight into role (e.g. more aware of management style)	7	2	=	9

(c) *Other:*	P	LM		Total
1. Increased command of basic facts about the organization	7	0	=	7
2. Better problem-solving/decision-making	4	3	=	7
3. Better planning/time management	3	0	=	3
4. Improved training skills	1	0	=	1
5. Reviewed career development/career planning	4	1	=	4

*   P = Participants in MSDGs.
** LM = Line managers of participants in MSDGs.

Space precludes giving specific examples of statements given by respondents in each of the categories in Table 16.1. However, illustrative words or phrases are given beside each heading (full details of statements are given in a report presenting the data findings. This report was, and as far as I am aware is still, available to members of the client organization should they want to see it). Table 16.1 shows that many of the participants felt that they had acquired personal strengths and insights from group participation. In particular, increases in self-confidence, self-awareness and assertiveness were mentioned. Increased interpersonal skills and insights are also a feature of the table.

It must be noted that four participants and five of the line managers who were interviewed mentioned that, for various reasons, they had not experienced or noticed any beneficial effects resulting from group membership.

Line managers do not appear to have noticed beneficial effects to the same degree as participants. While this might be expected by the nature of things, the degree of 'noticing' is also influenced by the closeness, observational skills, etc., of the relevant manager.

It was not really possible to 'cross confirm' responses of participants and their relevant line managers. The subjective nature of the research meant that respondents were using different concepts, different levels of generality and different frames of reference in their replies. There were also issues of confidentiality regarding the sharing of data.

Organizational Outcomes

Participants in their questionnaires were asked: 'Do you think that any of the changes mentioned have been of benefit to the department/organization? If yes, please indicate the benefits accruing to the department/organization.' Line managers at interview were asked the same question. Questionnaires sent to the remaining line managers asked them to give reasons for supporting/not supporting MSDGs.

The responses to these questions are given in Tables 16.2 and 16.3. Table 16.2(b) gives specific examples of changes made which were attributed to group participation. In Tables 16.2(a) and 16.3 I try to give a flavour of the nature of the responses relating to global 'climate' changes that were given by participants and line managers.

Table 16.2 Organizational changes.

(a) *Participant responses (global assertions of organizational climate change):*

1. Better understanding between each other.

2. Relationships developed and strengthened.

3. Improved relationships between staff and management.

4. Better working atmosphere.

Leading to:

5. Greater degree of trust, openness and honesty.

Leading to:

6. Clearer communications.

Used for:

7. Checking out ideas, resolving problems, etc.

(b) *Participant reponses (specific examples given of organizational changes):*

1. Changed supervisory practice.

2. Clarified roles (self and others).

3. Prompted to hold one-to-one interviews with staff.

4. Improved training and staff development in the department.

5. Increased involvement of area staff in processes/decisions.

6. Attempted change in section structure (support while doing).

7. Introduced small group discussions with staff.

8. Took steps to correct institutionalized racism.

Table 16.3 Line manager responses (global assertions of organizational changes).

(a) *Change in intra-department relationships:*

Improved quality of relationships

Leading to:	*Leading to:*
More co-operation	More openness (to what other parts of department are saying)
Makes it:	*Leading to:*
Easier to get work done	Reduced tension

Table 16.3 (cont.)

(b) *Change in culture/style:*

Pressure for culture change (intra-department)

Involving:

How conflict issues are handled

Also

How decisions are made
(more consultation/involvement desired)

Also

How participants behave toward
subordinates/peers/senior managers

Also

Style of middle management (more proactive)

Also

Use of non-hierarchical,
informal communication channels

May cause:

Conflict with senior management.

(c) *Change in interdepartment relationships:*

For example:

New networks, contacts developed.

2. Building of trust, knocking down departmental stereotypes.

(d) *Formation of 'in groups' and 'out groups':*

That is:

1. Development of shared identity by participants not shared by other
staff in the department.

Tables 16.2(a) and 16.3 give an impression of changes in climate or culture as felt by participants and line managers in one particular department where most of the group participants worked. Table 16.2(b) lists concrete changes made within this same department. Most of the responses of line managers and participants relating to changes in climate were positive as indicated in Tables 16.2 and 16.3. However, one senior line manager in this department expressed a more negative view. He thought that the outcome of group learning could cause a conflict of ethos with the prevailing management style between middle and senior management. He also thought that the use of groups on a large scale would cause 'in groups' and 'out groups' according to whether staff had attended the groups or not. Use of informal communication channels, he felt, could undermine the 'pastoral' role of the senior line manager. Again full details of statements made were included in the report referred to earlier.

Conclusions

I worked with the stakeholder steering group to interpret the findings, draw conclusions and make recommendations. Reports were then circulated to interested persons in the organization and presentations were made to relevant committees. Two reports were compiled, one showing details of all the data collected, the other the summarized findings, conclusions and recommendations. Only the latter was circulated.

It was relatively easy for sceptics to challenge the validity of the data and to question the degree to which generalizations could be made from it. The nature of the research, the existing organizational situation together with my own predilection caused the evaluation research to be non-experimental in design. Most threats to internal and external validity according to the alternative positivist, experimental approach are present.[6] Thus it is not possible to attribute cause and effect with any degree of certainty in this study and it is not possible to say with certainty that MSDGs alone caused the outcomes listed. However, the use of a qualitative, interpretive approach, I thought, was appropriate to the subject matter.

This approach focusses on the relevant stakeholders' 'definition of the situation'. I felt it was more likely to produce valid data than a positivist design (even if such a design were feasible). I drew certain conclusions from the findings. The objectives of the project from the point of view of the sponsor were given earlier. The first two objectives concerned the impacts of the groups on participants and the organization and the value of these impacts. Impacts have already been listed in Tables 16.1 to 16.3. Placing a value on these impacts is very difficult because of validity issues (already referred to), but also for other reasons indicated below:

(i) *Definition of managerial and organizational effectiveness* – there is no universal agreement concerning what managerial or organizational effectiveness consists of or what performance measure(s) can be used in assessing improvements in effectiveness. Related to this is the presence or absence of existing organizational procedures (e.g. appraisal and MBO systems) for assessing individual or organizational performance. In the authority under investigation there did not appear to be any such procedures.

(ii) *Subjectivity of values* – linked to the last set of problems is the subjectivity involved in valuing personal qualities and behaviours. What one person regards as a beneficial individual outcome may be regarded as dysfunctional by another. The organizational position or vantage point of the valuer is also important. Pedler *et al.*[4] note, in regard to the valuing of organizational outcomes, that 'he who defines organizational benefits is likely to be a member of the dominant coalition of power'.

The overall degree of impact of the programme is also difficult to value since little comparative data is available. The general extent and nature of the effects will be influenced by:

(i) *Transfer of learning barriers* – these may be due to the person receiving the development, the nature of the development activity and/or aspects of his/her environment. These factors make it very difficult to ascertain whether any lack of success in achieving outcomes is due to factors about the groups themselves and this method of development, or is due to barriers in the participants or the environment to which they return.

(ii) *Competence of line managers in observing their members of staff and identifying changes in attitudes or behaviour* – this relates both to the ability of line managers to notice change, and to the opportunity for them to observe change, i.e. either the participant or the line manager may leave or change position.

(iii) *Selection issues* – the type of outcomes reported may be a function of bias in the selection of staff to attend the groups (in this case participants were mainly from the Social Services Department).

(iv) *Self-justification* – it can be argued that group members need to report positive outcomes to vindicate their attendance in the groups and to continue to justify further attendance.

It must also be noted that a common approach to placing value on an activity is to try to assess how effective the activity has been in achieving certain goals. However, there did not appear to be any explicit objectives set for the groups by internal trainers or external facilitators. Perhaps the nature of self-development groups makes it impossible to set explicit objectives. I was not therefore able to use the achievement of given objectives as a measure of value.

Despite all the problems discussed above and keeping them in mind, it seems to me that it is possible to draw certain tentative conclusions regarding the value of MSDG outcomes. Participants and line managers made mostly positive statements about the outcomes they experienced or observed. Participants expressed a substantial degree of need/expectation satisfaction. A count of responses from both participants and line managers indicated a high level of continuing commitment to and support for the programme. The outcomes of the MSDGs were compared with models of self-actualizing individual (Burgoyne, Boydell and Pedler[7]), qualities of the effective manager (Burgoyne and Stuart;[8] Boyatzis[9]) and characteristics of effective organizations (French;[10] Bennis[11] and Burke[12]). In each case the outcomes seemed to reflect many aspects of the theoretical models. The organizational benefits seem to be in the area of improving organizational behaviour processes (Beer[13]) which, it can be hypothesized, may relate to improvements in harder measures of organizational performance.

The third objective of the project concerned recommendations regarding the future role and usage of the groups. It was recommended, based on the findings of the project, that the MSDG programme could be continued at least at its present level or at an increased level of activity. The findings concerning the organizations of the group programme and the context in which they operate led to relevant recommendations to try to improve those two aspects of the situation.

Returning to my own personal interest in the project, I noted that some respondents claimed that the groups had an impact on organizational culture/climate. Some (indeed most) respondents thought the impact was beneficial. It seems to be, however, that the use of MSDGs as an OD intervention may depend upon the level of management attending the groups, the number of groups in existence in the organization and the extent to which a 'critical mass' from one department attends the groups. Isolated individuals from one department attending a group may not be able to influence climate very much.

A worry I have concerning the use of MSDGs as an OD intervention is bound up with the notion of planned change. I feel that MSDG facilitators need to identify the appropriate organizational situations that can benefit from MSDG programmes. They should also be able to describe to the key stakeholders the probable outcomes that can be expected to occur in an organization given certain conditions. Otherwise the process and outcomes of a group programme may be unpredicted, unexpected or unwanted by organizational stakeholders. A further issue concerns the 'chicken and egg' situation of whether an appropriate climate is required to nurture MSDGs, or whether the impact of the groups creates the necessary climate. Some of these issues are explored in greater depth in the dissertation I have written on this topic.[14] However, more work still needs to be done on the use of MSDGs as an OD strategy.

Regarding the use of MSDGs as a means of individual manager development, I felt reassured about the benefits of using the approach. In fact, since completing the project I have myself initiated and facilitated self-development groups in the South-West regions and intend to continue to develop the approach in future.

Epilogue

I contacted the Central Training Officer of the local authority in March 1987 to find out what had happened to the MSDG programme in the authority subsequent to my report and its last presentation in July 1986. I was told that four of the six groups were continuing (without external facilitator support). No new groups had been started by the Central Training Department due to a change in position of the Central Trainer. A new trainer was to be appointed shortly. The job description of the new trainer includes the responsibility for continuing the MSDG programme. The trainer would be expected to maintain and support the programme and, in time, to act as an internal group facilitator. This could reduce the reliance on external facilitators. The intention is to start up at least two new groups each year through the Central Training Department. The effect of the research project was to consolidate support for the MSDG programme. It fostered a belief in the authority that the programme should continue as an important aspect of the management development strategy. It was thought that the programme in future might be offered to more senior managers in the authority. Other recommendations resulting from the project would be kept under consideration in the future development of the programme.

Contact with the Social Services Department (SSD) Training Section has confirmed that no new MSDGs have started since the finish of the project in July 1986. However, the two existing all-women's groups have been very proactive and have arranged meetings with senior management to discuss women's issues, in particular equal opportunities for women managers.

The Training Section is about to start a new phase in its MSDG programme. It currently has a waiting list of 68 staff (42 women and 26 men). The intention is to have two MSDGs running, by the summer, and possibly a further two by the autumn, of 1987. These groups will be given a more specific focus than the previous groups. They will be asked particularly to work on the issues involved in men and women working together. The groups will be separate men and women's groups but they will operate to some degree in tandem, i.e. they will have a 'start-up' two days together, then operate independently, then meet together again after an intervening period. Another change in the programme is the anticipated use of internal facilitators with pairs working as co-tutors to each group. They will have external facilitator support for their development and back-up. With regard to other recommendations in the report the climate of support for MSDGs in the SSD by senior management has increased. Policies for staff supervision and appraisal are under consideration and the role of the line manager in regard to MSDGs is being explored.

References

1. Rogers, C.R. (1969) *Freedom to Learn*. C.E. Merrill, Columbus, Ohio.
2. Patton, M.O. (1978) *Utilization Focussed Evaluation*. Sage, California.
3. Bunker, D.R. (1965) The effects of laboratory education upon individual behaviour. In Schein, E.H. and Bennis, W.C. (eds) *Personal and Organizational Change through Group Methods*. J. Wiley & Sons, New York.
4. Pedler, M.J., Boydell, T.H., Leary, M., Carlisle, J. and Cranwell, B. (1982) *Self-development groups for managers*. Manpower Services Commission, Sheffield, UK. (1982 (original) 1984 (published).)
5. Temporal, P.M.E. (1981) Creating the climate for self-development. In Boydell, T.H. and Pedler, M.J. (eds) *Management Self-Development: Concepts and Practices*. Gower, Farnborough, UK.
6. Kane, J.S. (1976) The evaluation of organizational training programmes. *Journal of European Training*, **5**, 6,1, pp.289–338.
7. Burgoyne, J., Boydell, T.H. and Pedler, M.J. (1978) *Self-development*. Association of Teachers of Management, London.
8. Burgoyne, J. and Stuart, R. (1976) The nature use and acquisition of managerial skills and other attributes. *Personnel Review* **5** (4) pp.19–29. (Autumn)
9. Boyatzis, R.E. (1982) *The Competent Manager: a Model for Effective Performance*. J. Wiley, New York.
10. French, W.L. (1969) Organization development: objectives, assumptions and strategies. *California Management Review* 12, pp.23–46.
11. Bennis, W. (1969) *The nature of organization development*. Addison Wesley, Reading, Mass.
12. Burke, W.W. (1982) *Organization development: Principles and Practices*. Little, Brown & Co., Boston, Mass.

13. Beer, M. (1980) *Organization Change and Development: A Systems View.* Goodyear, California.
14. Martin, P.C.W. (1986) Self-development as a means of management and organization development. Unpublished dissertation, Sheffield Polytechnic.

17

Envisioning the Learning Company

* * *

MIKE PEDLER AND JOHN BURGOYNE

Introduction

The time now seems ripe for trying to discover, in theory and practice, the usefulness of the 'learning company'. Individual managers and management development policy-makers have been stirred up by *In Search of Excellence*[1] and by Geoffrey Holland's vision of a management development plan for every company.[2] Organization level solutions are back in fashion. Theory has advanced and offers new tools for thought so that we have many new ways of thinking about organizations and we may now understand a little better collective self-development as opposed to individual self-development. Methodologies of group self-development, culture change, organization change, policy formation offer some approaches from which we can at least extrapolate to postulate ways of developing the 'learning company'.

It is nonetheless a voyage of discovery, a push into unknown territory. We can see an outline possibility but not the detailed shape and form. The 'voyage' metaphor breaks down for it is not out there waiting to be discovered; it can only be found by attempts to envision and create it. This chapter attempts to offer a starting point for this process and is in two parts. In the first we rehearse the argument that the learning company is the next frontier in development work. In the second we make four attempts, from different starting points, to get a glimpse of what a learning company might be like and what we might have to do to create one. As this chapter is very much a beginning rather than an ending, whatever strands are discovered will probably be left hanging loose, to be further woven by those of us who find the argument attractive.

The Learning Company as the Next Frontier?

The individual learner has provided the impetus for much recent thinking on management learning and development, and rightly so. Although there is a great deal we can say simply now about how people learn, there is also enough that is mysterious to keep us busy for a long time. Over the last half century, a great deal of attention has been given to groups of people as a source of power and development. We have gradually understood more of the influence which groups can have upon members' perceptions, motivations and learnings. Current designs in management development frequently employ group work as a central feature. Such designs, for example syndicates, teamwork, action-learning and self-development, typically involve small groups of four to eight members. Beyond this size 'airtime' and attention tend to become scarce and unequally distributed. There are ways of working with bigger groups, of forty or fifty people and more, of which the Tavistockian power and authority model is a well-known example. Others might include Quaker meetings, the familiar lecture plus questions and conferences as forums in which the learning design relies upon a larger rather than a smaller group of people.

It is at the group level – usually the smaller but sometimes the bigger variety – to which the term 'learning community' has been applied. We will use this term here as an intermediate concept to move beyond the individual focus for the organization of learning.

Our concern in this chapter is to establish a third level of learning and development design which attempts to take account of the pervasiveness and ubiquitousness of large scale organization. It has been suggested that the 'advanced' or 'developed' nations – USA, Russia, Japan, and those of Europe and Australasia – are 'organizational societies'. That is, despite many differences in national and local cultures, the lives of the citizen of Montreal and Moscow are likely to possess many similarities. Because of our membership of, and dependence upon, large organizations tending to have common cross-cultural characteristics, the assumption is that the manager in Osaka is likely to meet much the same pressures and problems in life as the one in Orleans. In everyday speech we are likely to condemn big organizations as prisons or extol them as havens; refer to them as machines or as amoeba-like; see them as enabling works of genius or as inventions of the Devil. The importance of big organizations in the current stage of societal development seems self-evident.

The theme of this book is the application of self-development – an idea which has been very much concerned with the individual and yet which has often utilized small group designs – to organizational processes and practices. We are trying to move up, using insights about how people learn and in what settings, to the design of organization. The learning company is an attempt at social invention – an image or metaphor of what this might look like. In one sense it is simply a pastiche of the various ideas in currency – self-appraisal, learning resources centres, self-development groups and so on. From another angle it is an act of invention – if we were to design an organization expressly to facilitate the learning and development of its members, and its own transformation, then what would it look like? Much of this book is concerned with the pursuit of the empirical – of the methods and technologies which exist and are being created. This chapter involves more the search for an adequate vision which will bring us one step closer to enactment.

Why the learning company? Because that seems to be the next step. We have understood the limitations of the training idea, which is as far as our horizons stretched in the 1960s, and the notion of self-development seems now well accepted. Beyond piecemeal applications there are calls for a wider vision. There is a swelling chorus for an increased organizational capacity to learn in response to rapid and accelerating changes. Geoffrey Holland of the Manpower Services Commission has called for a 'new management development initiative' in Britain which, by 1995, will create a 'tradition of learning companies' as part of a wider learning society (Holland,[2] paras 8–24).

Pointers to the Vision

Much contemporary thought on organizations centres on the notion that organizations are the products of the ways that we think about them, rather than things which exist independently of such thought (e.g. Morgan,[3] pp.11–17). This suggests that if we can change the ways in which we think about organizations, particularly in ways which are shared by the actors in them, then we may be much closer to changing them than we might otherwise have thought.

For the rest of this chapter we attempt four different ways of creating a vision of the learning company: lessons from the history of the learning community; developing the concept of the 'good company'; integrating systematic training and development into the company; and sketching some possible scenes from life in the learning company.

Lessons from the History of the Learning Community

The learning community has been seen primarily as a training design 'bringing together a group of people as peers to meet personal learning needs primarily through a sharing of resources and skills offered by those present' (Pedler, 1981[4]). The defining characteristics of this design include the twin responsibilities for members of articulating and meeting their own learning needs as well as helping others to do this via offering themselves as a flexible resource to the community.

A key feature is that all members are peers, implying not equality of knowledge or skill – indeed it is the very differences and diversity which create the potential of the design – but of equality in the political sense of equal rights, responsibilities and privileges. Membership is the core word. The learning community is more of a club or company of learners than a classroom. When it is working well it is a good company with only the one status, and a critical step in the development of the community is when participants begin to offer sessions to fellow participants, and when they choose not to take up offers from a staff person.

As a training design the learning community has been invoked by various practitioners including Roger Harrison in connection with changing the nature of college teaching;[5] Malcolm Knowles in his description of an approach to adult education;[6] by John Heron in his accounts of peer learning community and peer review audit;[7,8] by David Megginson and Mike Pedler as a programme for trainers;[9] by Reg Revans in his invention, the action learning set;[10] (Revans 1984); and most recently by Pauline Barrett in her management development programmes for housing managers.[11]

The current usage of learning community has its roots partly in the experiential group or T-group movement originating in the 1940s and also in the therapeutic community groups of Maxwell Jones and others in mental hospitals to encourage patients to act as therapists for each other. The therapeutic community turns out to have very similar aims to the current learning community as used in management education – 'a community whose goal is that each can learn how to be responsible for himself (sic) and is able to help himself through helping others' (Almond,[12] p.34). In turn we learn that the therapeutic community has its roots in a technique which was widespread in the nineteenth century known as 'moral treatment' which gives the patient the primary responsibility for her or his own development. Still older references to the learning community may of course be found, as in the mediaeval description of universities and monasteries as 'communities of scholars'.

The current concept has remained indicative and elusive rather than tightly defined. There are some advantages of this, not the least that an attractive idea may endure longer than a neat package. The idea of learning community is capable of far wider application beyond training course design. For example William Torbert has sought to create 'collaborative inquiry' in a series of public performances of his 'Theatre of Inquiry' in Boston in the winter of 1977/8. He has elsewhere concluded that 'schools of all kinds require post-bureaucratic structures if they are to educate rather than indoctrinate, for only the post-bureaucratic structures help members become aware of and take full responsibility for the way they structure their lives. The world as a whole must become a community of inquiry if our vast cultural differences are to be celebrated and reconciled rather than exploited, fought over and obliterated' (Torbert,[13] p.166). In a similar vein Fred Emery's 'search conferences' are designed to exclude or play down the role of expert so that 'common people' can gain confidence in their ability to know the world, trust their perceptions and invent theories in the same way as hitherto learned men have done.[14] At this point Emery could be speaking for Reg Revans who has strenuously applied his anti-expert stance to many aspects of management and government through the agency of 'action learning'.[10]

Malcolm Knowles has applied the concept of learning community directly to the conduct of professional associations.[15] The idea of 'learning exchanges' - motto: 'If you know it, share it' - stem from Ivan Illich's suggestions in *De-schooling Society*[16] where 'learning webs' replace formal institutions of education. However, such ideas can be traced back as far as Samuel Hartlib (1600–1662) who established an 'Office of Addresses' for organizing and communicating especially scientific learning among adults as well as putting forward schemes for comprehensive state-controlled education as the 'readiest way to reform both Church and Commonwealth'. Hartlib and his associates worked so closely together that they are 'all in a knot of one another's labours' and often published anonymously or collaboratively under one name. They called for a spectrum of alternative educational institutions by which 'all universities and eminent places of learning might be subtly undermined and made useless'.[17]

Donald Schon has provided perhaps the best text for the learning community writ large, although he has preferred the term 'learning system':

> We must, in other words, become adept at learning. We must become able not only to transform our institutions, in response to changing situations and requirements; we must invent and develop institutions which are 'learning systems', that is to say, systems capable of bringing about their own continuing transformation (p.30).[18]

Schon has further proposed the need for 'public learning' via the use of networks, sharing of resources, and the pooling of perceptions. His thesis rests upon a conception of the world as composed of a diversity of often contradictory perspectives which require the resolution of several apparent dichotomies, for example the need for self-reliance while recognizing one's inability to accomplish anything without engagement with others (pp.233–237).[18]

Developing the Concept of the Good Company

When working well the learning community is a good company, both in the sense of being composed of people we enjoy spending time with and of a group of people united in a productive enterprise. John Morris has written a number of largely unpublished papers on the theme of 'good company' on which the following comments are based.[19]

The good company is, first of all, 'everybody's business', contributed to and contributing to all stakeholders in an even-handed way. It aims to create quality for all investors rather than looking primarily to the financiers as is the current mode for so many companies. Success is defined as the creation of quality service for customers, quality of working life for members, quality of social responsibility to the public as well as the quality of business performance for the financial shareholders. In Morris's felicitous phrases, the good company is concerned with 'managing for mutual advantage' rather than 'just managing'.

'Mutuality' is as defined by Erikson as 'a relationship in which partners depend on each other for the development of their respective strengths'.[20] This defining characteristic both of the learning community and the good company is expressed beautifully by Morris:

> Good company is simply the condition of people in good relationship with one another; relationships that are personal and not forced or formal. *A good company is a state of affairs in which people can work together as persons who are naturally interested in the work they are doing together* (p.2).[19]

These are in part the design principles for the learning company, for the learning community and the good company are a relationship first and a set of outputs second. Of course, the two should not be too separated. As Revans has stressed in his action learning design, the intractable managerial problem, the person and the set of peers all require one another. The learning company must create both learning and development for its members *and* effective outputs in a competitive and not necessarily benign commercial world. Nevertheless, because we currently think too much in terms of outputs, profitability, performance, productivity and so on and neglect relationship, we must start to put that first as a necessary corrective. Our current thinking is overly 'male' as far as our concepts of work organization are concerned and the lack of 'female' qualities is causing a sterility which affects all the outputs of the good company.

This conscious celebration of the female principle is an aspect of what is being called 'new paradigm' thinking about work organization and which stresses among other things, 'organizational transformation' in which conscious thought and design are an essential part of bringing about our new world (Nicoll, 1984,[21] pp.4–16). Yet the elements of this so-called 'new paradigm' have always been available to us. An enduring example of good company is King Arthur's Knights of the Round Table which have exercised perhaps more influence than we realize upon English forms of organization, and which, in myth, began to fail when trust and companionship broke down. Revan's action learning set is a modern day descendant of these 'comrades in adversity' where it is the relationship – of peers, fellow members, fellow human beings – which is the first principle:

> When ordinary men (sic) like hard working managers are confused and uneasy, but nevertheless obliged by circumstances to get something done, it is not some intellectual explanation of their emergency that they seek, followed by a logical plan of action that will get them off the hook …At such times, borne down by responsibility, fear, confusion and helplessness, it is not argument one needs, but support, not analysis but example, not lucidity but warmth …Once the simple human aid has been given and the confidence starts creeping back, then may be the time to deploy the weapons of sophistication and dialectic (pp.289–290).[22]

Revan's essentially tragic view is balanced and yet echoed by this management consultant reflecting on his recent move to self-employment:

> Being a consultant in some ways gives you freedom …freedom for example to choose who you work with …being easy with those you work alongside and having fun with them is probably more important than the content of the work itself, which changes over time anyway, becomes less interesting, less useful, less remunerative …

Although we are here more concerned wth creating an image or metaphor of the learning company, it is worth noting that such notions are not entirely absent from today's commercial world. Mr Watson of IBM has announced upon more than one occasion that the main business of IBM is learning and development and that selling computers is a by-product of this. In Britain, Pedigree Petfoods avers that 'responsible self-management', which means allowing 'associates' (employees) to serve their customers and conduct their business in their own way with a commitment from the company to help associates develop their potential through learning new skills and subjects, is not incompatible with making money from selling petfood.[23]

Integrating Systematic Training and Development into the Company

Geoffrey Holland creates his vision of a learning company by listing ten features of training and development for such companies, such as individual training plans for all, systematic career management and so on.[2] The Mangham study[24] shows that about half of UK companies do some systematic management training (and half do not) and that there is absolutely no relationship between the amount of training and development activity and any measure of corporate performance used. This view, and this empirical finding, provide the background for one vision of the learning company that we find plausible, though of course they do not 'prove' it.

The vision is this: that a learning company does all the things that Geoffrey Holland's ten points imply in terms of individual and collective learning processes, but that it does them in an organic and integral way and not in a mechanistic/systems/bureaucratic way. That is to say, for example, that individuals have development plans in the sense that they and the people around them think about and discuss what that person could usefully learn and help to make it happen because it is a culturally accepted and socially normal thing to do, not because every manager gets a set of forms from the personnel office with a note saying it's time to do the annual development plans again in accordance with the company policy. Furthermore, individual initiatives in learning, development and career management, are not, in the learning company, just individually useful and locally beneficial tactics; they also add up to something in the organic process of organizational direction finding and taking, so that organizational transformation takes place. This is the organic equivalent of individual learning being systematically planned in the context of corporate and management development policy.

We must, however, be very careful here; both systems and procedures and formal policies do have a place in the learning company, but they must always be the means of facilitating the essential processes of learning and co-operation, not ends in themselves, and their perpetual tendency to become just this must be guarded against.

On the tactics and organizational integration of development activities, we believe that there is some value in a six level model of 'organizational maturity' towards becoming a learning company. The levels are perhaps most easily envisaged in terms of organizational systems and procedures that would represent them, but in our learning company, the processes would take place through organic and natural processes, with just the right amount of minimal and 'facilitating structure' to support and make them efficient:

Levels of organizational maturity towards integral development:

Level 6
As for Level 5, with the addition that the nature and quality of the processes of thought going into corporate direction choosing and taking is itself enhanced by processes of learning and development.

Level 5
As for Level 4, with the addition that conclusions about the cumulative human expertise and potential of the organizational membership, as revealed by processes 2–4, feed into the corporate direction choosing debate.

Level 4
As for Level 3, with the addition that the direction of career planning and choice of learning goals is informed by likely scenarios of corporate direction, and hence plays a part in the implementation of corporate policy.

Level 3
Integrated tactics of development and career management (i.e. development activities to help individuals pursue learning that is relevant to their thought through short- or long-term career futures).

Level 2
Piecemeal, unintegrated and uncoordinated tactical interventions either to facilitate learning, or to manage careers.

Level 1
No considered management of individuals' learning or careers.

It is our hunch that only a few small organic entrepreneurial organizations achieve a high level on this scale, and then only briefly. Success brings size, which increases the scale of the problem and makes it difficult to achieve the appropriate level of systematic procedure. Our feeling is that most organizations of any size currently, and at best, achieve Levels 3 to 4. The challenge of the learning company is to improve upon this.

Scenes from Organizational Life

A Learning Company?

Harvest Bakery employs 900 people and is one of the bigger plants in the Bakeries Division of Conglomerate Foods, a food manufacturing, catering and leisure group of companies. The following sketches were taken from a normal day shift last November . . .

. . .Down by the ovens, Laura McDonald, an 18–year-old telephonist, is showing a group from the local Townswomen's Guild around the plant. The smell of the newly baked bread is reminding everyone that they are getting close to that good time on every tour when they get to sample the products. Like everyone else at Harvest, Laura is wearing the standard white, one-piece worksuit, but she has her Christian name boldly and artistically embroidered on the shoulder flash. This degree of personalization is encouraged as part of the 'names not numbers' philosophy of the company.

Laura has elected to do the tour alone and without a more experienced 'shadow', and is finding that she can't answer some of the questions put to her. From time to time she asks one of the members working at the ovens to explain. One of the TWG members asks if this is Laura's job and Laura explains that everyone gets a chance to show visitors around if they want to on a 'jury system' rota, because it is believed that this makes everyone aware of the customers, what they want and what they look for. A number of heads nod wisely as the group heads for Despatch . . .

. . .Next to the Dining Room is the 'Learning Resources Centre' which contains books, tapes, magazines, films, handouts, computer programmes, distance learning materials as well as the 'hardware' and facilities for using these. The LRC is managed by Betty Ambler, a part-time member who works for 12 hours per week and who is available lunchtimes and at the evening shift changeover for consultation on anything members might wish to learn about. As well as the usual business-related materials, the LRC is well stocked with all sorts of information and sources on a wide range of hobbies and civic information. As well as following 'Open University'—type programmes members are investigating all manner of topics from how to rear mink to how to stand as a local councillor. Another part of the company's philosophy is that members who are learning anything – whether business related or not – are likely to remain more flexible and adaptable, more easily able to learn new things in the future and, hence, maintain the ability of the business to respond and develop.

Outside the LRC, where the corridor is at its widest are four carrels or booths which members can use to read or write in. There is also a small area of seating with pot plants and coffee tables which is a favourable spot for browsers and gossipers. The LRC remains open at all hours for use by members. When Betty is not there, borrowings have to be registered with reception . . .

. . .The members on Confectionery line B have scheduled a 45 minute break to get the whole team together to discuss quality and waste rates. There are no detailed disciplinary rules in the plant. All members have a general obligation to take responsibility for their own work *and* for the work of fellow members. It is assumed that members will act responsibly, solving their own problems if they can or calling for help if they can't.

Detailed issues such as time-keeping, ordering of materials and supplies, quality assurance, inspection safety and so on, are the responsibility of teams who elect a team leader to represent them to the co-ordinators. Any member is entitled to 10 days per year 'development' time and team leaders get another 5 for management training. Members are encouraged in appraisals to use all their development time and must prepare their own 'development plans' each year which are agreed with the relevant co-ordinator.

Confectionery team B have a problem with Bill Scott, a member of two years standing who has lost a great deal of time recently as well as being persistently late. Some members feel that quality is being affected and are saying that inspection is sometimes skimped when people are covering for Bill's absence. Everyone knows that Bill has had problems but . . .how long can things go on? Any team can, through the team leader request transfers, suspensions or other disciplinary action as they think fit. These requests are dealt with by the General Co-ordinator and are very few in number, amounting to two or three per year.

Because they know it will be a difficult meeting, Confectionery team B have called in a 'facilitator' to help them with their meeting. A facilitator is any member of the company who has been on the company's 'Facilitator Skills Training Programme' and has been trained to help groups deal with their business and problems. Almost 100 members of Harvest Bakery have undertaken this popular programme in their development time. Jean Vicks, a member from Mixing, will facilitate this meeting.

Jean sits and listens for the first twenty minutes, only then intervening to point out that, with only another twenty minutes or so left, perhaps a number of options could be clarified, following which an action plan for Bill Scott could be set . . .

. . .In the Members Dining Room (there is only one) Nigel Baines, the General Co-ordinator is having a cup of tea with two Departmental Co-ordinators (DCs), Jim Paul and Chris Mansur. They are discussing the forthcoming lunchtime meeting to decide on a new bonus scheme. Harvest Bakery follows the parent company line in paying everyone within a 3:1 ratio, that is the highest paid, who happens to be Nigel and the Despatch Co-ordinator, cannot earn more than three times the pay of the lowest paid member. In practice, the differential has been even less due to the old bonus being paid at a standard level. The proposal before the members this lunchtime is to gear the bonus to salary levels which will reward the co-ordinators significantly more while not reducing the share to the average member by that much.

Interestingly enough, this suggestion has not come from where one might expect it, but from a fortnightly 'Business Circle' in Despatch. After this meeting it circulated round the plant and got the necessary one-third of signatories to call a referendum. This will take place after the lunchtime meeting has allowed the debate to be heard.

Jim is of the opinion that the new system is long overdue. 'It's ridiculous that Nigel here should be taking home less than GCs of much smaller plants. None of us is paid enough but at least this is a start on rewarding those with the toughest jobs.'

But Chris disagrees. 'But it will lead to trouble I am telling you . . .niggles . . .the best pay system is a simple one that everyone can see is fair. We all get a decent wage here so why should we risk our good relationships by introducing differences . . .I can't see what those people are playing at . . .'

Nigel is inclined to agree with Chris but confesses to being surprised by the proposal having got this far. 'I agree with Chris in principle and you can bet that any disputes will end up you know where, together with any loss of goodwill or whatever. However, talking to people I'm surprised how many think the likes of us should get more than they do. They say things like "I don't take work home like you Nigel, you deserve it, mate" and things like that . . .I suppose what we have to remember is that most people are used to differentials, and much bigger ones than we have here.' . . .

. . .Outside the Dining Room, a group of young women and men are clustered around the notice boards, of which there are four. A small blackboard holds 'Business Notices' while a larger whiteboard announces forthcoming events. Some merriment and ribald comments are emerging in response to the end of shift talk to be given by the Sales Co-ordinator on 'Supermarket Merchandising'. Every month, someone at Harvest gives a talk on some aspect of their work and the Sales Co-ordinator is known to think highly of herself as well as Harvest's products. She is known for her 'hard selling' of most things! She is also very good at her job. Sessions last for an hour with about half of this devoted to questions and discussions. All members are invited and attendance has improved considerably since beer and sandwiches were introduced at the close of the session.

Also on the whiteboard are details of courses being attended and the dates and times at which people will be absent. The company supports members in going on most ouside courses, including qualification programmes, both in terms of finance and in time where this exceeds the '10 day allowance'. Harvest carries a permanent 2% overcapacity of members to cover development time which cannot be covered by work teams.

The two other boards in green and blue are headed 'Needs' and 'Offers'. Members can use these to post notices about all manner of things. These include requests or offers for lifts at weekends, books and cars for sale, or wanted tuition in many skills from piano to painting, as well as the quota of usually bogus 'lonely hearts' messages and anonymous declarations of admiration, etc. Maintaining the boards is the responsibility of the Development Working Party but, as ever, the jokers are more often on duty . . .

. . .In a small interview room by reception, two 'speaking partners' are working together. The parent company chairperson once exhorted members to 'admit mistakes joyfully' and this has been translated into a right which members have, if they wish, not only to admit mistakes openly in team meetings or in appraisal sessions, but to meet in one-to-one counselling sessions with a partner. Debbie Wells and George Payne could scarcely be more different. Debbie is a grandmother, George is 25; George was brought up in Malaysia, whereas Debbie has not often been outside of Lancashire. They work at opposite ends of the plant and yet both attended a counselling skills workshop together. Since then they have been meeting once every fortnight for an hour at a time. Each has half an hour to talk about and express their feelings about things that have happened to them – at work or at home. George is crying quietly and Debbie is holding his hand. A recent outburst at his team leader has brought back to George some painful sessions with his father . . .

. . . The bread delivery van driver is talking to a shopkeeper where he is leaving some trays of bread. He is asking about comments and complaints from the customers about the bread products, and also getting the shopkeeper's reaction to a new product idea which itself had its origins in the company's suggestion scheme. When he gets back there will be a de-briefing meeting with all the delivery drivers reporting on their findings. The driver makes less deliveries than before, talks more to shopkeepers on the rounds and to colleagues back at base, but the company no longer pays for market research surveys and the central complaints department needs fewer people.

There are bright new digital displays in the baking hall, wrapping and packing rooms. They show the throughput and rejection rates at the various quality control points. People glance up occasionally as if at a cricket scoreboard. Before this system was installed, managers got this information on a printout 24 hours after each shift, and occasionally called emergency shift meetings when things went seriously wrong. Now throughput and rejection ups and downs are discussed as a matter of course in quality circle meetings, but most importantly, problems get identified and looked at within minutes of them occurring . . .

. . . Paul, a YTS trainee and a health food fanatic, is talking with his parents and sisters over a meal. He is explaining how the company looks positively at the high fibre bread market and puts out various loss leaders in this area. He says 'we' when he talks about the company and mentions the newsletter, the company briefing sessions and in-company 'forum' events where he has been able to talk informally with research, marketing and accounting specialists about the economics, technology and marketing of health food products . . .

Perhaps we should add that people at Harvest Bakery work hard at producing bread as well as at their own development and that of the company. Of course, the company also has a reputation for an exciting range of products, which are good value for money, and its customers feel well looked after. If your reaction to this sketch was something like 'Well, it all sounds very well, but you can't run a business like this . . .' then that perhaps says as much about our current conception of work as of anything else. Work at Harvest Bakery is still hard work but it is much more about continuous development and learning than it used to be. There are costs involved – like the 2% development overhead – as well as in the wider aspects of employee development such as pay and benefits. A learning company needs new forms of relationship and managing as well as greater provision of development opportunities.

References

1. Peters, T. J. and Waterman, R.H. (1982) *In Search of Excellence*. Harper & Row, New York.
2. Holland, G. (1986) *Excellence in Industry*. Extracts of a speech at the Dorchester Hotel, London, 11th February, 1986. Manpower Services Commission, Sheffield, UK.
3. Morgan, G. (1986) Images of Organization. Sage, Beverly Hills, California.
4. Pedler, M. J. (1981) Developing the learning community. In Boydell, T. H. and Pedler, M. (eds) *Management Self-Development: Concepts and Practices*. Gower Press, Aldershot, UK.
5. Harrison, R. (1969) Classroom innovation: a design primer. In Runkel, R., Harrison, R. and Runkel, M. (eds) *The Changing College Classroom*. Jossey Bass, San Francisco, California.
6. Knowles, M. (1970) *The Modern Practice of Adult Education*. Association Press, New York.
7. Heron, J. (1974) *The Concept of a Peer Learning Community*. Human Potential Research Project, University of Surrey, UK. (March)
8. Heron, J. (1981) Self and peer assessment. In Boydell, T. H. and Pedler, M. (eds) *Management Self-Development: Concepts and Practices*. Gower Press, Aldershot, UK.
9. Megginson, D. F. and Pedler, M. J. (1976) Developing structures and technology for the learning community. *Journal of European Training* **5** (5). MCB, Bradford, UK.
10. Revans, R. W. (1982) *The Origins and Growth of Action Learning*. Chartwell Bratt, Bromley, UK.
11. Barrett, P. (1986) The learning community. *Industrial and Commercial Training* (March/April)
12. Almond, R. (1971) The therapeutic community. *Scientific American* (March)
13. Tobert, W. (1976) *Creating a Community of Inquiry: Conflict, Collaborations, Transformation*. Wiley, London.
14. Emery, F. E. (1982) Socio-technical foundations for a new industrial order. *Human Relations* **35** (12).
15. Knowles, M. (1979) The professional organization as a learning community. *Training and Development Journal* (May)
16. Illich, I. (1972) *De-Schoaling Society*. Penguin, Harmondsworth, UK.
17. Alexander, T. (1977) Learning exchange. *Ideas in Education*. University of Sussex. (January)
18. Schon, D. (1971) *Beyond the Stable State*. Random House, NY.

19. Morris, J. (1985; 1986) *Managing in a Changing Environment; Managing for Mutual Advantage; Just Managing and the Search for Excellence*. Unpublished papers, the Development Consortium, Manchester Business School, Manchester, UK.
20. Erikson, E. (1950) *Childhood and Society*. W. W. Norton, NY.
21. Nicoll, D. (1984) Grace beyond the rules: a new paradigm for lives on a human scale. In Adams, J.D. (ed.) *Transforming Work*. Miles River Press, Alexandria, Va.
22. Revans, R. W. (1980) *Action Learning: New Techniques for Managers*. Blond & Briggs, London.
23. Pedigree Petfoods (1987) Pedigree Petfoods. *Investing in People No. 3*. Manpower Services Commission, Sheffield, UK.
24. Mangham, I. L. and Silver, M. S. (1986) *Management in the UK*. Report to ESRC and the Department of Trade and Industry.

Index of Names

Index of Subjects